PLAIN MR. KNOX

Elizabeth Whitley

Christian Focus Publications

© Elizabeth Whitley

ISBN 1-85792-683-8

First published in 1960 and reprinted as paperback in
1972 by The Scottish Reformation Society,
17 George IV Bridge, Edinburgh EH1 1EE

This edition published in 2001
by
Christian Focus Publications, Geanies House,
Fearn, Ross-shire, IV20 1TW, Great Britain

www.christianfocus.com

Cover design by Owen Daily

Printed and bound in Great Britain
by Omnia, Glasgow

"*Nane have I corrupted, nane have I defraudit, merchandise have I not made of the glorious Evangel of Jesus Christ . . .*"

John Knox: Last Will and Testament

FOREWORD

Rev. Professor G. N. M. Collins, B.D., President

THE 400th anniversary of the death of John Knox provides a special occasion for the grateful remembrance of a man who, in the shrewd judgment of Thomas Carlyle, was "the one Scotchman to whom of all others his country and the world owe a debt." And the fact that 1972 is the centennial year of the Scottish Education Act makes it doubly Knox's year; for no man did more than he to bring the benefits of education to the common people.

In considering ways and means of marking the quartercentenary of Knox's passing, the Scottish Reformation Society set at the top of its programme the provision of a reliable and readable biography of the great Reformer; and the fact that such a biography was written, by Elizabeth Whitley, as recently as 1960 suggested to the Society the re-publication, in paper-back form, of this delightful book. So it comes about that, with the ready consent of Mrs. Whitley, *Plain Mr. Knox* goes again into circulation. Journalist and historian – aye, and politician too – meet in the cultured personality of the writer, who had the advantage also of sharing in the work of her husband's long ministry in Knox's famous church – the High Kirk of St. Giles. Her tribute to Knox in this fascinating biography has already brought corrective enlightenment to many; and we send forth this new edition with the prayer that Scotland may once again be induced to listen to the man who, more than any, laid the foundations of her democracy both in Church and State, and brought her a new sense of the sovereignty of God over the whole of life.

"John Knox's gospel is my gospel," declared Charles Haddon Spurgeon. "That which thundered through Scotland must thunder through England again." And to signify our agreement with this sentiment is simply to acknowledge that his message was the quintessence of New Testament Christianity – "the power of God, and the wisdom of God."

John Knox "being dead, yet speaketh". May it be given to our generation to hearken.

G. N. M. Collins.

Contents

viii

PROLOGUE

'The Flowers o' the Forest'

A s in our own lives, so in history there comes now and then a Marvellous Year: a vintage year of events by which all other years are dated.

In spring 1513 the Queen of France sent a ring to James IV, King of Scots, She begged him, if Henry VIII of England should attack France, to take 'but three paces into English ground'. James, greatest of the Stewarts but with their fatal streak, sent his messengers north, south, east and west to summon every able-bodied fighting man in Scotland.

In summer of 1513 young King Harry set sail for France, leaving the defence of England to his Queen, Katherine of Aragon. She was a passionate, headstrong young woman then, his elder brother's widow and his senior: but he was her devoted knight – 'Sir Loyall Hearte' – as embroidered on his surcoat and trappings in all the jousts.

Katherine heard the Scots were mustering, and gathered an army for the north, for which she and her ladies, as she wrote to Henry, 'were horribly busy sewing standards, banners and badges'.

In July 1513 his army almost complete, James IV went to the dedication of a new chapel to St. John in St. Giles', the Kirk of Edinburgh. The chapel had been given by Chepman, the King's printer and his friend: an on its roof you can see the sign of the apostle, the eagle holding the open book of John's Gospel: 'In the Beginning was the Word.' This was also Chepman's trademark.

In 1513 Erasmus of Rotterdam was a professor at Cambridge. Like a gentle ghost this priest's orphan drifts through all the scenes of violence: without family, without country – 'I am a citizen of the whole world' – without creed and without hate. He grumbles impartially at the salt fish, the thin ale, and the

A* 9

martyrs who 'send up the price of firewood'. Forced with cruelty into the priesthood as a boy, he stayed there: and interceded vehemently for Luther. He took no sides. 'Beasts do not fight, or only for food . . . but the justest war cannot commend itself to any reasonable man.' Yet through the hands of this quietist passed almost all the 'movers and shakers' of his times: Zwingli, Melanchthon, Calvin, a'Lasko of Poland, young Patrick Hamilton, cousin of the King of Scots, Geordie Buchanan, the poet and schoolmaster.

In 1513 Erasmus had already published his *In Praise of Folly*, dedicated to his friend and patron Sir Thomas More and later illustrated by Holbein. It brilliantly analysed the faults of his age. Now he was at work on the Greek New Testament that, three years later, became a landmark to scholars and a beacon-light to all Reformers. He fed, after all, one secret flame:

'Christ wished his mysteries to be published openly. I wish that even the weakest woman should read the Gospels – that they might be read and understood not only by Scots and Irishmen but by Turks and Saracens. I long that the farmer should sing them following the plough, the weaver hum them to the tune of his shuttle.'

In that year, 1513, there was among Erasmus's students a big, merry, open-handed lad, called Tyndale. He went home to Gloucester so filled with Erasmus's words that he said to an ignorant local priest:

'If God so spare my life, ere many years I will cause a boy that drives the plough to know more of Scripture than thou dost.'

In 1513 Pope Julius II died in great pomp and splendor. He was the last great dictator of totalitarian Christendom. To him is largely due the sunset glory of the Sistine Chapel, with its unrivalled ceiling to paint which Michael Angelo crouched 'chin on my belly like a Lombard cat, while the paint drips down my beard'. There are the Raphaels, the Botticellis, the Leonardos; the Peruginos, like Alpines in a hot-house: all that miraculous last flowering of a dying age.

And to build it Christ's truth was hawked, auctioned, bartered to all who would pay. Indulgences and relics were touted through

Europe: holy rags, bones, toe-nails, 'Virgin's milk' in little phials –
England alone had eight of these.

Against all this degradation stood one monk. Martin Luther:
driven three years later to his final repudiation of Rome: 'So help
me, I can no other'.

In August 1513 James marched south to the Borders with a
magnificent array: Highlanders, Lowlanders, fighting men from
the Western Isles to the East Neuk of Fife, the very flower of
Scotland's manhood. The English leader, Surrey, hurried north to
meet him with his army, Katherine following. On 9 September,
between the Twizel and the Till, the two armies met: long and
very bitter fighting followed. The result was decisive. 'The flowers
o' the forest were a' wede awa' '.

Katherine wrote jubilantly to Henry, on 16 September:

'This victory is the greatest honour that could be. The King
will not forget to thank God for it. I could not for haste send by
Rouge Cross the piece of the King of Scots coat which John
Glyn now bringeth. In this your Grace shall see how I can keep
my promise, sending you for your banners a King's coat. I
thought to send himself unto you, but our Englishmen's hearts
would not suffer it. It should have been better for him to have
been in peace than have this reward. All that God sendeth is for
the best.

In this letter is her Spanish cruelty and piety, and also her
disastrous tactlessness: for Henry's war in France at that moment
was not going nearly so well.

But for Scotland the war was over. Almost a whole generation
had been wiped out. Just why the English victory was so complete
is still debated: but the slaughter was terrible. The Scottish King
fell under his own banner 'a spear's length from Surrey' – the
English leader. His left hand was almost severed, his throat gashed,
his head cut. With him fell an illegitimate son, the gifted young
Archbishop of St. Andrews: the bishops of the Isles and of
Caithness, the abbots of Inchaffray and Kilwinning: the earls of
Montrose, Crawford, Argyle, Lennox, Glencairn, Cassilis, Bothwell: and Errol, hereditary High Constable: scores of lords and

knights and men of good family, including one Craig of Aberdeenshire, who left an infant son, and another called Spottiswood, who left two little boys: and many thousands of common men. Prisoners were few.

> The stubborn spearsmen still made good
> Their dark, impenetrable wood,
> Each stepping where the other stood
> The instant that he fell.

With that slaughter ended the brief Golden Age in Scotland that James had toiled so hard, and so brilliantly, to bring about. He had married Margaret Tudor, Henry VIII's sister: he had brought even the Isles into peace, and had sent his trading-ships far. The lovely lantern steeple of St. Giles' – 'the thistle crown' – belong to his reign: the poetry of Dunbar: the first printed books by Chepman: ship-building at Dumbarton. Of his son who fell that day Erasmus, once his tutor at Padua, wrote: 'What hadst thou to do with war, disciple of the Muses, and of Christ?'

James had been a faithful son of the Roman Church, but there was no oppression in his kingdom. In 1494, when Lollards from Kyle in Ayrshire were brought to trial before him, he had heard them with interest and pardoned them freely. There had been Lollards in Ayrshire for nearly two hundred years: since Scotsmen at Wyclif's day had brought his teaching home with them.

James had been passionately interested too in music, in drama, in medicine and explorations, and in the clumsy magic of his day. He had wished much for Scotland.

Now there was nothing left but chaos: an infant king, little James V, aged two, jumping in Lyon King's arms and ordering him to 'Play, Davie Lyndesay!'

> There was nae lilting at our yowe-milking,
>   Nae daffing or dawning at break o' the day,
> But sobbing and moaning on ilka green loaning,
>   The flowers o' the forest are a' wede away.

They carried the bloody corpse of James IV to Berwick and laid it in the little parish church, together with his banner, his sword and the harness for his thighs.

It was England's triumph; and Henry fortunately had a small victory in France. The papal envoy, Ammonio, wrote to Erasmus:

'The flight of the French was not more grateful than your three letters received in camp. . . . I send you a skin of Cretan wine. Carmelianus has lately produced an epitaph of the King of Scots stuffed with womanish curses. It will shortly be printed by Pinson. Carmelianus is vain enough about it, but if the writer had not warned, he would have made the first syllable of *pullulare* short. One wonders that anyone likes such stuff'.

And Erasmus in return, 25 November 1513:

'May all the Muses and Graces, and Letters in general, be as unpropitious to me as they are to Carmelianus, if anything has given me this year greater pleasure than your letter! That's an oath more binding than Styx! . . . I am as thankful as if I had received the wine! . . . and wonder you could trust such scoundrels. The plague will prevent me being in London before Christmas, and partly the robbers.

When I saw the word *pullalure*, I exclaimed: "Hic scabies!" and when I heard who was the author, "It's like him!"

For some months I've lived like a cockle, shut up in my shell, humming over my books. Cambridge is deserted for fear of the plague: and when all men are there, there is not much company. The expense is intolerable: the profits not a brass farthing. I will throw out my sheet anchor this winter. If it succeeds, I will make my nest. If not, I will flit.'

On Flodden's bloody field some twenty new English knights were made of those who had fought with conspicuous gallantry. They included one Ralph Bowes, whose sons Richard and Robert when they grew up, fought in their turn against the hated Scots.

On the other side the young Earl Bothwell who fell, aged twenty-one, left an infant son: and a kinsman called Sinclair who died with him left an infant daughter. When these two children grew up they married, and had a son James, Earl Bothwell – 'Mary's Bothwell'. Among their common foot-soldiers that day were many men from the Lothians, including two called Knox, father and son: and one Sinclair whose daughter had married the younger Knox. We know nothing else of them, except that they came from Haddington and that 'some of them' were killed under Bothwell's banner. Their bodies may have added to the great mound of common dead that day.

But this year 1513 which took away so much glory from Scotland, brought a still greater glory to it: for it saw the birth of a boy to that poor, and possibly stricken home, of the Knox's in Haddington. There was already one son, William, called after his father: and this one was called John. It was a favourite name of those years: perhaps because it was once the name of Scotland's patron saint; or perhaps because of the new chapel in St. Giles's. At any rate, it was a good name to give the boy who became so great a leader to his own people – 'a burning and a shining light': a preacher whose voice, serving the word of God, became a trumpet-call to which they rallied.

PART ONE

THE CHURCH OF ROME

1

Master Knox and his Bairns

THE story of John Knox is the story of the Reformation in Scotland: and therefore of much more than that. It is the story of a vision of democracy – of brotherhood, education, freedom of mind: of a people called to be a kirk, and a kirk that was to be the soul of a people. It was the splendid vision of this one dour little man – plain Master Knox till the end.

What his enemies could not achieve in his lifetime, his own country has accomplished after his death. His memory and his last resting-place are deliberately dishonoured, and all but obliterated today. Scottish school-children are almost never taught anything about him, unless a little abuse. Edinburgh, and perhaps even his own congregation of the High Kirk of St. Giles', are as ashamed today as they were four hundred years ago of his views on equality and his belief in the common man. Yet nothing can soften, as nothing can wholly destroy, the gospel of this lonely, dauntless figure.

. . . . .

Flodden wiped out Scottish prosperity, national as well as personal. The English chronicles of the battle make mention of the Scottish corpses: when stripped (according to custom) their well-nourished fatness was notable. But the years that followed were lean years. Scotland was leaderless: Henry VIII a perpetual menace on the Borders. The shrewd small boy called John Knox saw from his earliest years the wastefulness of these wars. The flat Lothian lands round Haddington gave the easiest access to both countries, and so were the first and worst sufferers in all the raids. He may well have had a hard boyhood.

The eldest boy, William Knox, went to sea. We hear of no younger brothers or sisters, which strengthens the possibility that it was the father who was killed at Flodden. John Knox was the gifted lad – 'the lad o' pairts' – intended for the priesthood. He stayed on at Haddington Grammar school, getting his Latin. From there he went to college at St. Andrews. There is no official record of his career: only a tradition that he was outstanding.

Yet he left without a degree. He may have refused the compulsory oath against Lollardry. But he accepted ordination in the Church of Rome, in his local church of the Greyfriars, Haddington.

So here, where he began, he continued for the greater part of his life. He said mass in family chapels, he witnessed documents as a notary, he was mildly famous as a teacher of children. He neither preached nor wrote nor fought, apparently. While the first Reformers struggled and died, his quiet youth went past without event.

It was George Wishart who touched and wakened him.

Wishart was at St. Andrews before Knox, about 1528. In that year young Patrick Hamilton, cousin of the King, was burned alive for heresy. This talented lad, who had written a small book of Devotions, and music for a mass, had studied under Erasmus at Louvain: and after with the Lutherans at Hesse. When he came home to preach at St. Michael's, Linlithgow, great crowds came to hear him. Cardinal Beaton, the real power in Scotland, invited him to 'dispute' in St. Andrews, and Hamilton accepted the challenge. In a day or two, Beaton pounced. In twenty-four hours he had him arrested, tried, condemned and fastened to a stake outside St. Salvator's gate.

Ghastly blundering followed. The wood was green, and lit three times without materially burning him. Gunpowder gave him 'a glaze, skrimpling his left side': yet still he lived. At last they brought straw in armfuls, and by six o' clock it was at length finished.

Wishart, tall and dark, 'comely of personage', as one of his students wrote, was also acutely sensitive. He would never have gone to witness this horror: but he could hardly escape the reek of it. Later it was said: 'The reek of Patrick Hamilton infected all it blew upon.' For soon, says Knox, all Scotland asked: 'Wherefore was Master Patrick burnt?'

After graduating, Wishart was ordained parish priest of Montrose. Here the laird, Erskine of Dun, had founded the first Greek school in Scotland. Here Wishart, once a pupil, was now also a teacher, happy and secure.

But ten years later he was on the run. He had given his Greek pupils Erasmus's gospel to translate. Summoned by Cardinal Beaton, he had smelt again 'the reek of Patrick Hamilton', and fled to England. For a while he taught in Cambridge, and met Latimer, Ridley, Barnes the friend of Luther, and the monk Coverdale. In spite of his Scots accent, a contemporary notes, he preached well: so Cranmer sent him to preach in the church of St. Nicholas, Bristol.

He was promptly arrested. A few weeks later the Act of Six Articles, reaffirming both Henry's supremacy and Roman doctrine, became law. All who could not conform came before courts run on Inquisition lines. They were tortured, they were burned alive. Quite a few so suffered in Bristol.

Before such a court Wishart was also brought. He recanted, denied his beliefs on oath and submitted to Mother Church. On two successive Sundays he 'carried his faggot' in public penance and humiliation, first to St. Nicholas and then to Christ Church. Then he fled overseas. But Barnes was burned alive with two others at Smithfield the following year.

These were cruel years. Henry had waded to his divorce through blood, and then shed blood again. Rome had her martyrs too. Queen Jane Seymour knelt in vain for mercy on the prisoners of the Pilgrimage of Grace – that rising in defence of monasteries in the north. But Henry made a horrible slaughter, including even wives: and had the leader, Roger Aske, hung alive in chains above York until he died.

Did Knox hear tell of this, as of something far away? Yet Roger Aske had a relative, Elizabeth Aske, a sensitive, deeply religious woman, married to that Richard Bowes whose father had been knighted on Flodden field. She already had several children, and about this time she had another daughter and called her Marjorie. In the years ahead, Marjorie Bowes was wife to John Knox.

On the Continent the Reformers' struggles continued. Calvin, fellow-student with Rabelais at Paris, had published his *Institutio*, that Charter of the Reformation, and gone into perpetual exile in Geneva. (But Rabelais became a priest!) Now Bullinger took the place of the butchered Zwingli as People's Pastor, and head of the Swiss Church. Tyndale was betrayed by a man who borrowed money of him ('for it was easy to be had of him, if he had any'), and strangled and burnt in the Low Countries.

In Scotland, James V was planning revenge: revenge, after nearly thirty years, for Flodden. He had lost two small sons: but now his French Queen, Mary of Guise, was expecting a new heir. All that spring and summer he had gathered troops: and rumours flew up and down the Debateable Land. The attack was expected by the usual route through Berwick; and a body of decoy troops sent to Haddington. Knox surely saw them ride through. Meanwhile, early one September morning, the main body slipped across the Solway in the west, picking their way through a huge boggy moss. When the sun rose, the English were appalled to see this great host.

But it was an army without leadership, without inspiration, without even real purpose. Finally, the King's banner was unfurled; but none knew whether to advance or retire. 'Slughorns blew, and all was confusion.' With all the vividness of one who has heard a survivor's account Knox conveys the dreamlike unreality of that dawn of a battle that never came off. For if the Scots were uncertain what it was all about, the invaded English were not. With the speed of righteous anger they swarmed out, and with every weapon that came to hand they fell upon the host. And the ranks wavered and broke, and disorder took them: and those who escaped the English were swallowed by the bog.

James was waiting, tense and eager, at Lochmaben ('some say, Carlaverock'), when the news was brought to him. He retired broken-hearted to Falkland Palace, and took to his bed. While he lay there, sick to death, they told him the Queen had had a child, but it was a daughter. 'The De'il take her,' he said: and perhaps someone murmured 'Alas!' for he added: 'It cam' wi' a lass, and it'll gang wi' a lass.' With this pun he turned his face to the wall, the first of five Stewart monarchs to die in his bed. (Of the next three, two died by the axe.)

A sister of James III, Mary Stewart, had married a Hamilton, Duke of Arran and their grandson, called 'the great Duke', was therefore part-royal. He was now proclaimed Governor. It was a blessed moment for those who longed for Reform, for at that time he supported it. He had as his chaplains John Rough and Friar Williams, preachers of Reformation. Williams had preached in Haddington and round about and Knox had heard him. Men like the Earl of Glencairn, from Finlayston on the Clyde, Sir Henry Balnaves of Hallhill, and Wishart's uncle, Learmonth, came to court: men who were statesmen as well as Reformers. They planned peace with England, to end the wasteful wars and devastations, and projected a marriage between the infant princess of Scotland and little Prince Edward of England. Henry himself was set on the arrangement: he drew up several suggested treaties, and as soon as the roads were open – it was an exceptionally hard winter – deputations came and went.

In that same year of 1543 the Bible in English became legal in Scotland. 'Then,' says Knox with sarcasm, 'might have been seen the Bible lying almost upon every gentleman's table. The New Testament was borne about in many man's hands. Some alas! profaned that blessed word: so some that perchance had never read ten sentences in it had it maist common in their hand; they would chop their familiars on the cheek with it, and say: "This has lain hid under my bed-foot these ten years!" Others would glory: "How oft have I been in danger for this book, or stolen from my wife at midnight to read upon it!" '

That spring a deputation led by Glencairn, Balnaves, and Learmonth went south to negotiate with Henry. Henry was perhaps a little mellower: he had just married his sixth wife, a really nice widow. He was Katherine Parr's third husband, and she was deeply in love with someone else – with Tom Seymour, the Lord High Admiral: but mercifully she was prepared to see in Henry the Will of God. Cranmer married them in English, and she promised to be 'bonair and buxom in bed and at board till death us depart'. Coverdale was her almoner, so Reformers breathed a little more freely; and Wishart slipped back to Cambridge to his students there.

Wishart had been in Germany, and down the Rhine to Switzerland. He had translated Bullinger's *Second Swiss Confession of Faith:* a book Knox surely read then or later. Now that the news was so good he joined his uncle, Learmonth, and the Scots commissioners on their way home, and Spottiswood, a young priest from Glasgow, came with them. They rode north through a May-time England green from end to end. Every good thing must have seemed within their grasp: peace, prosperity, free trade, and, at last, freedom of worship. Wishart went back to the family estates of Pitarrow, and settled down there.

But a year later he was out again preaching in Dundee. The hope of peace had passed again for another generation. Mary of Guise had pretended to agree to the English alliance: but her whole heart always was set on union with France. She had been gracious to Ralph Sadler, the English envoy; had had the baby princess brought and unwrapped 'out of her clouts' to show him how healthy and pretty a child she was. Sadler wrote to Henry that she was 'as goodly a child as any I have seen of her age, and as like to live, with the grace of God'. But Cardinal Beaton, nephew of Patrick Hamilton's killer, joined forces with the Queen Mother. Then Arran changed sides and went over to them. He did penance for his heresy and, supported by the earls of Argyle and Bothwell, attended mass and received communion again from the hands of the Cardinal.

Now that they had the power in their hands, Beaton and the Queen Mother lost no time. They rescinded the English Bible, and renewed the persecution of the Reformers. They renewed the alliance with France, and so slighted and temporized with Henry that he sent both an army and a fleet north with the orders: 'Sack, burn and slay.'

The orders were carried out with horrible precision. The English fought no army, but slaughtered civilians, women, children, and aged; devastating village and field to within six miles of Stirling, where the Queen Mother and the infant Queen had taken refuge. Next year the abbeys of Kelso, Melrose, Dryborough, and Coldingham were laid in ruins; even Edinburgh was burnt ('Woe worth the Cardinal!' cried the women, seeing this destruction, and knowing he had been first to fly). This 'rough wooing' ended all sympathy for an English alliance. 'There is not so little a boy but would cast a stone at it,' wrote an envoy at one point to Henry. Mary was crowned Queen in September 1543, the thirtieth anniversary of Flodden, when she was less than a year old. Thereafter she was moved from place to place, as Henry plotted to capture her and the Queen Mother plotted to get her to France. French troops had already been brought in, with a Papal legate: 'and what the English left, the French took'.

In the chaos and misery of these days Wishart preached the abiding love of God and the life eternal: and crowds of helpless people gathered to hear him. But 'heretics' were doubly suspect as 'English sympathizers' and Cardinal Beaton issued a political writ against him for 'unlawful assembly'.

Wishart fled to Kyle in Ayrshire, that 'receptacle of God's people of old', where Culdees and Lollards and the clean air of the moors had bred freedom of mind. But there he came up against the Archbishop of Glasgow, in whose see it was. So he was on the run again: but where? He heard that plague had broken out in Dundee, and went back there; preaching, teaching, healing, nursing and working among the very worst cases: till men whispered, that he sought death. But no such easy road opened.

After the plague died down, he went back to the family estate, to his books and painting. But the conflict went on in his mind. Once he broke out: 'What do I differ now from one dead, save that I eat and drink?'

At Christmas 1545 after two years of English destruction, Cardinal Beaton invited Wishart to Edinburgh, with the old bait of a public discussion there. Wishart set himself to go. The debate was put off to Haddington: and there, to that wonderful rose-red kirk by the river 'the Lamp of the Lothians', where Knox was reader, he came 'at the end of the Holy Days called Yule, in a most vehement frost'. This was Earl Bothwell's land, and he was in the trap at last.

One night at least he dined with Maitland of Lethington, father of Mary's Secretary Lethington. This one was a poet and politician; and a compromiser. Other nights he stayed with the Douglases at Longniddrie or with the Cockburns, who were both summoned later for 'resetting' him. John Knox, tutor to both these families, was now Wishart's bodyguard. He carried an old-fashioned two-handed sword, perhaps a relic of Flodden. The small priest, poor and plain-bred, with his big sword, must have been a quaint contrast to Wishart.

Wishart had already preached in Inveresk and Tranent 'with like grace and like confluence of people'. Here in Haddington he began a series of sermons: but fewer and fewer people came to the cold, dark church. They were afraid of their overlord Bothwell, father of Mary's Bothwell. This Earl divorced his wife when his son James was nine: and was now setting his cap at the widowed Queen Mother, Mary of Guise. To please her he would burn or sell every heretic in Scotland.

One evening a little before service a letter was brought to Wishart 'out of the West'. How far hoof-beat and foot-step must have carried in that flat, frozen land! This was to tell him that the lairds of Kyle in the west could not come to his support at that time. He was abandoned: and turned in bitterness to the tutor-priest saying: 'he wearied of the world, since men wearied of God'.

Knox did not understand. He was surprised that Wishart should want to talk before preaching, for such was never his custom: puzzled to see him pace up and down in an agony before the High Altar: 'his very visage did proclaim the grief and alteration of his mind'. (Did he consider a new flight?) When a handful of people had gathered out of the darkness, he broke off his usual theme, and preached judgement, and prophesied the destruction of Haddington.

But he was calm when they came to supper together. They sang an evening psalm, a Scots translation of Psalm 51, published in Wedderburn's *Guid and Godly Ballads*.

> Have mercy on me, God of might,
>   Of mercy Lord and King:
> For they mercy it is set full right
>   Above all earthly thing.

He took good night 'as it were for ever' from them all.
In the night Bothwell's men surrounded the house, calling for

his surrender. Then at last Knox understood the danger, and would have drawn his huge sword: but Wishart took it from him, saying: 'One life is enough for a sacrifice – gang back to your bairns, Maister Knox! And God bliss you!'

When Knox, long years after, began to write his *History of the Reformation*, it was at that moment in his life that he began his story.

2

The Call

BOTHWELL lodged Wishart briefly in Edinburgh Castle, and then handed him over to Cardinal Beaton, as a favour to the Queen Mother. Beaton had him brought over the Forth to his fortress at St. Andrews in Fife. There this Prince of the Papal church kept his men-at-arms, and his treasure, his wine, his women and his seven acknowledged bastards, some of whom married into the best families. There also, in the thick, chill sea-tower, he kept a bottle-dungeon for his enemies. This is shaped like a Burgundy bottle, seven feet wide at the top, and cut twenty-five feet into the sheer rock to the bottom, which slopes steeply towards the sides. You can see it still, lit now by electricity. Into this black dungeon in January 1546 went George Wishart, priest, scholar and something of an artist, aged thirty-two.

Beaton wanted the consent of the Archbishop of Glasgow to Wishart's disposal: and at first this was a little embarrassing, for they were not then on speaking terms. The summer before there had been a special High Mass in Glasgow Cathedral in honour of the arrival from France of Monsignor Lorge de Mongomery to command the French troops in Scotland. Beaton's procession and the Archbishop's had met head-on at the Cathedral door, and neither would give way. The awful bitterness of clerical pre-eminence had possessed them: 'then rochets were rent, tippets were torn, crowns were knappit, and side-gowns wantonly wagged' . . . Glasgow had loved it.

Now they made it up, and the trial proceeded. Sub-prior Winram, a man with a conscience, preached at it. He heard Wishart conduct his own defence at first with wisdom. Then to a charge that he had called the mass idolatry he said: 'Once when

I was sailing down the Rhine, I met a Jew. When I asked him why he would not admit Jesus as Messias, he gave first, that if He were He that should come, he should not suffer such want and poverty to be seen: for he was to set all things right (for though Jews be poor they be never beggars). And second, that Messias would not break the Law which forbad all graven images: but your temples (he said) are full of idols to whom ye pray, and ye even adore a piece of bread, calling it God.'

He was condemned to be strangled and burnt the next day, 1 March. At dawn, by his request, Winram heard his last confession and the jailor brought bread and wine so that he might for the last time give thanks and take, and give. Cannon were trained on the crowd to prevent interference: and to them Wishart called out not to be horrified by his death, but to watch his face 'for they would not see it change'.

Early one May morning ten weeks later the drawbridge of the castle was lowered for the bringing-in of lime and stone, for the building which was the Cardinal's hobby. A small party of men loitered in – Kirkcaldy of Grange, with four friends – and asked for the Cardinal who had not yet risen. In a little, another small group of callers lounged in: and then a third, under Norman Leslie, the leader. Now the porter took alarm, and would have raised the bridge: but it was too late – he was knocked on the head and dropped in the ditch, while the others hustled out the guards and secured the postern.

The Cardinal by now was roused and sought to barricade the door of his room with the help of his chamber-child. But with sword and threat of fire the raiders broke in and called him to account. He died in his chair crying, 'I am a priest – ye dare not kill a priest!'

For a while his body hung over the battlements: but, the weather being warm for the time of year, he grew offensive. So after discussion – they would neither bury nor burn him – they salted him well down and put him in his own oubliette.

The ale-houses sang his requiem:

> As for the Cardinal, I grant
> He was a man we weel could want,
> And we'll forget him soon.

And yet I think that, sooth to say,
Although the loon be well away,
The deed was foully done.

Having got inside the castle, the rebels found it safer to stay there. The news spread fast. By 28 May eight shillings was paid to 'ane boy to pass to my Lord Argyle with ane closit writing . . . to show the slaughter of the Cardinal'. To the Queen Mother, the death of the Cardinal was dolorous. 'In him perished faithfulness to France and comfort to all gentlewomen, especially wanton widows.' Fear of reprisals rallied all sorts of people to the castle. There was Sir Henry Balnaves, the statesman: Sir James Balfour: Kirkcaldy, laird of Grange, who came to be called 'the first soldier in Europe'. At the other end of the scale, there were broken men, outlaws and deserters who had been 'put to the horn'. Amongst those who came as 'known heretics' was John Rough, the Ayrshire preacher who had once been chaplain to Arran, in his Reforming days: and there was an impartial observer in Sir David Lyndesay of the Mount, Lord Lyon King at Arms.

Sir David, that colourful person, stood by the throne. He was also faithful to Rome, though no man ever did more to ridicule and denounce the abuses of that church in Scotland. On 24 November five shillings was charged in the treasurer's accounts for making a copy for the castle of 'the Grit Cursing raisit upon Norman Leslie, the Laird of Grange and 'complices.' But what odds? Curses could be bought from the priests by anyone who had missed as much as a porridge-spirtle. Lyndesay himself had already made one, for nothing, for a priest whose hen-roost had been robbed:

Black be their hour, black be their part,
For five fat geese of Sir John Rowlis
With capons, hens and other fowlis,
Baith the holders and concealers,
Resetters and the proven stealers,
And he that clutches, seizes and damns
Bewitch the Devil their guts and gams,
Their tongues, their teeth, their hands, their feet
And all their body, haill, complete. . . .

He wrote the common man's view of ritual in *Kitty's Confession:*

> And meikle Latin he did mummle
> But I heard nocht but hummle-bummle. . . .

His greatest play, *The Three Estates*, was first performed at Twelfth Night, 1540 at Linlithgow Palace, in the presence of James V and his Queen. It was a great success, and often repeated. In 1952 it was the triumph of the Edinburgh Festival in a shortened version by Robert Kemp, performed before the Queen Mother and Princess Margaret. Unforgettable was Duncan Macrae selling relics:

> I am Sir Robert Rome-maker
> A perfect public Pardoner
> Admitted by the Pope. . . .
> I give to the Devil with good intent
> This woeful, wicked New Testament
> With them that it translatit.
>
> Since laymen knew the verity
> Pardoners get no charity
> Without that they debate it.
> De'il fell the brain that has it wrought!
> So fall them that the Book home brought!
> Also, I pray the Rood,
> That Martin Luther, that false loon,
> Black Bullinger and Melancthon
> Had been smoored in their cude. (cradle)
>
> Here is a relic long and broad
> Of Finn MacCoul the right jaw-blade
> With teeth and all togidder.
> Of Colin's cow here is a horn
> For eating of MacConnel's corn
> Was slain into Balquidder. . . .

The siege of the castle began with a long lull. It can be seen yet how strongly built and well placed it was. Mary of Guise sent to

France for ships to attack it: and the castle sent Norman Leslie and Sir Henry Balnaves to London to ask help from Henry VIII.

But Henry was dying, with no time or money for the Scots. His heir, little Prince Edward aged nine, was seriously educated in Reform: and his guardian Uncle Edward Seymour, Lord Somerset, was also of the new faith: so hope remained, though time ran out. Both sides must have watched the sea for sails, throughout the winter and into spring again.

In the castle there was no single binding force or leader for such an odd mixture of people; until there arrived in spring the little priest from Haddington with his three schoolboys. Their fathers being outlawed, they had been in hiding: and were now 'wearied of removing from place to place'.

Knox was now about thirty-four. He was 'below middle height' in an age of smallish people: very dark, with a long face, long nose and deep-set piercing grey eyes. His voice was strong, deep and harsh: and Peter Young mentions his hands – preacher's hands, apparently, with long, expressive fingers. There is a whole controversial literature on Knox's beard, but one thing seems fairly clear: Besa's 'Santa Claus' beaver, so widely known, is a libel. Besa's *Portraits* contain many obvious errors: and even in later life Knox's beard was expressly reported neither long nor full by people who knew him. He was fond of music and good company.

He had really wanted at this point to go abroad to the Lutherans – 'The schools of Germany' – as Wishart had done: 'of England then he had no pleasure, by reason that the Pope's name being suppressed, his laws and corruptions remained in full vigour'. But since these boys were given to his charge he must abide by his duty.

So he settled down quietly in the castle with the 150 odd souls now gathered there: and like any good schoolmaster he carried on steadily with the boys' course of study from where he had been interrupted. He taught them 'grammar and other human authors', Latin, of course, and possibly Greek, of which he knew something. They also had private lectures in the castle chapel on St. John's Gospel, which was for Knox the heart of the matter. And they had public catechism on their faith and Bible knowledge in the parish church of St. Andrews. It quite possibly was Calvin's

Catechism that Knox was already using, for he always admired it. To give it in public was always part of Knox's design for he was a firm believer in reaching and teaching adults through children.

He soon also 'fortifyed the preacher by his pen'. John Rough, sincere and well-loved, was 'not of the most learned', and much troubled in his ministry there by the attacks of Dean Annan, Principal of St. Leonard's College in the town. Primed by Knox he could deal with him: but he was not the man to rest on others' labours. He and Sir Henry Balnaves had perhaps slipped in to listen to the lectures on St. John as others did. At any rate they saw the greatness in the man and 'earnestly travailed' with Knox that he would 'take the preaching place upon him'. But he utterly refused, alleging: 'that he would not run where God had not called him.' Meaning, that he would do nothing without 'a lawful vocation'.

If all that was necessary to let him fulfil his destiny was 'a lawful vocation', then a skilled playwright and producer like Sir David Lyndesay would manage one for him. Sir David, Sir Henry and John Rough laid their heads together in a godly conspiracy: and produced a dramatic incident worthy of *The Three Estates*, and incalculable in its effect.

On a certain Sunday Rough preached on the election of ministers: 'What power the congregation, however small, had over any man in whom they supposed and espied the gifts of God to be; and how dangerous it was to refuse, and not to hear the voice of such as desired to be instructed.' It must have been quite a long sermon, with several 'heads' to the argument. But the tension and the silence must have grown as the preacher reached the climax: and called upon Knox, who was taken completely by surprise:

'Brother, be not offended that I speak to you what I have in charge, even from all those present, which is this: In the name of God, and of his Son Jesus Christ, and in the name of these that presently calls you by my mouth, I charge you, that ye refuse not this holy vocation.'

Then he turned to the congregation, and asked them:

'Was not this your charge to me? And do ye not approve this vocation?

They answered: 'It was; and we approve it.'

They must have waited for Knox to reply; and surely he tried to answer. But the moment was too much for him. He broke down, into 'abundant tears', and fled to hide himself in his own room. 'His countenance and behaviour, from that day till the day that he was compelled to present himself to the public place of preaching, did sufficiently declare the grief and trouble of his heart; for no man saw any sign of mirth in him, neither yet had he pleasure to accompany any man, many days together.'

It was a call not only to difficulty and responsibility, but to persecution and exile and almost certainly to a death like Wishart's. That Knox greatly valued his vocation is shown in his lasting affection for St. Andrews 'where God first opened my mouth': and in his attitude towards his calling. He spoke years after of 'a reverential fear of my God, who called me, and was pleased of His Grace to make me a steward of divine mysteries, had such powerful effect as to make me utter whatever he put in my mouth, without any respect of persons.'

In the Book of Order at the Reformation, it is expressly stated with reference to calls that: 'the presentation of the people must be preferred'. No one was ever to be violently intruded or thrust upon a congregation: 'But this liberty with all care must be reserved till every several kirk'. In our cyclostyled world it is still one of the last independent and romantic quests to see some kirk's deputation set out, possibly disguised in un-Sunday clothes, to quarter Scotland for a promising preacher for their kirk.

Knox sometimes made a prophecy: and while generally these could be credited to his own discernment, he had flashes in later life of genuine second-sight. He valued this gift, as a sign that his calling was as real as that to the prophets of the Old Testament, of whom it was the peculiar function.

He was not long in consummating his call. One of the reasons he had to accept, he says, was because Dean Annan had finally entrenched himself behind the accepted sovereignty of the Roman Church: a full and final answer was called for. Preaching indeed was vital, for few of the people could read 'but all might hear'. The answer was to be made in a sermon in the parish church, under the liberal auspices of Sub-Prior Winram. There must have been a tremendous convocation of people, both from the town and from the castle, to hear this tussle. Besides Balnaves and

Rough and the Lord Lyon and Winram and 'many canons and friars of both orders', there was also the university contingent, including John Major, Knox's old professor. And this was, he says, the first time he had ever preached!

He took a text from Daniel, and demolished all Annan's argument in good style. It was a powerful sermon, of good Reformed doctrine: but it had not that sense of new horizons, of original authority, which is characteristic of his later preaching.

The congregation were gratified. Some said: 'Others sned the branches of the Papistry, but he strikes at the root.' Others: 'Maister George Wishart spake never so plainly, and yet was he burnt: even so will this one be.' The Laird of Nydie said: 'The Tyranny of the Cardinal made not his cause the better, neither yet the suffering of God's servant made his cause the worse. Therefore, we would counsel them to provide better defences than fire and sword: for men now have other eyes than they had.' Sir David Lyndesay turned the sermon into rhyme, and later put it into the mouth of one of his characters.

Shortly after this, Rough left the whole ministry in Knox's hands and left the castle to go south, possibly to stir up support. Knox then disputed in public in the town, with Winram in the chair and almost openly sympathetic. His opponent was one Friar Arbuckle, who became 'so wandered in the mist' (i.e. of his own arguments) 'that he fell in a foul mire'.

There was now a good measure of discipline within the castle, due to Knox and his preaching, and good relations with the town: though Winram was to receive complaints from his superiors for that. For the first recorded time in Scotland, Knox spread the Holy Table, first in the embattled castle and then openly, by will of the people, in the parish kirk: and priest and layman, noble and commoner, stout citizen and broken man, broke bread together and passed the common cup from hand to hand. This was the Table of the Lord, with its complete dignity and complete democracy: the expression of the belief of the worth of every man, the nothingness of any man. A meal not less a mystery for being made with common bread in common daylight, as was His own.

This was the true heart of the Scottish Reformation: as it has remained the true expression of the Scottish soul.

3

The Galley-Slave

IT was a pleasant day at the end of June 1547 when sails were at last sighted standing in from the North Sea. The excitement in the castle must have been intense: and bitter the disappointment when the Castilians made out, not the red cross of St. George of England, but the gold *fleur-de-lys* of France.

There were twenty-one galleys, under the command of Admiral Leone Strozzi, Prior of Cupua, who combined navigation for France with good works for the Church of Rome. He had brought the unwieldy fleet intact from Marseilles, a considerable feat.

The galleys waited for the Queen's troops to come overland, and then the assault began. At first those in the castle were quite cocksure. Somerset was raising an army, it might yet be in time: or his brother, Lord High Admiral Tom Seymour, might arrive any day with ships to their rescue. Knox had no such illusions and told them bluntly that they should make ready for the worst. Soon cannon were mounted on the steeple and towers of the abbey, and could fire right down on the castle, and the galleys attacked from the sea. Day after day, the besieged waited for the help which never came. Their one stroke of victory must have been the thing they remembered after with greatest horror: it was firing into a daring galley which came too close inshore and grounded, and which they nearly sank. They had a close and dreadfully clear view of what happened among the chained and crowded slaves on the rowers' benches when the shot smashed among them and the sea came in.

Plague broke out in the castle, and after holding out for two months they surrendered. Their treaty promised them a passage to France and freedom there. The Reformers had not looted the Cardinal's treasure, but the galleys wasted no time in loading everything moveable. They were so deep-laden when they sailed that they scraped on the back of the rock-ledges leaving the bay. The popular song in the ale-houses that summer had a chorus:

> Priesties, content ye noo, noo, noo, Priesties content ye noo,
> Norman and his company have filled the galleys fu'!

The galleys finally anchored in Rouen, and the treaty was not kept. The chief men were imprisoned in Mont Saint Michel, Cherburg, Brest; and Sir Henry Balnaves in the old castle up above Rouen. Lesser men and servants, including Knox, were chained as galley-slaves. They lay at anchor at Nantes on the Loire all winter 'miserably entreated'. The cold in mid-stream must have been intense. A galley-slave's shelter was his bench, his food the barest rations above starvation: there was no question of privacy or sanitation. The stench of the galleys was proverbial, and galley-fever prevalent. But slaves were expendable.

Yet, though heretics, the men were Scots, ancient allies against the English. Scots had fallen at Crécy, Poitiers, Agincourt: the Captain of the King's Guard was traditionally a Scot: a Scots High Constable of France had given Henry V his first defeat; Scots had marched in triumph to their own tune (ancestor of *Scots Wha Hae*) when Jeanne d' Arc crowned the Dauphin at Rheims: and a Scots page had gone with her to the market-place of this same Rouen when the English burnt her. Therefore these prisoners must be converted. Monks and priests 'travailed' incessantly with Balnaves, arguing, preaching, insisting, threatening. But he stood firm: and wrote a *Justification of Faith*, which he contrived to show Knox, and get his advice upon. Knox was delighted with it, helped in its final form, and was bitterly disappointed that it disappeared after being smuggled out of the country. It was not till after the deaths of both Balnaves and Knox that it was found again at Ormiston. Knox had written a *Summary and Epistle* to it 'as much as incommodity of place and imbecility of engine could allow'. It finished with this prayer:

> 'Hear. O Lord, and grant that as now with pen and ink, so shortly we may confess with voice and tongue the same before Thy congregation.'

It was dedicated to the faithful at St. Andrews: and its writing must have helped both men to get through that first weary winter.

In the castles of Cherburg and Mont St. Michel the Lesleys, who afterwards returned to Rome, and the Lairds of Grange and Pitmilly who remained Protestant, were all pressed to go to Mass, and all refused. The attempts to convert the galley-slaves were cruder. Knox's galley was called the *Notre Dame*, and dedicated to Our Lady. The galley-slaves were paraded in chains to hear Mass and Salve Regina's sung in her honour. They were threatened with flogging and torture if they did not bow down to the Mass. 'But they could never make the poorest of the company to give reverence to that idol.' Beyond question, it was Knox's spirit and the flame of Knox's conviction which gave them in time of trial that unity and comradeship which afterwards they lost. It was Knox, the children's tutor, who made and kept them Protestant at risk of their lives: it was to Knox they turned when, day after day and many times a day, they wondered if ever in years, or even in this life, they would be free? But the conviction in Knox was that he had not been called to die like a rat in a hole: and 'his answer ever was from the day that they entered in the galleys, that God would deliver them from that bondage, to His glory, even in this life'.

How much they instinctively turned to him is shown by the fact that somehow a message was smuggled through from the Laird of Grange and the younger Lesleys in Mont St. Michel, asking Knox if they might with safe conscience break their prison? Some of the other prisoners feared this might bring greater hardship on themselves: but Knox had no hesitation in saying that this was a selfish fear, and they might take any chance for freedom, provided only that no blood was shed, 'for to that he could never consent'. On Twelfth Night then, 'the Feast of Kings', the guard were so drunk the prisoners locked them all up and got out. But the French boy who helped them stole their money and went off to act as informer: so they had to change clothes and separate. It was over a year before they all 'in beggars' garments' managed to reach England.

In the galleys, Knox maintained his determined stand: not for defiance merely, but in loyalty to that Light he had seen. Knox can never be understood if it is not realized that first and last he was a

priest. To name these hell-ships after the mother of God was
blasphemy. To bring slaves by force to bow down to her image
was to degrade religion to crude idol-worship. To hang a likeness
of Mary with the Babe in her arms, simpering pleasantly down
on the agony of His brothers, was to make such nonsense of His
Gospel as shut men out from its truth for ever. Only men to
whom both Mary and Christ had become meaningless symbols
could have done such things. This was to Knox the unforgivable
sin of the Roman Church. This was in fact idolatry. Carlyle
said of Knox: 'He clung to sincerity as a drowning man to a
cliff.'

Once the 'patron' – captain – of the galley and his lieutenant
amused themselves urging the Scots heretics to kiss 'a glorious
painted lady' who had been brought aboard for adoration. Knox
steadily refused, so the 'painted brod' was forced between his
manacled hands: but he, snatching his chance, managed to toss
it overboard, crying, 'Let "our lady" save herself – she is licht
enough, let her swim!' This was not narrow-minded antipathy to
works of art: it was jealousy for the living God. After that, the
heretics were abandoned to their own damnation.

How, in fact, were Knox and Balnaves, and the other prisoners,
able to get in touch with each other in their various prisons?
Knox at least can have had little about him for bribes. There is a
possible solution in the autobiography of Sir James Melville.
Melville was sent to France by Mary of Guise about this time, to
be a page to the little Scots Queen, perhaps so that she would not
forget her Scots speech. When Melville reached court he was
taken into the train of Anne de Montmorenci, High Constable of
France: so that in fact he saw little of Mary. But he left the most
fascinating series of pictures: of himself, of France: and later of
Edinburgh and of Queen Elizabeth: and of Mary at Holyrood.
To read of the start of his career is like a Dumas novel, with all
the encounters at inns, the pretty girls, the narrow escapes. And
then the slow, cumbersome set-piece of mediaeval battles, lit by
flashes of chivalry: and quiet moments when one could sit down
at a barber's to have a wound dressed.

Melville hoped one day to make his name and his fortune: for
he had nothing when he went to France but his sword and his
boy's ambitions. He dared not openly support Reformers, and

when he did good deeds to fellow Scots in misfortune, he thought it wiser not to record them. So all he puts in his *Memoirs* is the tantalizing fragment: 'Mr. Henry Balnaves loved me as I had been his own son, by reason of some acquaintance I had with him in France, and small services I had done him there, during his banishment'. Possibly the services included the smuggling of notes and messages, and even of the *Justification of Faith*.

With the spring, the galleys were fitted out and put to sea: and they cruised north to the Scottish coasts again. It cannot have been easy for the small priest to bend, half-naked, to the great sweeps, under the lash of a whip that had no reason to pass him over. It was possibly still more bitter to find that their reason for going north was to cover fresh landings of French troops: to watch for the English shipping that might try to intercept them.

Somerset's looked-for army had reached Scotland just six weeks too late to save the Castle of St. Andrews. They won a savage battle at Pinkie, not far from Edinburgh itself: and made such a heavy slaughter that it finally determined the Scots against the possibility of an English marriage for their little Queen.

When the English danger was acute, she had been taken for safety with her 'four Maries' for playmates, to the island of Inchmaholme on Mentieth. After Pinkie, throughout that winter and into the spring when Knox's galley came north, French and English fought over Scotland. The French had some success too: and at one point, as Knox notes, Sir Robert Bowes of the Borders was defeated and made prisoner.

The English had made their headquarters in Haddington, and the French besieged it in force. The lovely 'Lamp of the Lothians', where Knox had been reader and Wishart had preached his last sermon, was battered half into ruins: and is so to this day. Mary of Guise had worked long and patiently to bring Scotland under France. At last, by the Treaty of Haddington, dated 29 June of that year 1548 the little Queen was betrothed to the Dauphin, eldest son of Henry II of France, and contracted to be brought up in France with her mother's people. The Scottish nobles finally agreed, though it was not exactly a free vote. 'Lord Elcho, a bloody man, sware with many God's Wounds that they wha wad not do so, wad do worse!' The French, having then 'gotten the bone for which the dog did bark', abandoned the siege. But not before all George Wishart's prophecies of death, destruction, fire and plague had been fulfilled on the unhappy little town.

Little Queen Mary, aged not quite six, was smuggled across to Dumbarton Castle, which is built on a volcanic plug that juts out into the Clyde, rather like a ship itself. The five little Maries must have enjoyed it thoroughly. That summer Admiral Villegaignon arrived in the Clyde with four galleys, and Mary of Guise received them on the Rock, and handed over the little Queen.

The galleys had to round the Mull of Kintyre, negotiate the west coast and the stormy north of Scotland, and so sail south again before they reached France, on 13 August. Mary, a pretty, lively child of high spirit is reported to have enjoyed the voyage: and, still more, the royal welcome King Henry II had arranged for her.

She was soon a favourite with the French King, who liked to talk to her and gave her the charming nickname of 'Reinette' – Queenlet. But his Queen, Catherine de Medici, saw in her a tool of the de Guises, the real rulers of France: and always hated her. Besides Mary's little fiancé, later Francis II, Catherine bore another six delicate children. Five of them were crowned, and all of them died childless.

Mary was seldom at Court as a child. She stayed with her grandmother, the Duchesse de Guise, on the vast family estates at Joinville. It cannot have been gay: but it would be tremendously grand. The de Guises were mortally proud, powerful, rich and religious. And what a religion! The Queen's grandfather was known as 'The Butcher of Alsace' for his massacre of the Huguenots there. One uncle, the soldier, fought to exterminate the Protestants wherever they could be found. The other, the Cardinal and Mary's chief adviser and mentor, was famed for his depravity, even in that age. It was he who later introduced the Inquisition into France, and was himself, presumably from choice, the Chief Inquisitor. He was too sophisticated to believe deeply in Rome: but he fully understood the menace of democratic Protestantism.

'And so,' wrote Knox, when an old, discouraged man: 'our Princess was sold to go to France, to the end that in her youth she should drink of that poison that should remain with her all her lifetime, for a plague to this realm and for her final destruction.'

If life was now formal, religious and strict for Mary, it was also sumptuous: she had abundance of the rich clothes she loved all her life, she had magnificent surroundings, and there were armies of abject servants to wait upon the de Guises. She was also admired, praised, flattered, for everything she said and did. Mary, who had once screamed at Cardinal Beaton in his robes, that he was the 'Red Etin' of the fierce north fairy-tales, was now brought up like a fairy-tale Princess.

In England, another little girl a few years older was brought up like the traditional step-daughter of the tales. Elizabeth Tudor's governess had written to Henry's chancellor, not so many years before, on behalf of the child who had neither 'gown nor kirtle, nor petticoat, nor no manner of linen, nor smocks, nor kerchiefs, nor vails, nor body stitchets, nor handkerchiefs, nor sleeves, nor mufflers, nor biggens.' But she had the gift of that most discerning fairy godmother: 'a little misfortune'.

Knox might have seen, (though probably didn't) Mary's galley slip past with its escort in August. Towards the end of that long summer's sweating at the oars he fell ill. It may have been typhoid or dysentery, or just some filth disease endemic to the galleys. He became so bad he was at last unchained and laid in the well of the ship, where he sank into such hopeless weakness and lethargy that everyone, himself included, expected he would shortly die. In this black well of despair he made the cry of the psalmist his own:

'Have mercy upon me, O Lord; for I am weak: O Lord, heal me; for my bones are sore vexed.

'My soul is also sore vexed: but thou, O Lord, how long?

'Return, O Lord, deliver my soul: oh save me for thy mercies' sake.'

Years after, writing on prayer, he said: 'This was not written for David only, but for all such as shall suffer tribulation to the end of the world. For I, the writer hereof, in anguish of mind and vehement tribulation and affliction, called to the Lord when not only the ungodly, but even my faithful brother, yea and my own self, judge it my cause to be irremediable.' And again: 'If we call constantly to God, beyond expectation of all men He shall deliver. The cause I am so long and tedious in this matter is, I know how hard the battle is . . . I know the grudging and murmuring complaints of the flesh . . . I know the anger and indignation against God, calling all his promises in doubt . . . against which rests only faith, wherein if we earnestlie continue, He shall turn all to gladness: for with experience I write this and speak.'

Did the slave-master signal Knox out for special contempt, that he speaks so bitterly of 'the ungodly'? It is very possible. The 'faithful brother' that he speaks of was a fellow Scot, James Balfour. He after proved a complete opportunist, ready to sell body or soul, or anyone else, to the highest bidder: and when chased from Scotland came to a bad end in Sweden. But as a fellow-prisoner he had been a loyal friend. Apparently he too had been released from his oar, to tend his comrade in extremis. In an attempt to rouse him from his deadly lethargy, he raised him up to a port hole and asked, pointing over the endless billows, 'if he knew where the was?' Perhaps the sound of bells carried faintly to them from the steeples of far St. Andrews town.

'Yes, I know it well,' whispered the prisoner, 'for I see the steeple of that place where God first opened my mouth in public to His glory; and I am fully persuaded, how weak so-ever I appear, that I shall not depart this life till that my tongue shall glorify His godly name in the same place.'

From that hour he began to live: and steadily recovered, though shattered in health, and in constant pain and weakness for the rest of his life.

In his work on prayer he also says that there are some to whom God 'gives to drink, before the maturity of age, the bitter cup of corporal death, that thereby they may receive medicine, and cure from all infirmity'. This fellowship of suffering, of those who have passed through the dark valley, is a mystery and a hidden strength. Knox's physical loss, in weakness and in pain, was outweighed by the gain of a rock-bedded faith. He could look thereafter on all the terrors and the treasures of this world with changed eyes.

This then was the true birth of the Kirk of Scotland, in the stinking hold of the French galley *Notre Dame*, rolling in the grey North Sea.

PART TWO

THE CHURCH OF ENGLAND

4

Chaplain to Berwick

VERY early in 1549 Knox was released, probably in an exchange of prisoners, and made his way to England. There the reign of young Edward VI, Henry VIII's only son, made a little bright patch of toleration: a sweet 'taste of freedom'. Later, Knox called it 'that great rest'.

Edward VI had been crowned in London in February 1547 aged nine and a half. He wore white velvet and silver brocade, and rode a white pony. Delicate though he was said to be, Tudor determination, of which he had his full share, carried him through the exhausting coronation service. At the same time his uncle Edward Seymour, Lord Somerset, had himself installed as Protector, also with the most elaborate ceremony. The people of England watched: and since nothing in particular was done for them they helped themselves as best they could. For between Westminster Abbey and Westminster Hall Edward rode over 'fine cloth, at least twenty lengths': but after he had passed, and before the foremost nobles in the procession could reach it, it disappeared: 'for whosoever could cut a piece off, took it for himself'.

That was Somerset's best year, when he rode north with his army: too late to save the castle of St. Andrews, but still able, though largely by luck, to win the battle of Pinkie with its heavy losses to the Scots. He was hailed as a hero in return, though indeed he had gained nothing in the north but fresh hatred.

The Protector's brother Tom, the Lord High Admiral, had also an eye to power. He made the widowed Queen his mistress and then his wife. She had always been deeply in love with him. Then he collected the young princesses Mary and Elizabeth, and the Lady Jane Grey. It must for a while have been a happy household. But, being Tom Seymour, he had to start flirting with red-headed Elizabeth. It began in fun, Katherine knowing: but she came on them one day in each other's arms, and sent Elizabeth packing.

Not long after, Katherine had a daughter, her first child by four husbands: and a few days later she died. Then Tom seemed to lose all sense and discretion. He plotted madly, he was discovered and condemned. By the time Knox reached London he was in the Tower: and in March he died: 'very dangerously, irksomely and horribly', as Latimer put it in a funeral denunciation: for he cursed all religions impartially on the scaffold, and fought the headsman with his bare hands while he chopped with his axe.

Elizabeth, implicated in part, was closely watched and constantly questioned. She said nothing. Her inquisitors told her of Tom's death, testing her: but the girl who had learnt so much so fast looked unmoved, saying only, after a little, 'This day died a man of much wit but little wisdom.'

In spite of that short, bitter struggle for power, Knox would find the little King genuinely bent on making his father's church a living reality. Somerset, too, was sincere in his belief in Reformation: he had written a religious book and Calvin had dedicated a Commentary to him, but the vital inspiration was that of the King – 'Such a one for his age as the world has never seen', wrote Knox. When his beloved tutor, Sir John Cheke, was seriously ill and thought to be dying, Edward announced at breakfast: 'He will not die. I have begged his life from God, in my prayers this morning, and have obtained it.' When Bucer, one of the religious refugees, whose wife and children had died of the plague, felt the cold bitterly in the Cambridge winter, Edward sent him 100 crowns out of his own very scanty pocket-money to buy a stove. Said Knox, 'What gravity above age, what wisdom surpassing all expectation of man and what dexterity in answering all questions proposed were in that excellent Prince the ambassadors of all countries, even mortal enemies . . . as the Queen Dowager of Scotland could and did testify.'

There was a measure at last of toleration: the Princess Mary was allowed to keep her Mass, but everywhere Reformers were welcome to preach. The Cambridge men breathed freely, taught widely: Archbishop Cranmer, Bishops Latimer and Ridley, Coverdale, the translator of the Bible who had once been Barnes's monk and then Katherine Parr's almoner: and now another 'Schottish-man born' – John Knox to take the place of George Wishart.

Religious refugees flocked in, such as Peter Martyr of Florence, John a'Lasco (Laski?) of Poland, Bucer and Ullmer, Fagius and Tremellius the Jew: and other Scots like MacBriar, and Willock the ex-Franciscan, both of Ayrshire, and John Rough, lately chaplain to the castle at St. Andrews: Seton was now a London preacher, McAlpine a canon of Salisbury Cathedral, and McDowall a bishop's chaplain there. Williams was preacher in Bristol. Schoolmen like Aylmer, Roger Ascham and Grindal taught King Edward and Princess Elizabeth and Lady Jane Grey. Bishop Hooper returned from overseas with a wife. Foxe married, and Parker, Master of Corpus, sought out the incomparable Margaret to whom he had been silently vowed for seven long years. Even Mrs. Cranmer emerged from seclusion, if not literally from a chest.

It was probably Sir Henry Balnaves who took Knox in in London, and clothed him, and recommended him to the King. Sir Henry would be well known at Court for his many embassies there. It is possible that Lyon King, Sir David Lyndesay of the Mount, Knox's old admirer and impresario, was at Court too as Ambassador to speak for him. In any case, the new Church was desperately short of real preachers: so very shortly Knox was appointed chaplain to Berwick, that border town whose medieval walls are still whole and complete. Here once again he was treading in John Rough's footsteps, for he had been preacher there, and had married a Scotswoman: but now he had gone to a new living in Hull.

Knox found this, his first real charge, a meeting-place for trouble. Berwick has changed hands several times, being finally ceded to England seventy years before. It was full of the broken men of both nations, and it had a large unruly garrison of over six hundred men. One of Somerset's correspondents wrote at this time: 'There is better order among the Tartars than in this town . . . no man can have anything unstolen'. He goes on to describe

how soldiers stole from townsfolk, and they in return shut their
doors in the faces of the war-wounded and crippled, and left them
to die in the streets. The continuing war between Scotland and
England must have added to the bitterness; for Berwick was near
enough to the scene of Somerset's massacre at Pinkie two years
before. And it was still only thirty-six years from Flodden, from
whose bloody field the corpse of James IV had been carried 'with
his sword, his banner and the harness for his thighs', to lie in this
same little parish church where Knox was now preacher. Englishmen in green-and-white coats mixed with Scots conscripts from the
Lothians, at present in English hands, wearing red St. George
crosses back and breasts. There must have been plenty of hatred on
both sides. And the north had always been loyal to the Pope. It
had heard the bells ring backwards for the Pilgrimage of Grace in
Henry's time, and had never forgotten the horrible cruelty with
which it had been put down.

Yet in a comparatively short time the small Scot from the
galleys had brought a measure of order and unity among them, by
the sheer power of his word. In one of his rare boasts he said
years later to Mary Queen of Scots, when accused of trouble-
making:

'In England I was resident only five years: the places were
Berwick, where I abode two years; so long in the Newcastle: and a
year in London. . . . I shame not, Madame, further to affirm that
God so blessed my weak labours that in Berwick (where commonly before there used to be slaughter by reason of quarrels
arising among the soldiers) there was as great quietness all the time
that I remained there as there is this day in Edinburgh.'

To Knox, delivered out of prison and out of despair, that first
green English spring must have been like a new heaven and a new
earth. Surely he preached as a man inspired, a man redeemed: a
man new-born into a miraculous world.

And he offered them a new religion: for he, a salaried clergyman
of the Church of England, spread before them for the first time
(and soon also for the last time), the Table of the Lord's Supper,
as he had served it in the besieged castle of St. Andrews. They
passed the common cup from hand to hand, they broke together
the common, everyday bread: English and Scot, citizen and
prisoner of war, owner and outcast, 'minister and congregation

sitting both at ane table, with no difference betwixt them . . . for at the Lord's Supper all are equal'.

To this period of Knox's preaching with power belongs his treatise on prayer, which is so vivid and so readable: so filled still with his profound experience in the galleys. And with it was a brief summary, no more than an outline, of his communion service, and it, too, is full of striking things.

By earthly and visible things set before us, He lifts up up to Heavenly and invisible things . . . herewith the Lord Jesus gathereth us unto ane visible body, so that we be members ane of another and make all together one body, whereof Jesus Christ is only head. . . .' And again: 'It is not His presence in the bread that can save us, but His presence in our hearts. . . .'

This last was a bold statement, for Edward's first prayer-book brought out that same spring, left the whole doctrine of the mass and real presence untouched, substituting only English for Latin. Indeed, it looked at that point as if the English Church would be merely a Roman Church without Rome. As Bishop Hooper put it: 'That which was the Mass of the Blessed Virgin Mary is now but the Communion of the same.' It was in the nature of the English genius to conserve: but Knox was feeling his way out to a wider horizon.

Baptism too, the other sacrament, was 'in face of the congregation', the whole family of God 'assisting' – Knox used the word in the French sense: and for both sacraments he insisted on the fullest instruction.

What Sunday, one wonders, did Knox first see a great lady come among his people with her servants and at least one of her daughters, Marjorie? Mrs. Bowes, wife of Richard Bowes, Warden of Norham Castle, sister-in-law of Sir Robert Bowes, Warden of the Marches; daughter-in-law of Sir Ralph Bowes of stately Streatham who was knighted on Flodden Field for his share in the slaughter of the Scots. She herself was daughter and heiress of the Askes of Aske, that ancient house which had supported the Pilgrimage of Grace. That Mrs. Bowes came to hear Knox at all was remarkable: that she became one of his disciples and ultimately gave up everything for the Reformed faith suggests that in sheer courage she was worthy of her breeding. She was a woman well over fifty then, with a grown family of at least twelve children:

George the heir, Robert the second son, who became a notable Ambassador, and ten daughters. The fullest genealogical account gives four daughters unmarried, five married into good families – and Marjorie.

Mrs. Bowes was a deeply religious woman who suffered from depression. She was seeking soul in a mist of doubts, who had too good a brain to accept any easy evasive answer. When Knox called her progress 'a very mirror to my own', he was perhaps thinking of the early happiness and security they had both known in the nursery of the Roman faith. When he argues with her it is as with an equal, and he uses the language of the mystics of the Early Church, whose writings they would both know. He told her once he had always delighted in her company ... 'for I find a congruence betwixt us in spirit'. His own unwavering faith was to her a rock in a weary land, and she clung to it with all her strength.

On her part she showed Knox a kindness and graciousness he had probably never known in all his life. After the rough and homeless years the sheer beauty and dignity of the great houses where she lived, and the way of life in them, must have been a revelation to him. He never to his dying day forgot 'the motherly kindness ye have shown as me at all times'.

Mrs. Bowes's eldest son George inherited Streatham, the magnificent mansion with its turrets and deer-parks. Here his descendants lived for two hundred years until another Bowes's heiress married John Lyon, Earl of Strathmore, and so founded the Bowes-Lyon family, a daughter of which married into the British royal house in the twentieth century, when Elizabeth Bowes-Lyon became Queen to George VI, and mother of Queen Elizabeth II.

Against the background of these great and lovely homes, and the magic of this first spring of freedom, there is another girl: Marjorie Bowes, the girl whose face we can never see. She too must have felt the compelling power of a born leader of men, and she too was part of his Vita Nuova.

5

'Dearlibelovit'

BUT for Wishart, Knox might never have left the Church of
Rome, which he had served for so long, Now, in the old
enemy-land of England, he came to love the English people and
English Church, so that he could easily have settled down there.

Life was sweet to him now as never before, in spite of the after-
marks of the galleys. In this lull of freedom he could preach; and
he felt the power of the word he was preaching. This his first
congregation was one he loved to the end of his life. And he must
often have been at Norham Castle, reading and expounding to
Mrs. Bowes, or walking under the apple-blossom with Marjorie.

In April 1550 he was summoned by his bishop – 'dreamy
Durham' – to a special public preachment at Newcastle. Knox
had written a 'Vindication of the Doctrine that the Mass is
Idolatry', and he may have been preaching in defence of this. It
was a great social occasion, held in the church of St. Nicholas
(which is still in use). The council of the north, part of the privy
council of the realm, attended: the Earls of Shrewsbury, Westmorland and Cumberland; Lords Wharton, Conyers and Dacres
of the north; Sir Robert Brandling, Lord Mayor of Newcastle;
and a great concourse of knights and their ladies, with the name
of Sir Robert Bowes high up on the list.

Knox was not intimidated. He preached with conviction and
boldness. Why did wide vision shrink to narrow cult? What made
liberating teaching grow into idolatry?

'Who burdened us with all these ceremonies, prescribed fasting,
compelled chastity, unlawful vows, invocation of saints and with
the idolatry of the Mass? The devil, the devil, brethren. . . .'

Mass became a magic spell, a pagan sacrifice, celebrated for
divers causes; some for peace in time of war, some for rain, some
for fair weather, some (alas, my heart abhorreth sic abominations!)

47

for sickness of bestial . . . the sacrifice of Christ's body and blood should not be used for taking away the toothache, or that our oxen should not take the lowing-ill, our horse the spavin, all manner diseases our cattle . . . yea, why was it wherefore ye would not say Mass, perversit priests?'

In the Papist Mass the priests are placed by themselves at one altar. They must be clad in a several habit whereof no mention is made in the New Testament. Is this necessary that things be "done decently and in order"? Dare they affirm that the supper of Jesus Christ was done without order and undecently wherein were seen no "disguisit vestments"? Should not all be taught by the plain word?

'In the supper of the Lord the bread was broken, the cup distributed amongst all according to hoiy commandment. In the Papist Mass the congregation get nothing except the beholding of your joukings, noddings, crossings, turnings, upliftings, which are nothing but a diabolical profanation of Christ's supper. Now jouk, nod, cross as ye list, they are but your own inventions . . . and finally brethren ye gat nothing but gazed and beheld while that one did eat and drink all.'

'It shall not excuse you to say the congregation is participant spiritually. O wickit Anti-Christs! Sayeth not Jesus Christ, "Eat of this, and drink of this, all do this in remembrance of Me?" Christ commandeth not that we should gaze upon it, bow, jouk and beck thereto, but that we should eat and drink thereof ourselves, and not that we should behold others do the same, unless we would confess the death of Christ Jesus to appertain nothing to us. . . .'

'Judge, brethren, what comfort hath this taken from us, whilk will that the sight thereof shall be sufficient. I would ask first, if the sight of corporal meat or drink doth feed or nourish the body? I think they will say Nay. And I affirm that no more profit receiveth the soul in beholding ane other eat and drink and their receiving no part thereof.'

'Neither hatred nor favour to any causeth me this day to speak, but only the obedience which I owe unto God.'

Were Knox's congregation riveted to their seats, if only with horror? Some, perhaps many, paid only lip service to Reformation, and returned obligingly to Rome under Mary. Durham, a real Bishop of Bray, argued on both sides and died a Papist. Wharton never forgave Knox, nor Brandling, nor Sir Robert Bowes: and Westmorland was hostile, If for that sermon alone his life was now forfeit in England as much as in Scotland should the Roman Church have power again.

But for those who groped, like Mrs. Bowes, for a living Lord among the dead-clothes of creed and policy, his voice rang as a trumpet-call in a new dawn. Its notes sounded throughout England, and echoed across the Border into Scotland. From now on men looked to him, listened to him: he was a marked man, if only because the common people came eagerly to hear him.

How reckless it was to speak out at that point Knox probably knew better than anyone: for he watched the political situation. 'Simple Somerset', Knox once called the Protector: and indeed Edward Seymour had good intentions towards the people; but he failed to solve the economic miseries of over-taxation and enclosures. First the Cornishmen rose. (They also disliked the new Prayer Book 'because it was in English' – they spoke Cornish). After they were subdued Jack Ket, a landowner, led a far bigger revolt in the north, where the landless men were even worse off. For a while he organized his army of the dispossessed successfully from 'the giant oak in Mousehold Heath', defeating mercenary troops. Then a bigger army, led by Dudley (later Duke of Northumberland) routed the rebels, and they were mostly hanged.

Dudley rode back to London a hero: and made a glorious figure in his great scarlet riding-cloak, his tall sons riding behind him. His father had risen from obscurity as one of Henry VII's tax-gatherers, but had lost his head, by popular demand, on that king's death. Dudley grew up poor in a rich man's household; and married his lord's daughter, who loved him devotedly. He had limitless ambition: and from this time began to take the centre of the stage.

By late autumn, Somerset fled by night to Windsor, taking the little King, whose chest suffered. Yet between bouts of coughing he came out to save the Protector from a hungry, angry mob. 'I pray you, good people, be good to mine uncle and ourselves.'

For a time Somerset was in the Tower. By the April that Knox preached in Newcastle he was free again, but his power had gone. He was building Somerset House with the passion of one who feels his time is short. Even his church had lost meaning to him. 'He became so cold in hearing God's word that . . . he would go visit his masons, and would not deny himself to go from his gallery to his hall for hearing of a sermon.'

Dudley was now the rising star: and he was not a Reformer but an opportunist. Most men took care to trim their sails.

That autumn the Queen Regent of Scotland landed in England, with a safe conduct. She had been visiting her little daughter the Queen of Scots in France: and also begging more men and money to repress her stormy kingdom. 'She maketh all at this Court weary from the high to the low,' wrote the English ambassador at Paris: 'such an importunate beggar she is'. . . . She was most graciously received by Edward, who still would have married the little Queen Mary Stewart: and she owned herself impressed.

These happy, quick years sped. In Knox's last spring in Berwick there was a sense of crisis in the air. A deadly epidemic, the sweating sickness, swept the country: and people died with startling suddenness. (Dudley lost a beloved daughter. 'The night before,' he wrote, 'she was as merrie as any child might be.') There was more unrest and discontent among the growing army of the poor. 'Old Father Latimer', preaching before the King and a great crowd in London, vividly described the miseries of the times. And it was after this particular sermon that Edward took steps to found hospitals and schools. Latimer was tumultuously popular, as witness an entry at St. Margarets, Westminster, of one and six-pence: 'for mending divers pews that were broken when Doctor Latimer did preach'.

At the end of May, Berwick had a great stir of excitement as troops and horsemen came pouring in. 'The Marquis of Suffolk' (Lady Jane Grey's father, later Duke) 'is gone into Scotland with 300 cavalry and some good preachers with a view of instructing and enlightening those parts of the country subdued within the last few years.' This was an optimistic term for the ravaged Borders and Lothians, who had their own ideas both of submission and religion.

Two of the preachers were ab Ullmis, the refugee; and Willock, the ex-Franciscan friar from Ayr, who had been one of the Marquis's household at Bradgate. Knox and Willock were close friends: and though soon separated for years and by thousands of miles, they remained friends and fellow workers till they saw the Scottish Reformation established in 1560. Now perhaps they had hopes to share, as they spoke of Scotland: and the parish church must have heard a rousing word from his pulpit.

Some hopes were justified. Both ab Ullmis and Willock often wrote to Bullinger at Zurich, the leading Protestant authority. (Willock's letters begin crisply: 'Health in Christ!'). Soon, ab Ullmis writes with surprise that they found many of the Scots people well-instructed in doctrine already! But whereas in England the new faith was mostly supported by the wealthy upper classes, they found that in Scotland it was the common people who treasured it. The Queen Regent and the nobles held by the Auld Alliance with France and the Pope, but the commons of Scotland were feeling their way to a soul of their own.

But yet any established Reformation in Scotland must have seemed at that time more distant than a dream; and meantime Knox had a church, a ministry ever growing in scope and power, and an English girl to be his true-love and his wife. For sometime late in that death-shadowed spring he, the low-born Scot, the middle-aged nobody, was handfasted before witnesses to Marjorie, daughter of the Bowes of Streatham and descendant of the Askes of Aske.

Their love-affair remains their secret. Knox, with his dour, pad-locked reserve, would have had it so. But some facts are clear enough. Marjorie must have been very deeply in love to make this secret contract, unknown to father, uncle and probably brothers. Marriage contracts were big business to the Tudors, and daughters at their parents absolute disposal. They were better to die virgin than to cheapen the family by marrying 'beneath them'. Marjorie's loyalty and devotion are unquestioned. Having risked so much to marry Knox, she followed him to exile and poverty; her sons were born in a strange land, and she was beside him through the last desperate campaign of the Reformation.

None of Knox's personal letters to Marjorie, to which he refers, have survived. Mrs. Bowes kept all hers, which her husband could have read from end to end with no other feeling but boredom. But whatever Knox wrote to Marjorie it was surely not spiritual exhortation. One letter of his to Marjorie Mrs. Bowes kept, because it dealt chiefly with her own doubts and fears: but it also gives a glimpse of Knox's touchy Scots pride. He wrote:

'The place of James teaches us, beloved sister, that in Jesus Christ all that unfeignedly profess Him are equal before Him and that riches nor worldly honours are nothing regardit in his sight; and therefore willed the Spirit of God, speaking in the Apostle, that such as are true Christians should have mair respect to the spiritual gifts wherewith God has dowered his messengers, not to external riches, which oft-times the wicked possess: the having whereof makes man either noble nor godlie, albeit so judge the blind affections of men. The apostle damns such as prefer a man with a golden chain to the poor: but hereof will I speak no more.'

He adds: 'I think this be the first letter that ever I wrait to you.' It is signed, 'your Brother, John Knox'.

Marjorie eventually brought a small dowry with her – 100 marks – yet Knox never touched a penny of it, leaving it intact to their sons when he died, adding: 'I of my poverty extended (it) to £500 Scots'.

The many letters to Mrs. Bowes have been made a ground for scandal against Knox, by detractors lacking better material. After she was dead, and he a done old man near dying, he sat down with disgust to refute those of his own day: to 'declare to the world what was the cause of our great familiarity and long acquaintance, which was neither flesh nor blood, but a troubled conscience upon her part, which never suffered her to rest but when she was in the company of the faithful, of whom (from the first hearing of the Word at my mouth) she judged me to be one'.

He goes on revealingly: 'Her company to me was comfortable, (yea, honourable and profitable, for she was to me and mine a mother), but yet it was not without some cross; for besides trouble and fasherie of body sustained for her, my mind was seldom quiet, for doing somewhat for the comfort of her troubled conscience, whereof this rude letter is the least and of basest argument, among many which lie beside me. . . .'

Perhaps his 'mother's' assistance in his secret marriage helped repay Knox for all his patience with her.

When and how did Knox marry Marjorie? We shall never know. Presumably it was before he moved on, late that summer of 1551, to the more important charge of Newcastle. There he preached in the church of St. Nicholas, and travelled round a wide area as far as Holy Isle, where Aidan from Scotland had first brought Christianity 900 years before. From there too he could still visit Marjorie. Were their handfast vows – legal Scots marriage – their only ceremony? Or, more likely, did Willock marry them some still summer dusk or dawn in the private family chapel?

There is a small clue that could be read as confirmation of this. The following year, newly returned to Oxford from a visit to Knox's district, Willock and ab Ullmis sent an urgent query to Bullinger. They asked: 'Whether that be a legitimate and true marriage which is contracted without the knowledge or consent of parents: and whether those persons can be said to live piously and lawfully in holy matrimony, who being so married continue in the same?'

True marriage it surely was. Whittinghame and Goodman, colleagues of Knox in Geneva, constantly asked to be remembered to Marjorie in their letters to Scotland. Calvin, when she died, wrote to Knox that she was 'one of the very sweetest of women, and 'a wife such as one seldom finds'.

As to what she meant to Knox himself, one can read a little between the lines. 'Dearlibelovit', he called her, and she 'who of earthly creatures is most dear'. She was in fact the one person in the world who really belonged to him. She was his harbour, his refuge; the only home he had on earth. So, in the middle of an acrimonious argument in State dispatches with Queen Elizabeth over the *Blast* – which he would not retract and she could never forgive – he suddenly breaks down to plead most humbly for her.

'I wrote unto you before in favours of my wife, beseeching you eftsoons to grant her free and ready passage, for my wicked carcase, now presently labouring in the fevers, needeth her service. I beseech you to grant unto the other men that cometh for my wife, passport to repair towards her for her better conducting.'

(Did Elizabeth accept that as a tacit victory for women?)

At the end, Mrs. Bowes rested her own people in English soil. One of Marjories' sons (perhaps both) lies buried in the beautiful great court of John's College, Cambridge: but her gallant dust lies somewhere beneath the hurly-burly of traffic that ebbs and flows round the High Kirk of Edinburgh. Her grave is unhonoured and, unless it lies with her husband's, unmarked.

The words of Ruth could have been hers: '. . . whither thou goest, I will go: and where thou lodgest, I will lodge: thy people shall be my people, and thy God, my God. Where thou diest, I will die, and there will I be buried. . . .'

Hers was indeed a Pilgrimage of Grace.

6

Chaplain to the King

K NOX's preaching in Newcastle brought him fame, not only in the north but throughout England. In December, less than six months after he went there, he was appointed one of the six special chaplains to the King, of whom Edward made personal note in his diary.

In the happy early years of Edward's reign Somerset had abolished all tortures, and burning for heresy. Cranmer had a spell of peace in which to draw up his incomparably beautiful prayer book. In the last two years of the reign the political climate changed but the fundamentals of the Anglican Church were still being laid down: and John Knox was one of those who helped to shape them.

This was not due to any policy on Knox's part. The autumn that he moved to Newcastle, Somerset was again in the Tower, and Dudley, Duke of Northumberland, now head of State. Yet on All-Saints' Day, 1 November, Knox dared to stand up for the fallen man, and savagely attacked the charges.

This must further have annoyed the Bowes men, for Sir Robert the elder brother was climbing with Dudley. That very autumn he was made Privy Councillor, and the next he was Master of the Rolls: and in some way Knox clearly helped him on, perhaps by a 'word at Court'. But now, even the most earnest Reformers doubted Knox's wisdom over this sermon. Was not Dudley a 'good Protestant'? He was far harder to the Romans than 'simple Somerset' had ever been: heresy-hunts and burning were revived, missals and stained-glass windows widely destroyed, the Princess Mary's Mass forbidden.

But to Knox the faith came first, policy second. He knew perfectly that to Dudley and Bowes and those like them the reverse was true: and if necessary they would change that faith to suit their policy. So he boldly preached 'a lamentation at the destruction of the vineyard of the Lord', and attacked the 'mortal hatred among those which ought most assuredly be knit together by Christian charity and by benefits received'.

In December Somerset was tried, and the people cheered as they saw the axe carried behind him with the blade reversed. But though cleared of treason he had been convicted of felony, for which the penalty was also death. Dudley was hard pressed for time: the Council met on 23 January and he dared not wait till then. Yet he did not care to disturb a specially merry Yule with an execution. Somerset had been tried without defence under a special Bill, tortured in the Tower – he who had abolished torture! – and moved twice under cover of darkness. It was actually the cold dark morning of 22 January that he was brought out to die. To the last the crowd did not believe it, 'Pardon! Pardon!' they shouted, seeing a horseman ride up, and began cheering. It fell to Somerset himself to say: 'There is no such thing, good people, there is no such thing.' And with 'Lord Jesus, have mercy', he laid his head on the block.

Edward has been blamed for not fighting for his uncle's life. The boy was never, as Knox saw clearly, 'lord of his own will'. He had to hold his own against skilled and ruthless schemers. Even his diary is carefully non-committal. Knox was a shrewd judge of boys; and it is good to see his own high opinion of Edward vindicated by a modern historian, Hester Chapman, in her book, *The Last Tudor King*.

Dudley now styled himself: 'Highness'. In June 1552 he rode north to inspect the Borders with the Earls of Pembroke and Huntingdon and so magnificent a train that, as he explained to Cecil ,whose people were plain, he tried not to stay with friends in case he ruined them. He heard Knox preach several times, and was clearly impressed by his native power. Impressed and also made uneasy. Here was one man in England not afraid to stand up and say what he himself believed right. There must have been great crowds to hear him, and many Scots slipping back and forth over the Border.

In autumn 1552 Dudley brought Knox south with him, riding in his great train of nobles and notables, and with an ack- nowledged place in it. Edward's revised Prayer Book was just going to press, containing a stricter demand for uniformity in compulsory kneeling to receive the sacrament. Knox's first sermon at court was a ringing attack on this. Why bring back compulsory idolatry and banish the fellowship of the common bread?

He caused a sensation. Printing was suspended, and the other royal chaplains were all consulted. There were great discussions: and finally a rubric, after called the Black Rubric, was inserted, to explain that kneeling did not mean worship of the bread. 'A runagate Scot did take away the adoration or worship of Christ in the Sacrament, by whose procurement that heresy was put into the last Common Book. So much did that one man's authority prevail at that time.' Cox, Cranmer's secretary, Dean of Windsor and passionate ritualist, hated Knox bitterly from thenceforth. His enemies were increasing with his fame.

The forty-five articles were now being drawn up, and were gradually reduced to thirty-nine. Here again Knox was consulted and had a hand in modifying parts. He preached constantly before the King, at Hampton, Windsor and Westminster, and was a favourite of the royal boy. He was given letters of recommendation from the Council to the shires, notably Bucks., and a trading-patent granted to his brother William, who now had a ship of his own of 100 tons burthen. In October, Dudley, who did not wish Knox back in the north, wrote to Cecil from his house in Chelsea:

'I would to God it might please the King's Majesty to appoint Mr. Knokke's to the office of Rochester Bishopric.' He gives four good reasons. 'First, to be a whetstone, to quicken and sharp the Bishop of Canturbury,' (Cranmer) 'whereof he hath need: and to be a confounder of the Anabaptists in Kent. Third, he should not continue the ministrations in the north contrary to this set forth here.' i.e. in the new Prayer Book. 'Also that the family of Scots, now inhabiting in Newcastle, chiefly for his fellowship, would thereafter not continue there, wherein many resort to him out of Scotland, which is not requisite.'

It was an excellent scheme, but like Dudley's other greater schemes it had one fatal flaw: it ignored the human factor. Knox did the incredible thing: he refused the Bishopric! Cecil, who through each changing regime of power-seekers had managed to remain a key man, must have been much amused. Dudley returned to the matter in November:

'And further, I have thought good to put you, and so my Lords, in memory that some order be taken for Knokke's, otherwise you shall not avoid the Scotts from out of Newcastle, which all things considered, methinks should not be forgotten.'

Early in December he wrote again, peevishly, to Cecil:

'Mr. Knox being here to speak with me saying that he was so willed by you, I do return him again, because I love not to have to do with men which be neither grateful nor pleasable. I assure you I mind to have no more to do with him but to wish him well.'

For once his judgement was sound, and Cecil must have chuckled. So there was one man in England not to be bought! From then on Cecil and Knox seem to have had a genuine respect, even affection, for each other.

In all his busy and important work, Knox worried about his flock in Berwick and Newcastle. He heard they were wondering if they must give up their own sacraments: wondering if, now that he was one of the great ones himself, he did not care. He wrote to them:

'Touching my life and conversation, I am even such yet in heart as I was in your presence, when I walked before you, not as a hypocrite, counterfeiting gravity yet lacking God's fear, but trembling for my sins I accompanied with you as your common brother, like the common sort of God's elect children . . . which my frailty I never yet concealed from you, nor yet pretended to advance myself other than God had appointed by preaching his truth.'

'Be not moved with every wind of doctrine, nor yet that ye doubt the virtue of that religion . . . preached amongst you by a wretched, weak and most feeble man. . . . To this gospel stick fast, brethren, come what trouble, chance or variety that even happen amongst men.'

'To touch the point, kneeling at the Lord's Supper I have proved no convenient gesture . . . but, because I am but one, and have in my contrar magistrates, Common Order and judgements of many learned I am not minded for that one thing to gainstand ... besides the breach of charity which always is to be avoided.'

He asks only that it be clearly explained that no superstition is involved.

'With life and death, dear brethren, I am at point; they are before me in equal balances.'
'These things I tell you that ye be not slandered and offended, as if some spirit of pride was late creepin in to me. Not so, dear brethren, I praise God of his gift and with tears pray for the continuance of the same.'

So much for fame. Then he adds bitterly:

'This day I am more vile and of low repute in my own eyes than I was the day my feet were chained in the prison of dolour (the galleys, I mean): or yet the day that I was delivered by His only providence. For better now I am taught of my own infirmity which, as it compelleth me frequentlie to groan, so God be praised it is a scourge and bridle that admonishes me never to glory in the flesh. ...'

But it was not pain and weakness alone which made him miserable at court: nor was it unkindness, for the King held him in personal regard and wished him in higher office; but the Court itself sickened him. It was heart-rotten. The placeseekers round Dudley were bad enough: it was a poor consolation to reflect that the papist party, quietly gathering strength in the background, were probably worse. There was old Lord Norfolk who kept his mistress in the same house as his wife, and who offered his friend, as soon as he should tire of his wife, a maid with pretty proper tettins'. There were Rich and Wriothesley, who had disjointed little Ann Askew: and others no better. Treachery was everywhere. Once more a knock on the door could spell death, with torture, dishonour, ruin: and no one was safe. The men who fawned on Dudley now were soon to sell him. While they all swore love and loyalty to the King they were counting his days as he coughed the winter out: counting their chances when he would cough his last.

Knox got back to Newcastle for Christmas Day, and preached a rousing sermon that echoed through England. He damned disloyalty, treachery, power-seeking and power-mongering, corruption in the high places: and all those hidden papists who only waited a change of authority to change once more their faith. He preached fearlessly in spite of Sir Robert Brandling, Mayor of Newcastle, wriggling with rage in his pew. 'For that wretched (alas!) and miserable Northumberland could not be satisfied till such time as Simple Somerset most unjustly was bereft of his life.' It was not the first time he had preached of judgement due for Somerset's blood. 'I was compelled of conscience oftener than once to affirm that such as saw and invented the means how the one should be taken away, saw and should find the means also to take away the other.' ... and again: 'What the Devil and his members meant by his taking-away, God compelled my tongue to speak in more places than one: and especially before you, and in the Newcastle, as Sir Robert Brandling did not forget of long time after (God grant he may understand all as fully. . . .)'

Brandling understood all right. He accused Knox to Lord Wharton, and the ominous summons now came to Knox's door. He had barely even time to scribble to Mrs. Bowes and Marjorie, for what might well have been the last time:

'Urgent necessity will not suffer that I testify my mind unto you. My Lord of Westmorland has written unto me this Wednesday, at six of the clock at night, immediately thereafter to repair unto him, as I will answer at my peril. I could not obtain license to remain the time of the sermon upon the morrow.'

Were these not the trials the Gospel promised?

'Rejoice, sister for the same word . . . doth certify us of the glory consequent. As for myself, albeit the extremity should now apprehend me, it is not come unlooked for. But alas! I fear that yet I be not ripe nor able to glorify Christ by my death: but what lacketh now, God shall perform in his own time. Be sure I will not forget you and your company, so long as mortal man may remember any earthly creature.'

That was as much as he dared say, lest his letter be seized and Marjorie dragged down with him. He had to answer 'as to an action for treason'. He had written his defence to Dudley, who sent it on to Cecil with a most amusingly patronising note. Dudley could afford to be generous, to indulge the King's preferences now with the end so near. He sent Cecil various documents:

'. . . also a letter from poor Knox by which you may perceive what perplexity the poor soul remaineth in at this present. The which, in my poor opinion, should not do amiss to be remembered by the rest of my Lords, that some order might be taken by their Wisdoms for his re-comfort. And as I would not wish his abode should be of great continuance in those parts' (i.e. the north) 'but to come and go . . . . so do I think it very expedient that his Highness' pleasure should be known, as well to the Lord Wharton as to those of Newcastle that his Highness hath the poor man and his doings in gracious favour. . . .

'I pray you that the King's Majesty's good contentation towards the poor man and his proceedings . . . be indelayedly certifyed to the said Lord Wharton . . . and that something might be written to the Mayor for his greedy accusation of the poor man, wherein he hath, in my poor opinion, uttered his malicious stomach towards the King's proceedings. . . .'

He closes with a pious flourish:

'. . . as knoweth God, to whose infinite goodness let us pray that all things may prosper to his glory, and to the honour and surety of the King's Majesty.'

Brandling had reason to remember, and no doubt to regret, his rash complaint. Knox was cleared. 'Heinous were the delations laid against me', he wrote to Mrs. Bowes amd Marjorie: 'and many are the lies that are made to the council. But God one day shall destroy all lying tongues, and shall deliver his servants from calamity. I look but one day or other to fall in their hands: for more and more rageth the members of the Devil against me . . . I look not to depart from Newcastle before Easter: my daily labours must now increase, and therefore spare me as much as ye may. My old malady troubles me sore, and nothing is more contrarious to my health than writing. Think not that I (ever) weary to visit you: but unless my pain shall cease, I will altogether become unprofitable.'

Knox had gone straight back to Newcastle from London, in spite of Dudley. Not only was it by the King's favour that he was cleared of the charges, but also it was apparently by the King's own wish that he was offered, while in the south, the city living of All-Hallows, Bread Street. But this also he refused.

Yet he came north again a man both ill and deeply distressed. He writes again to Mrs. Bowes: 'The pain of my head and stomach troubles me greatly: daily I find my body decay, but the providence of my God shall not be frustrate. I am charged to be at Widderington upon Sunday, where I think I shall also remain Monday. The spirit of the Lord rest with you. Desire such faithful as with whom ye communicate your mind, to pray, that at the pleasure of our good God, my dolour, both of body and spirit, may be relieved somewhat, for presently it is very bitter.'

And again: 'Your messenger found me in bed, after a sore trouble and most dolorous night, and so dolour may complain to dolour when we two meet. . . . But dear Sister, I am even of mind with faithful Job, yet more sore tormented, that my pain shall have no end in this life. The power of God may, against the purpose of my heart, alter such things as appear not to be altered, as he did unto Job; but dolour and pain, with sore anguish, crys the contrary. And this is more plain than ever I spake, to let ye know ye have a fellow and companion in trouble.'

Knox was suffering from more than the pain of his battered body. In London he had seen death in the young King's face: and the wolf-pack gathering, ever bolder. He knew the end was in sight.

7

'The Great Shipwreck'

THE second Sunday in April 1553 the last Tudor King of England went to hear, for the last time, one of his favourite preachers in Westminster Abbey. All the glitter and jingle of a medieval court was there; the glorious, flashing colour, the shields and banners, the velvet and miniver. His Highness Dudley, Duke of Northumberland, a gorgeous figure, famous as a jouster, with his tall handsome sons: Paulet, Marquess of Winchester, the perfect time-server, who was Comptroller, Secretary and Lord Treasurer to Edward, who cursed Mary as a bastard, yet lived to 'crouch and kneel' successfully to her in turn; all the dukes and earls and jewelled ladies were there: for sermons were high fashion for the moment, in England.

Knox, the dour little Scotsman, rising to preach, perhaps looked round from the white-faced boy to the jealous lords: and gave out his text from the Gospel of St. John xiii. 15: 'He that eateth bread with me hath lifted up his heel against me.'

These words, used by the Lord at the Last Supper, are quoted from Psalm 41, v. 9, in which David laments the treachery of Achitophel. Knox turned back to read again those incomparable stories of treachery and heroism in Isaiah, in 2 Samuel xvi and xvii, 2 Kings xviii; stories of three different sorts of traitors: of Shebna the traitor who wormed his way into King Hezekiah's confidence, becoming comptroller, secretary and treasurer – did the congregation prick up their ears? Of Achitophel who rose to be the highest in the land while he plotted with Absalom to supplant David: whose counsel 'was as the oracles of God': of Judas who sold his friend.

The preacher's voice rose to a climax: 'Was David and Hezekiah, princes of great and godly gifts and experience, abused by crafty counsellors and dissembling hypocrites? What wonder is it then, that a young and innocent King be deceived by crafty, covetous, wicked and ungodly counsellors? I am afraid greatly that Achitophel be counsellor, that Judas bear the purse and the Shebna be scribe, comptroller and treasurer.'

There must have been a wave of anger – perhaps of laughter – along the gorgeously dressed congregation. Was there too a flicker of satisfaction over the white face of the little King? But whether or not he was the King's favourite, this sermon went a little too near the bone: Knox was summoned before the Privy Council of England on 14 April.

There were present at this Council, Cranmer, Archbishop of Canterbury, the Lord Chancellor, the Earls of Bedford, Northampton and Shrewsbury; the Lord Treasurer ('Shebna'), and the Lord Chamberlain, and two Secretaries of State. For obvious reasons, they did not take him up on the sermon; but instead brought up the old complaints against him. Why had he refused preferment? Why had he objections to kneeling, to the special wafer instead of common bread, and the like? Knox had answers ready for all their points: so in the end they 'dismissed him with fair words', saying only 'they were sorry to understand he was of a contrary mind to the Common Order.'

He 'was more sorry to understand', answered Knox, 'that the Common Order should be contrary to Christ's institution'.

But he did not get back to Newcastle. The Council had been in touch with Wharton again that spring for 'the avoiding of the Scots in Newcastle'. There must have been a large, probably increasing number all through Knox's ministry there, to make them so nervous.

Knox was sent to preach that summer in Kent and Buckinghamshire, and found a congenial congregation in that most English corner of England, the village of Amersham. This was a 'right pretty market town on Fridays', according to a quaint old description: and it was also a corner where the soil had been tilled, long before, by Wycliff, and where this later sowing fell gratefully.

His enemies could afford to wait a little. The sands were clearly running out for Edward. Youth had ceased to fight with death: his days were numbered.

Dudley, Duke of Northumberland, saw that too. The throne

would soon be empty: he had a chance, if he hurried. He coveted to 'establish it to his posterity', as Knox put it. Little Lady Jane Grey's parents sent for her, from her beloved books. They told her she was to marry Dudley's son Guildford, a large, handsome, rather childish young man. It would probably have been the dashing Robin, later Elizabeth's adored Leicester, but he had already been married off to an heiress, Amy Robsart. Jane was appalled. She protested with all the obstinacy of cornered weakness. She had been promised to the son of dead Somerset: her loyalty was there. Her parents had no time to waste on sentiment. Her mother yelled and cursed at her, her father struck her 'several shrewd blows' in the face before them all. Her collapse was taken as assent, and the happy arrangements duly proceeded. Dudley's plans were now laid.

In May or June of that year the marriage took place, with the utmost magnificence: the two fathers-in-law keeping open house to the whole city of London for three days together. Guildford was apparently fond of his tiny bride: but Jane never willingly endured him.

Because of her open aversion, and the King fast coughing his lungs out, Dudley saw it was no good leaving the succession, as Edward had done, to 'The L.' Jane's heirs male'. It must be altered to: 'The L.' Jane and heirs male'. This the King agreed, determined to preserve the Church which had been the achievement of his brief life. He got the consent of the Council, with some difficulty. Only Cecil tried to wriggle out, being seized with a providential illness. So convincing were his protestations, that an elderly councillor sent him his favourite prescription. It deserves recording:

'Take a sow pig 9 days old, distill with one handful of red fennel, one handful of liverwort, half a handful of red neeps, half a handful of celery, 9 dates, clean picked and pared, 9 great raisins and pick out the stones, ¼ ounce mace, 2 sticks good cinnamon. Set in the sun 9 days: and' (a fine gesture) 'drink 9 spoonfuls together *when you list.*'

This new will was Edward's last effort for his Church, and also Dudley's last point secured for his scheme. Mary and Elizabeth

C

were still branded as bastards and passed over, as they had been by their father before this.

The last weeks ran out fast. By the beginning of July Edward was reported dead, but they dressed him in his velvet state robes and brought him to the window to show to the crowd: a pitiful, infinitely lonely little figure. Not long after, hearing him murmur, they ran to prop him up lest he had words of importance: but he smiled and said only, 'I was praying.' On 6 July he died.

Dudley hid his death to gain time. They must first secure Mary and Elizabeth, rallying points for disaffection: and he sent them pathetic summonses from 'their dying brother'. Simple Mary started at once: but was warned by a secret messenger, and rode for her life. Elizabeth, crafty as Cecil in the art of survival, promptly retired to bed also: 'Too ill to be moved'.

Knox was at Amersham when the news was at last confirmed. He broke out in passionate lamentation, not only for the death of a sovereign he admired, a boy who had been his friend, but for England: its new Church, its new peace. To him this was 'the great shipwreck' of all their hopes and achievements. He foresaw nothing but ruin and bloodshed.

Jane was proclaimed Queen in London on 10 July; looking pretty at last, according to ambassadors, in a magnificent dress of green and silver, her dark red hair braided and her shoes built up to make her a little taller. She accepted the fate, but utterly, unexpectedly and tenaciously refused to allow Guildford to be King, as his father had planned. It was not right, and she would not do it.

Meanwhile forces, had been quietly, ceaselessly gathering round Mary. Dudley rode out to meet them, his last hope a pitched battle, for he had always been a brave and brilliant soldier. But 'his men's feet marched forward but their hearts marched backwards'. Once again, for the last time, he had discounted the human element. The people of England possibly hated papacy, but they hated injustice more. His army melted away to Mary, his sworn friends handed him over: he came back to London a prisoner, his scarlet cloak mud-spattered by the crowd, his plumed hat perforce in his hand, the name of Somerset thrown at him. Knox's words were come true.

On Sunday 19 July there were bonfires and banqueting in the

streets of London, dancing and rejoicing for Mary the Cinderella princess, brought home to reign by the will of her people. No doubt they enjoyed the fun, enjoyed the feeling of wrong righted: no doubt Knox was unpopular when he cried that Sunday 'in more places than one' in London that long and bitterly would they rue it. Queen Jane herself laid aside royal trappings thankfully and said to her father: 'Can we go home now?'

Knox had friends in London, and apparently quite a congregation of his own: including 'three honest poor women' who wept with him over Mrs. Bowes's afflictions. Among the more wealthy, the Hickmans were supporters: and, more especially, the Lockes of Cheapside Street. Mrs. Locke became a constant correspondent, sending and demanding news. Knox probably stayed with her and her husband while the foolish were 'skipping the streets for joy' over Mary's restoration. He himself was full of the darkest foreboding; he began to warn his congregations that they must be prepared to stand trial for their faith.

'The last trumpet is blowing within the realm of England, and therefore ought everyone to prepare himself for battle. For if the trumpet shall altogether be put to silence, then shall it never blow again with the like force within the said realm till the coming of the Lord Jesus.'

Yet Mary's reign actually began with leniency and mercy. All heretics were to be given full time to recant. First to take advantage of that was Dudley, Duke of Northumberland, who became a penitential papist; and indeed declared he had been one all the time. 'But seeing a new religion start, run dog, run devil, he must after it.' He beseeched Mary for life 'if but that of a dog', and abjectly craved pardon for his heresy.

('Pardon!' cried little Jane in the Tower, 'Woe worth him!')

Dudley was executed on 22 August. Mary, refusing all advice, kept Jane and Guildford alive.

But the religious refugees prepared to take up the weary trail again. Among the first to leave was a'Lasco, sailing from Gravesend with 175 of his congregation, on 15 September.

During these summer months, Knox had a crisis in his personal affairs too. He had been trying to get the Bowes to recognize his marriage to Marjorie. It was Marjorie herself who seems to have initiated this; either because she wished to be with him in the coming trouble, or because her father was insisting that she and her mother return to the Roman Church, as he had done.

The time could hardly have been less propitious. The repeal of all clerical marriages was already being urged. And the Bowes had fallen with Dudley. Sir Robert had resigned his Master-of-the-Rolls, and must have felt his whole position precarious. Knox was never more unwanted.

He had gone from London to preach in Kent at the end of summer. Did he, unwitting, help to fan there a smouldering fire of resentment against Mary and her papacy? He prayed publicly:

'Take not from us the light of Thy evangel, and suffer Thou no papistry to prevail in this realm. Illumine the heart of our sovereign lady, Queen Mary, with pregnant gifts of Thy Holy Ghost. And inflame the hearts of her Council with Thy true fear and love. Repress thou the pride of those that would rebel. . . . But O Lord let us never revolt or turn back to idolatry again.'

On 20 September back in London he wrote to 'his Mother and his Spouse', 'After the writing of my other letters, which have lain beside me of a long time for want of a bearer, I received your letters as I returned from Kent, where I was labouring before the receit thereof. I was assured of your trouble, and of the battle of my own flesh, before God: and I suspect a greater to lie upon you both than that your letters declares me to.' Then after a long dissertation on Mrs. Bowes's 'spiritual cross', he returns to the problem: 'My great labours, wherein I desire your daily prayers, will not suffer me to satisfy my mind touching all the process between your husband and you, touching my matter concerning his daughter. I praise God heartily, both for your boldness and constancy. But I beseech you, mother, trouble not your self too much therewith. It becomes me now to jeopard my life for the comfort and deliverance of my own flesh, as that I will do by God's grace; both fear and friendship of all earthly creature laid aside. I have written to your husband, the contents whereof I trust our brother Harry will declair to you and to my Wife. If I escape sickness and imprisonment, be sure to see you soon.'

Knox believed that he was risking his life when he appealed to Sir Robert Bowes, Marjorie's uncle, to help them; he clearly did so because he had done Sir Robert some favour in the past years, and Mrs. Bowes thought he had a right to his support. In November he wrote:

'Dear Mother,

So may and will I call you, not only for the tender affection I bear unto you in Christ, but also for the motherly kindness ye have shown unto me at all times since our first acquaintance: albeit such things as I have desired (if it had pleased God), and ye and others have long desired, are never like to come to pass, yet shall ye be sure that my love and care toward you shall never abate, so long as I can care for any earthly creature.

'Ye shall understand that this 6th of November I spake with Sir Robert Bowes on the matter ye know, according to your request, whose disdainful, yea, despiteful words have so pierced my heart that my life is bitter unto me. I bear a good countenance with a sore troubled heart; while he that ought to consider matters with a deep judgement is become not only a despiser but a taunter of God's messengers. God be merciful unto him. Among other his most unpleasing words, while that I was about to have declared my part in the whole matter, he said: "Away with your rhetorical reasons, for I will not be persuaded with them." God knows I did use no rhetoric or coloured speech, but would have spoken the truth, and that in most simple manner. I am not a good orator in my own cause.'

Whether or not Sir Robert then informed against him – as is possible – Knox left London abruptly in early December. He preached steadily as he went, making for Newcastle: in pain and weakness, in the darkest foreboding: and above all 'in very dolour and anguish of heart' from his treatment from the Bowes. He got letters from a servant of Mrs. Bowes on 19 December and messages from a married daughter of hers whom he visited.

'Upon Monunday, I was with your daughter Bowes, who hath her heartily commendit unto you, and unto our sister Marjorie. She forgot none of your directions, but did declare unto me both your grief and her own, which I find both to proceed from one fountain. Praise be unto God, I left her in good comfort, referring thanks unto God for all his benefits. I was not, as yet I am, in good case to have travelled: for I had lain Thursday at night, and Friday all day, sore troubled in the gravel. I know the cause and original, but I can not remedy: but He who willeth me to suffer, shall at his pleasure. It will be after the Twelfth Day before I can be at Berwick, and almost I am determinate not to come at all; ye know the cause. God be more merciful unto some, than they are equitable unto me in judgement. The testimony of my conscience absolves me, before His face who looks not upon the presence of man.'

The testimony of his conscience did not absolve him from the attentions of his enemies. Here in the north both Wharton and Brandling, as well as the Bowes, must have been itching to lay hands on him now their chance had come. Mary's amnesty for heretics expired on 20 December, yet Knox dates this letter, 'With troubled heart and weak body, at Newcastle, this Tuesday, 22nd of December, 1533'; and adds a postscript, 'I may not answer the places of Scripture, nor yet write the Exposition of the Sixth Psalm for every day of this week must I preach, if the wicked carcase will permit.'

Shortly after this his servant was seized, and the letters written to Mrs. Bowes confiscated. (Was this servant Jamie Campbell, who was with him for so many years afterwards?) He was really afraid now lest Marjorie and her mother might have been seized too, and tried to make a secret dash for Berwick, at least to say farewell to Marjorie. But the hunt was up and he was too well known to be easily hidden. Even to carry his messages was to risk one's life.

He realized it was hopeless, and sat down to write a farewell letter:

'Dear Mother and Spouse unfeignedly belovit in the bowels of our Saviour Christ Jesus, with my very heartily commendations:

I perusit both your letters, not only directed to me, but also it that sorrowfully complains upon the unthankfulness of your brother as also of mine, that ye should not have been equally made privy to my coming in the country with others, whereof the enemy would persuade you . . . that we judge you not to be of our number.

Dear Mother, be not so suddenly moved, he is your enemy that so would persuade you. God I take to record in my conscience, that none is this day within the Realm of England with whom I would more gladly speak (only she whom God hath offered unto me, and commanded me to love as my own flesh expected), than with you. For your causes principally enterprisit I this journey: for hearing my servant to be stayed, and his letters to be taken, I could no-ways be pacified (for the most part of my letters was for your instruction and comfort), till further knowledge of your estate: and that ye were no sooner advertised, only want of a faithful messenger was the cause; for my coming to the country was so soon noised abroad, that with great difficulty could I be convoyed from one place to another. I knew of no such danger as was suspected by my brethren. For as for my letters, in them is nothing contained except exhortation to constancy . . . but the cause moving me that for a time I would have been close was, that I purposed (if so had been possible) to have spoken with my wife, which now I perceive is nothing apparent, until God offer some better occasion. . . .'

He finishes with ghostly consolation, and thanks Mrs. Bowes for her offers of help:

'Ye may be sure that I would be bold upon you, for of your good heart I am persuaded, but of your power and ability I greatly doubt. I will not make you privy how rich I am, but off London I departed with less money than ten groats: but God has since provided, and will provide, I doubt not, hereafter abundantly for this life. Either the Queen's Majesty or some Treasurer will be XL pounds richer by me, for so meikle lack I duty of my patents.' (i.e., as royal chaplain whose salary was £40 per year). 'But that little troubles me. Rest in Christ Jesus.'

Some time late that month of January Knox was smuggled aboard a ship for France. It may have been brother William's boat, for he had called regularly at Newcastle when Knox was there. As he left, Wyatt's rebellion flared up in Kent: that rebellion which so nearly succeeded, ending only in the streets of London itself; but which, failing, sealed 'Queen Jane's' death-warrant.

Jane and Guildford were executed on 9 February. Guildford, young and spoilt, cried at the block; but tiny Jane, except for a momentary terror at the huge scarlet-clad headsman, was composed enough. 'Jane Dudley bids you a long farewell,' she said to the crowd; and to the headsman: 'I pray you, dispatch me quickly.' She was just sixteen. Because her mother, who had a new lover, did not care, and because she was a heretic, her little body lay half-naked in a great pool of blood for the rest of the day.

It was the end of that little drama of policy, that curtain-raiser for England's Grand Guignol years of horror piled on horror. It was the end too of Mary's mercy. Gallows went up all over London, and numbers of people were hanged.

Among those who fled like Knox into exile were Grindal, Lever, Haddon, Foxe, Gilbey, Cole and old Coverdale; also MacBriar and Willock, and Rough who later came back. Parker and his Margaret hid, and were never caught. Cheke, the late King's tutor, re-canted in the Tower for terror, and died next year of a broken heart at the age of forty-four. Perne, who had been briefly a royal chaplain, was, as a contemporary put it: 'Papist, Protestant, Protestant, Papist – but always Andrew Perne'.

Among those who stayed and suffered were Cranmer, Latimer, Ridley, old Hooper, Bradford, Rowland Taylor and a host of ordinary parsons and their people.

PART THREE

THE GENEVAN CHURCH

8

The Failure

L ANDED in Dieppe, Knox knew an overwhelming reaction of depression and remorse. Would it not have been better to have stayed and died with those who had become his own people? It could almost have seemed easier than trying to start life again from the bottom of the ladder: a homeless foreigner, tired, ill, beggared, and no longer young.

'I cannot express the pain which I think I might suffer,' he writes to Mrs. Bowes almost on landing, 'to have the presence of you, and of others that be like troubled, but a few days. . . . My daily prayer is, for the sore afflicted in those quarters. Sometimes I have thought that impossible it had been so to have removed my affection from the Realm of Scotland, that any Realm or Nation could have been equal dear unto me. But God I take to record in my conscience, that the troubles present (and appearing to be) in the Realm of England, are double more dolourous unto my heart, than ever were the troubles of Scotland.'

He had known his first great happiness in England, and come to love it: and his whole hope and prayer must have been one day to return to it.

With his letter to Mrs. Bowes he sent her the exposition on the 6th Psalm, that psalm which had so comforted him in the galleys; he had been working on it in snatches during the past weeks, and it was now a full treatise of comfort for those in adversity.

At the end of it he writes, he says, 'as though I should take from you my last good-night on earth'. Neither fear of death nor the rage of the devil alone could hinder him from trying to see her:

yet it is uncertain, he has to admit, 'if ever we shall meet in this corporal life'. He is tormented still by conscience over his flight: 'And albeit that I have in the beginning of this battle, appeared to play the faint-hearted and feeble soldier (the cause I remit to God), yet my prayer is, that I may be restored to the battle again.' He prays he may obtain such mercy that 'I shall be so encouraged to fight, that England and Scotland shall both know that I am ready to suffer more than either poverty or exile, for the profession of that doctrine, and that heavenly religion, whereof it has pleased His merciful providence to make me, among others, a simple soldier and witness-bearer unto men'.

At the same time Knox sent a pastoral letter to 'The Faithful in London, Newcastle and Berwick', his three congregations. It is dated the last day of February 'from a sore troubled heart, upon my departure from Dieppe, whither God knoweth'. In this he quoted freely from Jeremiah who also was a prophet in troubled times, whose book, so full of battle-cries and trumpets, had come alive to Knox. Yet, he reflects, 'by all likelihood then, there were some Cob Carles, that were not pleased with the prophet, neither yet with his preachings'. He had reason to know!

'What was said in Newcastle and Berwick before the Sweating-sickness, I trust some in these parts yet bears in mind. And upon the day of All-Saints (as they call it) the year the Duke of Somerset was last apprehended, let Newcastle witness! What before him that was then Duke of Northumberland, in more places nor one. What before the King's Majesty, whom God has called from wordly misery for our offences, at Windsor, Hampton Court and Westminster. And finally, what was spoken in London, in more places nor one, when fires of joy and riotous banqueting were at the proclamation of Marie, your queen. If men will not speak, yet shall the stones and timber of these places cry in fire and bear record that the truth was spoken. . . .'

Knox saw that as the true office of the prophet, to which the servant of God's word was called. He must, at whatever cost or danger to himself, or however unwilling the people, hold out the

Eternal Truth of God; so that the racing tide of events could be seen and judged against it. Jeremiah had known how to blow 'the trumpet of the Lord': and he knew too how people shut their ears to talk of judgement, and shout it down. 'What reverence and audience, I say, was given to the preachers this last Lent by such as then was in authority?... assuredly, even such as by the wicked Princes of Juda was given to Jeremiah.'

Amongst those who did 'prophesy and plainly speak' had been Grindal, now in exile, who 'plainly spak the death of the King's Majesty': Lever, who 'spak the desolation of the common-weal': Bradford (then in prison, burnt at Smithfield in July, 1555) who 'spared not the proudest'. It was Bradford who had taken the Duke of Somerset as his example of growing coldness and sudden judgement: '*Judicium Domini*! *Judicium Domini*! The judgement of the Lord, the judgement of the Lord! lamentably cried he, with weeping tears.' Haddon, the Latin scholar, too had affirmed that 'worse was to follow unless repentance be found'.

So Knox, with all the force of his overwhelming sincerity urges them to hold fast to the faith they had professed: 'by blood planted, by blood keepit in mind, by blood increased and fructifyed'. For if they all recant and go back, through fear, to the idolatry of Rome, what inheritance shall be left to their children? Revelations are not given twice. It is not the 'marvels of Merlin' which lead him to prophesy this, but 'the plain truth of God's word, the invincible justice of the everlasting God'. Knox's agony of mind was very real: but he had to speak what he had been given.

'I wish myself to be accursit of God, as touching all earthly pleasures ... I sob and groan, I call and pray, that in that point I may be deceivit. But I am commanded to stand content for it is God himself that performs the word of his own true messengers. His justice and order cannot be perverted.

'The sun keepeth his ordinary course, and starteth not back from West to the South. And so it is with the light of the Gospel. Most evident it is that where the light of God's word for the unthankfulness of men has been taken away, that there it is not to this day restored again. Witness whole Israel and all the countries of the Gentiles, where the apostles first preached. What is in Asia? Ignorance of God. What in Africa? Abnegation of the very

Saviour, of our Lord Jesus. What in those notable churches of the Grecians where Christ Jesus was planted by Paul, and long after watered by others? Mahomet and his false sect. Hath God punished the nations forenamed and shall he spare us?'

The Mohammedan Turks at that time had swept right over Greece and reached the very gates of Vienna.

National sin and national judgement Knox could see: and it is a doctrine uncomfortably real to our own atomic age. The right to rebel he could not yet see: but in this hour of crisis he grappled with it. How far might the true shepherd defend his sheep, without defying lawful authority? Or did the crux of the matter lie in this unnatural supremacy of women? Mary Tudor in England and Mary of Guise in Scotland seemed to sum up all the disasters of the times. And what of the 'crowns matrimonial' which they had the right to bestow? Could it be just that because of their sex a Spaniard might be King of England, a Frenchman King of Scotland?

Knox made his way to Geneva, where Calvin was now a fountain-head of Reformed doctrine. We remember Calvin's name chiefly in a derogatory adjective today. But Knox included some of his sermons in French in his daily reading till his death: and they were personal friends. Calvin had once written: 'We are not forbidden to laugh or to drink wine.' And again: 'The little singing birds are singing of God: the beasts cry unto Him: the elements are in awe of Him: the mountains echo his name. Waves and fountains glance at Him, grass and flowers laugh out to Him.'

Calvin sent Knox on to Bullinger at Zurich, that Father of the Faith to whom Willock and ab Ullmis had once appealed on secret marriages. Bullinger sent back to Calvin an account of the questions, and the answers he made to 'the Scotsman you commended to me'. The first question was on the rightful succession of Edward VI, (and therefore his right to leave the crown to his chosen heir). The second asked, 'Whether a Female can preside over, and rule a kingdom by divine right, and so transfer the right of sovereignty to her husband?'

The third question began: 'Whether obedience is to be rendered to a magistrate who enforces idolatry and condemns true religion?' and the fourth asked, 'To which party must Godly persons attach themselves in the case of a religious Nobility resisting an idolatrous Sovereign?'

Bullinger's answers all counselled patience and endurance: but Knox seems at that time to have had hopes of returning to England with some national revolt. He made his way back to Dieppe at the beginning of May, and from there he wrote two 'comfortable epistles to the afflicted Brethren in England.' In the first one, dated 10 May, he mentions that he has 'travelled through all the congregations of Helvetia, has reasoned with all the Pastors and many other excellently learned men upon sich matters as now I can not commit to writing: . . . if I thought that I might have your presence, and the presence of some other assured men, I would jeopard my own life to let men see what may be done with a safe conscience in these dolorous and dangerous days; but seeing it can not be done instantly without danger to others than to me, I will abide the time that God shall appoint.' He adds the hope that 'if by any means I may, intend to speak with you or it be long.'

Those who have left no stone unturned to throw at Knox have accused him of writing inflammatory pamphlets while he himself sat in safety. But both this letter and the sadder one he wrote at the end of the month were exhortations to constancy only. 'There falls no thing to you, nor yet to the flock of Christ Jesus this day within the miserable realm of England, which did not fall on Christ's true and beloved disciples before and after His death.' His one fiery pamphlet, the *Admonition to the Faithful*, rebounded on his own head. Indeed, it was not so much that Knox said or wrote more than many of his contemporaries; but rather that all his words had an added impact of their own.

The news in Dieppe that May 1554 was worse than ever. In Scotland to hasten on her life-long policy of bringing the country wholly under France, now that her daughter was formally betrothed to the Dauphin, Mary of Guise took on herself the sole Regency of the country. 'As comely a sight,' comments Knox, 'as if a saddle had been placed on an old unrewly cow.' To buy off the great Duke, who had been regent until then, he was given the French title of Duc de Chatelherault, which the Hamilton family still bears.

In England, Mary Tudor had pressed through her Marriage

Bill: and Philip of Spain was preparing to sail from Corunna, with an escort of 150 ships, to marry her that wet summer at Westminster. Parliament had hesitated long at passing the old anti-Lollard Heresy Laws: but Mary pressed for the election of members of 'a wise, grave and Catholic sort'; and next winter they went through. Cranmer and Ridley were now on trial at Oxford. Steadily the stream of homeless refugees poured into France. Knox was perhaps already drawing up that catalogue of those victimized for their faith, which he afterwards published. Some of the London names were apparently known to him, by his marginal comments. Another exile, Foxe, was later to fill a book with a full and dreadful account of the martyrs.

Against this darkening background Knox published in July his *Admonition*. Part of it is a rather beautiful sermon, likening again the Commonwealth of England to a ship on a voyage. Like the disciples, so dreadful is the storm that they think only a miracle could save them: 'to have had the heavens opened or else that the winds and raging waves of the sea suddenly should have ceased'. But the only sign granted was 'his comfortable word and lively voice. It is I, your Master, yea, your Master most familiar'. Very movingly he writes of those whose faith wavers through fear: he agonises with them.

But he accuses himself too, as one who had broken the bread of life to them: 'It is not in my knowledge nor judgement to define . . . what portion every man received of this bread, neither yet how that which they received agreed with their stomachs. But of this I am assured, that the benediction of Christ Jesus so multiplied the portion that I received of his hands, that during that banquet . . . the bread never failed when the hungry soul craved or cried for food: and at the end . . . my hands gathered up the crumbs that were left in such abundance that my basket was full among the rest. Yet how small was my learning, and how weak I was of judgement, when Christ Jesus called me to be His steward . . . alas! how blinded was my heart and how little I did consider the dignity of that office, and the power of God that then multiplied and blessed the bread which the people received of my hands. . . .'

Again: 'peradventure my rude plainness displeased some, who did complain . . . but alas! this day my conscience accuseth me, that I spake not so plainly as my duty was to have done: for I ought to have said to the wicked man expressedly by his name: "Thou shalt die the death".'

He had worse still to confess.

'For, in preaching Christ's Gospel, albeit mine eye (as knoweth God) was not much upon wordly promotion, yet the love of friends and carnal affection of some men with whom I was most familiar, allured me to make more residence in one place than in another, having more respect to the pleasure of a few, than to the necessity of many. That day I thought I had not sinned, if I had not been idle; but this day I know it was my duty to have had consideration how long I had remained in one place, and how many hungry souls were in other places, to whom, alas! none took pain to break and distribute the bread of life.

'Moreover, remaining in one place I was not so diligent as mine office required; but sometime, by counsel of carnal friends, I spared the body; sometimes I spent in wordly busyness of particular friends; and sometime in taking recreation and pastime by exercise of the body.'

Knox is still the shepherd and the mystic: urging the persecuted: 'If your communication be of Christ, assuredly he will come before you be 'ware. His word is like unto sweet smelling ointment, or fragrant flowers, which never can be moved nor handled, but forth goeth the odour, to the comfort of those that standeth by: which is nothing so delectable if the ointment remain within the box, or the flowers stand or lie without touching or motion.'

But then follows his fiery rhetoric. Vehemently he attacks 'bloody Bonner', Shebna the turncoat treasurer; and Gardner who had once accepted Henry's supremacy, but who now took such a savage and personal lead in the persecutions and burnings: 'son of Satan, brother to Cain and fellow to Judas the traitor'. There is a passing reference to the Emperor, Charles V ('no less enemy to Christ than was Nero'), but most bitterly of all Knox denounces Mary, the cruel, the unnatural: 'an open traitress to the Imperial Crown of England, contrary to the just laws of the realm, to bring in a stranger and make a proud Spaniard king'. He added the phrase that has stuck, even to the history books of today: 'Under an English name she beareth a Spaniard's heart.'

This was published on 20 July, the day Philip set sail for England. After it, Knox set forth wearily again. 'My own estate I cannot well declare, but God shall guide the footsteps of him that is wilsome, and will feed him in trouble that never greatly solicited for the world. If any collection might be made among the faithful, it were no shame for me to receive that which Paul refused not in the time of his trouble. But all I remit to His providence who ever careth for His own.'

At this low ebb in Knox's hopes and fortunes, he received a call. Many of the English refugees had settled in Frankfort-am-Maine, where they had the use of a French Reformed church on condition that their services conformed to its usages. Knox had no sooner found his way back to Geneva, than he received a call to become one of their three pastors. At first he hesitated to accept: and he humbly consulted Calvin, as he later did on most calls and decisions. Calvin urged him to accept, and so he went. It was a long, long journey from Geneva, and presumably he walked all the way through the towering mountains and high passes.

Among those who subscribed this call of 20 September 1554 were John MacBriar the Galloway preacher, lately fled from England, who was to end up as vicar of St. Nicholas, Newcastle, where Knox had so vehemently preached: and William Whittinghame, a non-conformist student from Cambridge; and Lever, once one of the Court preachers, now a colleague of Knox. The third man asked was Haddon, chaplain once with Willock to Jane Grey's father: but he refused.

For there had already been some trouble at Frankfort. Other exiles in Zurich refused to join them unless they used the English Prayer Book. Strasbourg exiles joined in the argument: and the congregation was rent in two by the time Knox arrived in November.

He was unwilling to give communion until they were at peace. He would not give it in the Genevan form against the will of part of them: and if they all preferred the Anglican form, he would preach only. Otherwise, he begged to be released: but to this they would in no wise consent'.

So Knox, Whittinghame, Foxe (of the *Martyrs*) and Gilby and Cole drew up a summary of the Prayer Book for Calvin's judgement and sent it to him at Christmas. Pending that, they produced an order that was in fact a first draft of Knox's Book of Common Order. Calvin's answer eventually arrived rather disapproving of 'popish dregs'; so a committee then appointed reached agreement on a modified English liturgy without further trouble. This was agreed by all, and was to be given fair trial till the end of April. Public thanks were given for the healing of the strife, and communion was taken together.

But long before April there arrived a fresh batch of refugees, including Dr. Cox, ex-canon of Windsor, part-author of the Prayer Book and old and bitter enemy of Knox for his Black Rubric. In less than three weeks he had him outed.

The refugees came truculent. On their very first Sunday they broke out into loud responses during the service: being admonished by the elders they said 'they would have the face of an English Church'. 'The Lord grant it to have the face of Christ's Church,' said Knox.

Next Sunday, before a preacher could arrive, one of them entered the pulpit and began to chant the litany, to which the others loudly responded. But it was Knox's turn to preach in the afternoon. He had been doing a course on Genesis, on the origins of law and authority: and had most timeously reached disobedience and disunity. The fuel was all too ready to his hand. He knew the men before him as a shepherd knows the troublemakers of his flock. There had been time to reform in England, and it had not been done: there had been those happy in pluralities who had neglected God's needy: there had been those, now so bold, who had lately bowed the knee to papacy. . . . Every bullet found a billet. The King's Chaplain was heard again in full power, and they were all obliged to listen.

Cox then demanded his party's right to vote: Knox, ever a believer in rights, insisted on his having it. They then joined forces with Lever's conservatives and voted Knox out of office. Whittinghame's party, in fury, had recourse to the civil Senate of Frankfort, who ordered them curtly to adhere to their original agreement – that is, to the French Reformed services – or to give up the church.

Cox agreed: and produced his trump card, as it were from up his sleeve. It was a copy of Knox's *Admonition* in which he not only fiercely denounced Mary but had made that passing reference to the Emperor as 'no less enemy to Christ than was Nero'. This, Cox and his supporters claimed, was treason; and they accused Knox before the magistrates of the city: an ugly little piece of malice. It put the magistrates in a dilemma: they were sympathetic to Knox, but they could not risk accusation of harbouring traitors to the Emperor, or for that matter to the Queen of England. The Diet of Augsburg was already sitting, arranging peace. Whittinghame spoke up boldly for Knox: and another ex-royal chaplain, Grindal, wrote from Strasbourg to Ridley in his prison; and Ridley wrote back that Knox was a man 'of wit and learning', but added that he marvelled how 'he can or dare avouch such views before Englishmen'. (Besides the communion order, what Knox chiefly disliked in the English Church was private baptism and the litany). He must have hated to be so meanly worsted, and by such a man as Cox: but as a parish priest he knew the evil of 'the breach of charity' within the flock. He gave in, for the Church's sake, and agreed to go.

His last Sunday in Frankfort, Knox went humbly to church, to worship with the ordinary folk. But even that was not allowed. Cox and his party raised an outcry against him and walked out, leaving chaos behind. On 25 March he took prayers in his lodgings for about fifty people, speaking on 'the death and resurrection of Christ and of the unspeakable joys which were prepared for God's elect, which in this life suffer trouble and persecution for the testimony of His blessed name'. Early next morning many of them came out to see him off with tears: a lonely, black figure of failure.

Most of the Reformed churches in Europe were excited about 'the Troubles in Frankfort', taking sides and rushing into print about it. As a good-going ecclesiastical row it lasted some time. Knox himself once wrote his own account, but then thought it not worth printing. After Knox had agreed to go, Whittinghame wrote furiously to Calvin, on 24 March 1555:

'For Master Knox, being most unjustly charged before the Magistrates with High Treason, has been ordered to quit the place, not without the regret of all good men, and even of the Magistrate himself. He is therefore on his way to you, and will explain the whole matter in order. This only I can speak from experience, that nothing ever occasioned greater distress and shame to good men than this wickedness has done.'

Calvin himself wrote sharply to Cox, after Knox's return, giving his opinion that Knox had been 'neither godly nor brotherly dealt withal', and that it would have been better for Cox to have stayed at home than to have come abroad as a firebrand. (Ultimately a neat judgement fell on Cox: for when he was restored to office in Elizabeth's Court she put a crucifix in her chapel, and he objected to that as violently as once he had wanted a litany; he even had to fall back on Knox's own arguments to defend his views.)

Meanwhile Frankfort got itself a real bishop with surplices; and with that and a litany some were happy at last. Others, led by Whittinghame, rose and followed Knox to Geneva, where they eventually became part of his 'most faithful little flock': so the dissension continued.

The chief result of this failure was that Knox lost for ever his place in the English Church. Even if it lived again he was cut off from it: he was as homeless, rootless, churchless as ever he had been.

9

Reveille

IF the Lord then had no more active use for him, he would turn his back on the world and study. He settled down in Geneva, and it was almost certainly Hebrew that engaged him: he had had 'a fervent thirst' to learn it for years, knowing already Latin and Greek, A new translation of the Bible was in hand, the 'Geneva Bible'; and various people in England sent him small sums, enough to keep him on the edge of existence. He seemed content: a humble member of the Reformed Church, a private student sharing in a great work and at rest at last. He can have had little desire ever again to tramp the weary roads, or risk an ugly death in strife: or indeed ever again to leave, as he wrote, 'the den of mine own ease, the rest of quiet study'. Perhaps he was growing old.

But less than six months later there came a disturbing echo out of the past: a letter from Mrs. Bowes more urgent, more definitely demanding than before. Sir Robert Bowes, the ambitious uncle, died that March: and her husband had apparently relented a little in hostility to Knox. Though not a great deal: when he died three years later he left money only to his three unmarried daughters, and then only if they did not marry against their brother's wishes. However, Mrs. Bowes now begged him to come and rescue both Marjorie and herself from Mary Tudor's England.

Knox found this idea 'most contrar to my own judgement'. Not only did he risk death, but how could he support a wife, much less a mother-in-law? It was a long, dangerous way to go to add to his burdens, and only poverty to offer them. But 'every word of the faithful ought to be keepit', he once wrote: and he never refused a call. He set off again on what he may have hoped was his last journey: but it was really the beginning of his story.

He reached Berwick in late summer, and was touched and

pleased by his welcome. Perhaps he re-captured something of the happiness he had once known, his first spring there, with Marjorie's love, the unfaltering kindness of his 'belovit mother' and the loyalty of a congregation which, in spite of the persecution, seemed still firm. Here too he got encouraging news from Scotland. Quietly but steadily the people were rejecting the hopelessly decadent Church of Rome: and this in spite of the political triumph of Mary of Guise, and of Mary Tudor in England.

'Thus did light and darkness strive within the realm of Scotland,' Knox was to write, 'the darkness ever before the world suppressing the light, from the death of that notable servant of God, Master Patrick Hamilton, unto the death of Edward the Saxt, that most godly and most virtuous King . . . Satan intended nothing less than the light of Jesus Christ utterly to have been extinguished. . . .' But 'first came a simple man, William Harlaw', preaching diligently: and then Willock the Ayrshireman came back openly. He had escaped from England to Emden, where he practised as a doctor. Now Anna, Duchess of Friesland, sent him home to Scotland to conduct her trade negotiations – and to spread the Reformation.

'And lastly, at the end of hairst, came John Knox.'

'At the end of harvest' was a wonderfully descriptive phrase: for he came to sow, and had mainly to reap. It was more than eight years since he had been in Scotland: but so far from forgetting him, his own people had made of him a legend: a distant but still glimmering star they could look to in the darkness.

He slipped over the Border, and came secretly to Edinburgh where he lodged either with John Syme, burgess, or with the wealthy Barron, Dean of Guild, in the High Street near St. Giles'. And through the dark of these steep-pitched, narrow streets, sharp with the first frosts, a throng of folk came silently: the Dean of Guild, the Town Clerk and a great crowd of common men and women. His whispered name ran like magic through the tall 'lands' – the towering tenements of the Royal Mile: and still they came, and still they listened.

'The ways of men are not in his own power,' Knox wrote to Mrs. Bowes: 'Albeit my journey towards Scotland, belovit mother, was maist contrarious to my awn judgement, before I did enterprise the same: yet this day I praise God for them who were the cause external of my resort to these quarters. . . . If I had not seen it with my eyes, in my own country, I could not have believed it! Yea, mother, their fervency doth so ravish me, that I cannot but accuse and condemn my slothful coldness. God grant them their heart's desire! Comfort yourself in God's promises, and be assured that God stirs up more friends than we be 'ware of. My commendation to all your company. In great haste, the 4 November, 1555. From Scotland. Your son, John Knox.'

Knox saw now that this was far more than a revolt from the corruptions of Rome. It was an overwhelming hunger for a new and cleaner communion. The first step was to cut off the last rags of superstition. The mass was already dead to the people: but it took courage to break off the thousand-year-old habit of it. Knox took on himself the responsibility of making the break with Roman ritual and all its accretions. 'With Popes, Purgatory, penances, pilgrimages, salt and oil for bairns and all sic-like baggage!' He went back to the great law-giving of Deuteronomy, and applied it to the Gospel: 'Add nothing to it, take nothing from it.' He would have them all receive the Gospel in its naked simplicity: delivered first to plain unlettered men: and therefore theirs for the taking in every age.

Some of the lairds who had now come forward were uncertain of this, and they thrashed the matter out, in platonic tradition, at a supper party in Edinburgh that winter. The host was Erskine of Dun, honourable, gentle and wise, who had been a friend of Wishart's and yet was respected by the other side. He brought another of Wishart's old friends there, David Forres. There was Willock, of course: and young Maitland of Lethington, son of the poet, already wordly-wise and witty. He, ever for compromise, was one of those who protested. What harm could it do to go to Mass, as well as follow the reformed doctrine? Did not St. Paul, at the commandment of James and of the elders . . . pass to the temple and feigned himself to pay his vow with others?

There is all Scotland in Knox's answer; first, he gives an excellent show of logic as to why the two cases are totally different: and then he adds: 'Secondly, I greatly doubt whether either James's commandment or Paul's obedience proceeded from the Holy Ghost.'

'To argue with Knox,' sighed Maitland, 'is like a foretaste of Judgement Day. We see perfectly, that our shifts will serve nothing before God, seeing that they stand us in so small stead before man!'

With Erskine, Knox crossed the Forth and went up into Angus and the Mearns. All that stretch of bien farming land heard him gladly, but were cautious to commit themselves, as their nature was. He came back from there to lodge with another good friend of the Reformed Faith: old Lord Sandilands of Calder House, that tree-encrusted mansion barely ten miles west of Edinburgh. Sandilands, who was also prior of the Knights of St. John (the Knights Hospitaller), had presented the living of Calder-comitis to Spottiswood, after the latter's return from England. Sandilands was nephew to Lady Cockburn of Ormiston, and had himself barely escaped through a window of her house on the night of Wishart's arrest. So here again Knox's preaching was a harvesting.

At Calder House Knox first met the men who might be leaders of the nation: Archibald, Lord Lorne, heir to the Duke of Argyle: Erskine, later Earl of Mar and Regent: and young James Stewart, later Earl of Moray and Regent, illegitimate half-brother to the young Queen in France, full cousin to Erskine of Dun. This young 'Lord James', as he was called, had been prior of St. Andrews – over Winram – since infancy: he had already met Knox at the English Court as a lad, and may have heard him preach there and so been influenced. Ablest of all James V's children, he would have made an excellent King.

Knox won these men. They were so moved by his preaching they 'wished it could be public'. He spent the rest of the winter between Edinburgh and Mid Calder; and set off after Yule to Kyle, the traditional 'receptacle of God's people'. There he preached in Barr and Kinyeancleuch and in Ayr itself: and in the houses of Gadgirth, and of Ochiltree: 'and in some of them he ministered the Lord's Table'.

But it was at Finlayston, at that still lovely point above the river Clyde, opposite Dumbarton Rock, that he was first publicly and specially called to give Communion. Finlayston was the seat of the Earl of Glencairn, and he and his wife and two of his sons were present. Across the then shallow salmon-river were French soldiers, the garrison of Dumbarton Castle on the Rock and not many miles upstream was Paisley, with its rich abbey and powerful abbot. Probably out of reverence they did not use any domestic goblet, but unscrewed and reversed two great hollow silver candlesticks to serve as chalices. For over three hundred years these candlesticks continued to be so used, being sent up to the parish kirk of Kilmacolm twice a year at the sacrament season; until some time at the end of the nineteenth century they disappeared.

Knox went back to Calder, where again the Lord's Table was spread, and many came from the country round about, and from Edinburgh. Tradition sometimes places these celebrations in the open air, for now it was spring.

From Calder he went again with the Laird of Dun up the east coast, where he was joyfully welcomed, and begged to give the Sacrament there too: 'whereof were partakers the most part of the gentlemen of the Mearns'. Having made up their minds to join him they did so wholeheartedly, making a vow in public 'to maintain to the uttermost of their powers the true preaching of the evangel of Jesus Christ, as God should offer unto them preachers and opportunity'. Knox was now not only preaching a faith, he was founding the Kirk.

The bruit of all this, to use his own Franco-Scots word, had run through the country. The Queen Regent had already asked, if it were some refugee Englishman who was preaching? And a bishop answered her: 'Nay, no Englishman, but Knox, that knave!' Out of their bitterness the Black Friars rashly summoned him to answer charges of heresy in Edinburgh. Perhaps they did not think he would come: but come he did, promptly and most willingly, escorted by Erskine of Dun and 'divers other gentlemen', saying he wished 'no other armour but the power of God's word and the liberty of his tongue'. It was too much for the friars, who hurriedly withdrew their charges: but Knox was already installed in the Bishop of Dunkeld's 'great lodging', and saw no reason to hurry away. He preached there twice a day, with reckless boldness, to 'a greater audience than ever before he had done in that town'.

To Berwick he wrote:

'Belovit Mother, with my maist heartily commendation in the Lord Jesus Christ – albeit I was fully purposit to have visited

you before this time, yet hath God laid impediments, which I
could not avoid. They are such as I doubt not are to his glory,
and to the comfort of many here. The trumpet blew the old
sound three days together till private houses of indifferent
largeness could not contain the voice of it. God, for Christ his
son's sake grant me to be mindful that the sobbs of my heart
hath not been in vane, nor neglected in the presence of his
Majesty. O! Sweet were the death that should follow sic forty
days in Edinburgh, as here I have had three! Rejoice mother;
the time of our deliverance approacheth . . . I can write no more
to you at this present. The grace of the Lord Jesus rest with you.
In haste – this Monunday – your son, John Knox.'

Glencairn brought the Earl Marischal to hear the preaching one
night. Both were deeply impressed. Knox's words seemed to
clothe their faith with a visible body, till they could almost see the
shape of a national church. Anything seemed possible in that year
of miraculous harvest: even an open and legal sanction of their
faith. At their pressing, Knox sat down to write a letter to the
Queen Regent, pleading for a settlement for the new kirk.

Knox wrote this letter with his very heart's blood, and in utter
sincerity. If there was any chance that it might succeed it would
not be lost for him. He humbled himself to the dust to write it, as
one of whom the Regent could have heard nothing but ill. 'I am
traduced as a heretic, accused as a false teacher and seducer of the
people, and more beside.' So it might appear 'foolish to many that
he, a worm most wretched, a man of base state and condition,
dare enterprise' such a letter. Nevertheless, he pleads for the
people of Scotland to this Frenchwoman, and draws a picture of
the ideal ruler, whose charge rests on God: and he warns that
failure to recognize this brings judgement. If she will not listen
to this heart-cry of her people 'then shall ye suddenly feel the
depressing hand of Him who hath exalted you. Ye will be
compelled to know, will ye nil ye, that He is Eternal against
whom ye address your battle. . . . Lay the Book of God before
your eyes and let it be judge. . . . I confess I desire your Grace to
enter into a strange and grievous battle . . . yet shall your reward
be great in this world, and immortality with joy inestimable shall
be your portion.'

It was not perhaps so very tactful after all: Knox was at his worst in diplomacy. But there could be no mistaking its passionate sincerity. Glencairn delivered the letter to the Regent, and they waited in vain for an answer. Knox heard afterwards that, having glanced through it, she had handed it over to the Archbishop of Glasgow, Cardinal Beaton's nephew, with the remark: 'Please you, my Lord, to read a pasquil!' (i.e. an April Fool). He was bitterly hurt, savagely disappointed. All their brief, bright dream vanished in the daylight: they saw all too plainly how fantastic it had been.

There was no question of armed resistance. Bloody Mary Tudor over the Border was reaching a climax of cruelty against the Protestants: France was behind the Regent. It was a complete check.

At this point Knox received a call from the English Church in Geneva, of which he had been an ordinary member after 'the troubles at Frankfort'. Now they asked him to come back to be their pastor, jointly with Christopher Goodman. He accepted, and sent off in advance Marjorie and her mother and his servant Jamie Campbell and 'Patrick his pupil'. He himself lingered to take a last flying farewell of the new congregations. This time he went with young Lord of Lorne to his father's court at Castle Campbell: for MacCailin Mor was unofficial but absolute monarch of his own considerable kingdom of Argyle. He must have been a formidable despot to impress: but impressed he was, and a loyal supporter from then on, and his people with him.

Perhaps it was their ancient tradition which made the westward lands of Lorne take so quickly and so firmly to the Reformed faith. For all that country is dotted still with traces of the Church first planted by the little saints who followed Columba; and it is passionately kirk-minded to this day.

Knox wrote a letter to the Commons of Scotland after his return to Geneva that is, like the Gettysburg address, one of the great human documents of history.

'Neither would I that ye should esteem the reformation and care of religion less to appertain to you, because ye are no kings, rulers, judges, nobles nor in authority. Beloved brethren, ye are God's creatures, created and formed to his own image and similitude: for whose redemption was shed the most precious blood of the only beloved Son of God: to whom he hath commanded his Gospel and glad tidings to be preached; and for whom he hath prepared the heavenly inheritance. . . .

And this is the point wherein I say, All men are equal: that as all be descended from Adam, by whose sin and inobedience did Death enter into the world, so it behoves all that shall obtain life to be ingrafted in one, that is in the Lord Jesus who being a just servant doth by his knowledge justify many. . . .'

In Exodus xxx, the same oblation was asked of all the men of Israel, from the richest to the poorest. 'If this equality was commanded by God for maintainance of that transitory tabernacle . . . is not the same required of us, who now have the verity? For as the price which was given for man's redemption is one, so God requireth of all that shall be partakers of the benefits of the same a like duty. . . . Of the prince, that he refuse himself and that he follow Christ Jesus; of the subject he craveth the same.'

'And this is that equality which is between the kings and subjects the most rich and noble, and betwixt the poorest and men of low estate; to wit, that as the one is obliged to believe in heart, and with the mouth to confess the Lord Jesus to be the only Saviour of the world, so is the other. Neither is there any of God's children of years of discretion so poor but he hath this much to bestow . . . neither is there any so rich of whose hand God requireth any more.'

10

The Stickit Minister

KNOX was a parson in the Church of England for five years, in Geneva for barely two. Yet he was rarely happy in his Swiss charge, pasturing his 'most precious little flock' between the eternal snows of Mont Blanc and the blue water of Lake Leman. He had a happy home of his own, and a congregation of some of the best minds and most dedicated men of the day, with whom, he said, 'I would be content to end my days, if so it might stand with God's good pleasure. I can give no reason that I should so desire, other than that my heart so thirsteth.'

Here was published the *Book of Order* based on the draft he and Whittinghame had drawn up in Frankfort: and Goodman and probably others also collaborated in it. Here he shared in Coverdale and Whittinghame's new translation of the Bible, and some Scots words crept into it. (It became the Elizabethan's Bible: and was infinitely the best till the authorized version.)

John Bale, one of those who signed the Frankfort call and then followed Knox to Geneva, wrote of the town at this time:

'Geneva seemeth to me to be the wonderful miracle of the whole world: so many from all countries come thither, as it were into a sanctuary, not to father riches but to live in poverty . . . is it not wonderful that Spaniards, Italians, Scots, Englishmen, Frenchmen, Germans, disagreeing in manners, speech and apparel, sheep and wolves, bulls and bears, being coupled with the only yoke of Christ, should live so lovingly and friendly? . . .'

Knox himself had written, in the autumn of his return, to his London friend Mrs. Locke, who was anxious not to recant, but very afraid of burning. He advised her rather to leave her possessions and fly abroad than do either.

'In my heart I could have wished, yea, and cannot cease to
wish that it might please God to guide and conduct yourself to
this place where, I neither fear nor eshame to say, is the most
perfect school of Christ that ever was in the earth since the
days of the apostles. In other places I confess Christ to be
preached, but manners and religion to be so sincerely reformed,
I have not yet seen in any other place beside.'

Mrs. Locke, with her husband and family, took Knox's advice,
and they reached Frankfort about December.

That spring was especially blessed to Knox. For when the
snows melted and the tide of spring flowers rushed up the Alps,
his first son was born. Surely it was bending over the cradle in
tenderness that prompted the quotation: 'Behold, an Israelite
indeed in whom there is no guile'! For he was called Nathaniel:
and christened in May, with Whittinghame as godfather. As the
roads opened up again Mrs. Locke came on to Geneva with her
two children, in time for the christening.

That March, Knox had written to two loyal women in
Edinburgh:

'My own motion and daily prayer is, not only that I may visit
you, but also that with joy I may end my battle among you.
And assure yourself of this, that whenever a greater number
among you shall call upon me than now hath bound me to
serve them' – (in Geneva) – 'by His grace it shall not be the
fear of punishment, neither yet of the death temporal that
shall impede my coming to you.'

His call was nearer to hand than perhaps he realized. That same
May there arrived in Geneva the Edinburgh Dean of Guild Mr.
Barron with Mr. Syme. They had come all that way to bring a
letter calling Knox back to Scotland: and it was signed by
Glencairn, James Stewart, Erskine and Lorne. It was a most clear
and lawful calling:

'Grace, Mercy and Peace for Salutation:
Dearly Beloved in the Lord, the Faithful that are of your
aquaintance in thir parts (thanks be to God), are steadfast in

the belief whereunto you left them, and has ane godly thirst and desire, day by day, of your presence again; which if the Spirit of God will so move and permit time unto you, we will heartily desire you, in the name of the Lord, that ye will return again in thir parts, where ye shall find all faithful that ye left behind you, not only glad to hear your doctrine, but will be ready to jeopard lives and goods in the forward-setting of the glory of God. . . . The rest of our minds this faithful bearer will show you at length. This, fare ye weel in the Lord.'

Knox courteously consulted Calvin and the other ministers: 'who all with one consent said that he could not refuse that vocation unless he would declare himself rebellious unto his God, and unmerciful to his country'. So he sent off letters home, by whatever messengers could be found – by the burgesses, perhaps? – accepting the call, and promising to come. Owing to the troubled times, he got no answer.

Meanwhile, Mrs. Locke's little daughter died, which must have grieved them all. Her son survived, and became the great-uncle of Locke the philosopher. Knox's successor had to be chosen: and since the congregation chose Whittinghame, he had also to be ordained. It was almost certainly Knox who ordained him, and no doubt he did so with both pride and affection. After Mary Tudor's death, when the little flocks all scattered home to England, Whittinghame became chaplain to the Earl of Warwick during the defence of Havre (1562 and 1563): there he did so well and so loyally that Warwick – the eldest surviving Dudley – wrote home both to Cecil and to his brother Robin – (Elizabeth's Leicester) – praising and recommending him. The year after, he was made Dean of Durham: and on his ordination being questioned, the Dean of York said that he was 'ordained in a better manner than even the Archbishop himself'. The Lord President said he could not in conscience agree to allow 'Popish massing priests in our ministry, and to disallow ministers made in a Reformed church'. So Knox's ordination was valid in the Church of England, and Whittinghame remained Dean without further ceremony.

Knox probably waited for further word from Scotland; for it was more than three months before he finally set off. Perhaps he felt in his bones that the times were wrong. He had always keenly watched the political situation, and his prophecies were often his shrewd judgements of it. Now the times could hardly be worse for his venture. The long rivalry between France and Spain had come to a head in war: Mary Tudor, to please Philip, had dragged England in against France on 7 June. France was moving closer to Scotland as her old ally, and Mary of Guise, Queen Regent, saw her aim of bringing Scotland wholly under France at last a possibility. The de Guises in France were determined to stamp out Huguenots once for all: the Inquisition had been set up there in April, with Mary Stewart's uncle as Chief Inquisitor, and persecution was bitter.

But Knox had had a call: and although he got no further news, and although his own judgement may have been against it, he obeyed. Before he took a long and most moving farewell of his 'dear flock' he may have officiated at three baptisms for them on 17 August. On that day were christened Zacharie Whittinghame, son of the new minister, Zacharie Bodley, son of John Bodley, whose descendant founded Oxford's Bodleian Library: and Susanne, daughter of John Barron, (not the Burgess, but a divinity student). This last child unfortunately died.

At last, at the end of summer he set out. There must have been some secret 'underground' line by which a man so well marked for death as Knox could pass across France: And the strain on it at that time was particularly heavy. Since the Edict of Compiégne against heretics that July, death stalked them. At any time the weakest link in the chain of safety might give way. That summer too the Spanish army gave the French, under the High Constable Anne de Montmorenci, a crushing defeat at St. Quentin. The constable was taken prisoner. His Scots squire, James Melville, who was there, heard him say: 'it was against his profession and occupation to fly'. Melville himself barely escaped on a captured horse, that bolted and tore through a guarded bridgehead. The cardinal gave it out that heretics were in league with the English, and were therefore traitors: he also put it about that their secret meetings were really obscene love-feasts. So when the priests betrayed to him one of their meetings in rue St. Jacques in Paris that September, he had a lynching mob ready to his hand.

Knox in September was at least near enough to the scene of this acute danger to know of it all: and he reports on the burnings that followed. The cardinal wished to kill all the prisoners: which was logical. Protestantism was largely stamped out in Spain by the *auto-da-fé* the year before at Valladolid. Mary's uncle pressed hard for the same simple, wholesale slaughter in France. It was the King, Henry II, who refused. They burnt only a few, including one young gentlewoman with a face '*vermeille d'une excellent beauté*'; and a lad of sixteen.

It was October when Knox at last reached Dieppe, after his secret and most dangerous journey; and there a bitter blow awaited him. There were, at last, two letters from Scotland: one advising delay, the other bluntly advising him not to come at all. The writer had 'communed with some that were most frack and fervent in the matter, and in none did he find such boldness and constancy as was requisite for such an enterprise: but some did repent that ever any such thing were moved: some were partly ashamed: and others were able to deny that ever they did consent to any such purpose, if any trial or question should be taken thereof'.

Knox wrote back 'To the Lords and others' that, when he had at last taken this in, 'I partly was confounded and partly was pierced with anguish and sorrow'. Confounded, for had he not consulted 'the most godly and most learned of this day'? And now it must 'redound either to your shame or mine: for either it shall appear that I was marvellous vain', seeking advice where none was required; or else that his counsellors were in error, lacking 'ripeness of judgements'. 'To some it may appear a small and light matter that I have cast off and as it were abandoned alswell my particular care as my public office and charge: leaving my house and poor family destitute of all head save God only, and committing that small (but to Christ dearlie belovit) flock, over the which I was appointed one of the ministers, to the charge of ane other. This, I say, to worldly men may appear a small matter, but to me it was and yet is such that more worldly substance that I will express could not have caused me willingly behold the eyes of so many grave men weep at once for my cause as that I did, in taking of my last good night of them. To whom, if it please God that I return, and question be demanded, what

D

was the cause of my purposed journey? judge now what I shall answer.'

Then Knox adds impassioned expostulation, which has a most revealing climax:

'God open your eyes, that ye may espy and consider your own miserable estate! My words shall appear to some sharp and undiscreetly spoken: but as charity ought to interpret all things to the best, so ought wise men to understand, that a true friend can not be a flatterer, especially when the questions of salvation, both of body and soul, are moved: and that not of one or two, but as it were of a whole realm and nation.'

Was it news to the lords that Knox now saw the Kirk in terms of the 'whole realm and nation'? Perhaps it was new to him too, in the sudden, startling realization of all that he had lost. He ended with the cry that, unless they were 'dead with the blind world', it was their clear duty to defend the oppressed, even to the risk of their lives: for that was their true title to nobility; not birth, nor name, nor lands.

The trumpet-note rang even through Knox's written word, and they rallied, when the letter was received and read out in Scotland. In December the lords met in Edinburgh and drew up a Common Bond: but Knox heard nothing of it. His letter, and other letters following it, went out into the void: no answer came, no news, no hope.

He wrote again on 1 December, a milder letter to his 'Brethren and others', warning them against discouragement and the troublesome small sects of the day: particularly against the pharisees and unco' guid, for the Church was for sinners; and from it 'ought no man to separate himself, notwithstanding that in the same the darnel and cockle appear to surmount the good seed'.

By now the Channel ports were closed, and brother William presumably could make no contact. Whatever the secret chain of communication from Scotland, somewhere a link had broken. Perhaps some smuggler found it safer to ditch the answers Knox never got. All he heard from Scotland, gathered from the papists, was of the increased power of the French there: the Queen Regent's jeering comment on his last year's letter appealing for freedom of worship: and that he had been condemned and burnt in effigy at the town cross outside St. Giles' the previous summer. Also a persistent rumour that the lords, hoping to make good terms, were supporting Mary of Guise in her demand for the Crown Matrimonial for France. On 17 December Knox wrote a long letter to combat that.

His letter began with a long appeal to scripture: showing how God could raise up leaders, even 'from the very dung-hill'. At the end, he gets down to brass tacks. He had seen once for all in Dudley's day what happened to those who tried by politics to further the kingdom. They were, now and always, to 'fly all confederacy'. And they were not to trust the Great Duke (Hamilton) – who, if he could be bought over, could also be bought back. Knox remembered his vacillations from boyhood. Yet, though holding aloof, they were not to revolt but to 'give lawful obedience to the Authority . . . for a great difference there is betwixt lawful obedience and an fearfull flattering of Princes. . . .'

Still no answer came. In England things were blacker still: no tidings came –

> Save that the night grows darker still
> And the tide rises higher.

Mary, still believing she was pregnant and that Philip might be won back if she had a child, and England expiated its heresy, burned and tortured, tortured and burned. The total number of her victims has been estimated at 300 in three years! and they include old men and girls, married couples, blind and halt, rich and poor. In the Channel Islands they burned a pregnant woman whose baby, 'a fair man-child', born in the flames, was burned with her.

Knox kept a careful list, as he got news. Many of the names he must have known: as when he adds to 'Cuthbert Symson' that he was 'one of the Deacons first chosen in the congregation in London'. Among the earliest names he catalogued were those of previous years. In 1554 Dr. Rowland Taylor, the saintly scholar, was martyred in his own town of Hadley: and old Bishop Hooper was burned outside Gloucester Cathedral, in the presence of his own wife, family and people. When this beloved old man was moved from his foul and solitary dungeon in the Fleet to Newgate, they did it by night and 'put out the coster-mongers' candles' for fear of outcry. He met his end with courage and great dignity, crying out only, 'For God's love, let me have more fire'.

The liquid-filled human body is horribly incombustible. Old Bishop Latimer and Bishop Ridley were tried and condemned next autumn. Throughout the trial Latimer, original to the last, wore several old-fashioned woollen nightcaps with earflaps tied under his chin, to save him the irritation of hearing the 'evidence'. His other clothes were 'an old Bristol frieze gown girded to his body with a penny leather girdle, at which hung by a long string his New Testament and his spectacles without a case, depending about his neck on his breast'. . . . Cranmer, afraid of the fire, recanted again and signed his denial of faith. When the other two were taken out they were chained to a single stake – the 'candle' Latimer meant, in a last jeer at Rome, when he cried: 'Play the man, Master Ridley! We shall this day light such a candle as I trust by God's grace shall never be put out!' He was himself eighty-two and once the gunpowder tied round him exploded, he was fortunate to die almost at once. But poor Ridley, standing in a tar-barrel, had his legs almost burnt off and was driven to drag himself towards the hottest part, crying: 'I cannot burn!'

The reprieved Cranmer had meanwhile gone through the most intensive brain-washing in prison. He was brought out for a final public recantation in Oxford in March 1556. He was a pitiful sight. The timid, brilliant scholar who had been terrorized by his schoolmaster and again by Henry VIII, was now completely broken. Trembling, dirty-bearded, 'he that late was Archbishop, Metropolitan, Primate of All England and King's Privy Counsellor, now in a bare and ragged gown, and ill-favouredly clothed, with an old square cap', was exposed to all men's scorn or pity. Sometimes, during the long denunciatory sermon that followed the *nunc dimittis* this 'living figure of perfect sorrow' leaned against the pillar, praying: 'and more than twenty times the tears gushed out'.

The sermon reached its climax, which was an appeal to him to have courage amidst the flames. Slowly, there penetrated to the darkened chaos of his mind the fact that though he had recanted he was not after all to escape. Slowly, perhaps, he straightened and the tears ceased to run down.

'Lest any doubt of his earnest conversion,' cried the preacher in conclusion, '. . . I pray you, Master Cranmer, openly to express the true profession of your faith, that all men may understand that you are a Catholic indeed.'

'I will do it,' said the broken man, 'and that with a good will.'

The clergy assembled must have hushed to hear him: and must have been stunned with astonishment as his voice gathered strength, and the words poured out, reaching a triumphant peak:

'. . . now I come to the great thing, which so much troubleth my conscience more than anything that ever I did or said in my whole life and that is the setting abroad of a writing contrary to the truth; which now here I renounce and refuse as things written with my hand, contrary to the truth which I thought in my heart, and written for fear of death, and to save my life if it might be . . . my hand shall first be punished there-fore: for, may I come to the fire, it shall be first burned.'

So, gloriously, he died.

Nor was there need for ecumenical movements in the flames. John Rough, Knox's old colleague and the instrument of his calling at St. Andrews, had been living secure with his wife and children in Friesland. They earned their livings making stockings and other knitted goods: and Rough ventured over to London to sell a consignment and to take further orders. Some of the London congregation and their preachers had been caught and burned at this time – probably in April, 1556, when several were burned at once. Some sympathizers, lurking in a dark lane near the ghastly spectacle, recognized Rough stealing past and asked him, 'Where had he been?'

'Where, quotha',' said Rough, 'but to learn the way.'

He stepped into the shoes of the martyred man, and became pastor to the remnant in London. A year later he too was caught, and that very December Knox chafed at Dieppe he was taken out to Smithfield and died at the stake, three days before Christmas, 1557. So ended John Rough 'not of the most learned', yet one of the Glorious Company for all that.

Knox had not sat idle while he waited in his no-man's-land, hearing nothing but bad news. He had preached in French and

ministered to the Huguenot congregation in the rue d'Ecosse in
Dieppe. And he so strengthened and inspired them that they
began for the first time to have 'the face of a kirk'. Their records
still bear witness to his work. He also began a translation of an
Apology for the French Protestants the de Guises had caught,
and against whom they had made abominable charges. 'Our
cause is one this day with the primitive kirk', wrote Knox
remembering Nero, who had spread the same tales against the
early Christians. This work had to be finished by someone else,
he himself was so busy. He preached and baptized also in La
Rochelle.

And so the winter wore away with never a word from Scotland.
That December the Queen Regent had 'left no point of the
compass unsailed' to gain her end – the granting of the Crown
Matrimonial to France. She made such verbal promises to the
lords of freedom of worship that they went temporarily over to
her side. The Scottish Parliament of that month granted the
Crown Matrimonial to France when Mary should marry the
Dauphin; and so the Regent's life's ambition was realized.

In January, England lost Calais, her last French possession:
and Scotland began to fill up with French troops, Frenchmen
taking over all the high offices, including that of the Great Seal
of the Realm. Henry II began to press for the marriage of Mary
and the Dauphin, so that very month commissioners for the
marriage were appointed in Scotland. They sailed from Leith,
the port of Edinburgh, on 9 February and landed at Dieppe.

Did Knox watch from behind some latticed wooden shutter,
and see the bustle and sensation of their arrival, and of their
escorted state departure? It must have been a great occasion:
with all the horses and outriders and pennons, the glorious
colours of the silk and velvet clothes, the bugles and plumes, the
embroidered harness and horse-trappings, the glitter and jingle
of sword and spur and wrought bit: and the shouts and cheers of
all the excited crowds. And to Knox all this happy excitement
must have been the bitterest dregs of disappointment: for foremost
among those gay riders to the Court of France were James
Stewart and Erskine of Dun, two who had signed his call to
Scotland.

11

The 'Blast'

NEWS of Knox's unhappy suspension had worked back to Geneva; and on 16 December, at a meeting of the English congregation there, they had re-elected him as their minister, along with Christopher Goodman. It says volumes for Knox's popularity that they should have gone so far out of their way to call him back. Word of their calling must have got through to Knox; for after the Scots lords had ridden through he put his pride in his pocket and set off on the weary, dangerous road back.

It was more, this time, than just one more failure in a life-time of failures. He went in the bitterness of a despair that counted this as final. He was turning his back, once for all, on his dream of Reformed Scotland.

He reached Geneva in March 1558. There he poured out his grief and confusion to one of the good ladies of the Edinburgh congregation probably thinking them safer correspondents and more likely to receive his letters. He signed his letters to them 'John Sinclair', using his mother's name: and he asked them to pass the letters round. In this first one he cried that surely Satan had hindered him, as he had impeded Paul to go to Thessalonica!

'. . . Only this dare I say, that sometimes (seldom, alas!) I feel a sob and groan, willing that Christ Jesus might openly be preached in my native country, and with a certain desire that my ears might hear it, though it should be with the loss of this wretched life. . . . the cause of my stop do I not to this day clearly understand. I most suspect my own wickedness, who am not worthy of so great a joy and comfort, as to hear Christ Jesus truly preached where my heart most thirsteth. . . .'

Yet he had to admit another reason.

'I heard such troubles as appeared in that realm: I began to dispute with myself as followeth: "Shall Christ Jesus, the Author of Peace, be preached where war is proclaimed? What comfort canst thou have, to see the one half of the people rise up against the other? Yea, to jeopard the one, to murder and destroy the other? But above all, what joy shall it be to thy heart to behold with thy eyes thy native country betrayed into the hands of strangers which to no man's judgement can be avoided?" . . .'

Yet now he had abandoned the call he was in an agony of remorse: 'almost as without comfort and without counsel'. 'Desiring you . . . unfeignedly to call to God for me. . . .' He also will not cease to pray that they may continue steadfastly, 'leaving unto your posterity such testimony of your perfect faith. . . . Then whatsoever shall become of this wretched carcase, I am most certainly persuaded that the invincible power of Him . . . shall perform that good work which He has began amongst you.'

In that final paragraph he betrays his despair. He now thought that the moment for Reformation had passed for his generation. He could only hope that the light would not be utterly extinguished. To leave a clear record for those who would come after, he published in the next few months a new edition of his letter appealing for freedom of worship to the Queen Regent, adding a biting commentary in the margin: and also an *Appellation to the Nobility and Estates* against his condemnation and burning. In July he published the second half of this Appellation, addressed to the Commons of Scotland: this was the glorious piece of writing, quoted in the previous chapter, that might almost have been Knox's last will and testament to his own folk.

That April, the week after Knox had written his heart-broken letter to Edinburgh, there was a royal wedding in the Cathedral of Notre Dame in Paris. Very lovely, very moving must have been that tremendous and historic occasion, when the Crown Matrimonial of Scotland passed to France: and before all the great and the splendid Princes of the Blood and the Princes of the Church, a tall girl of sixteen was married to a pale boy three months younger. It was one of the most magnificent weddings that France had ever celebrated.

And behind the music and the magic, the beauty and the incense, the ugly facts: before she signed the marriage treaty with the Scots commissioners, Mary signed three secret treaties. In these her rights to the Scottish and English crowns were pledged to France if she died without issue: to be held till France was repaid 'for Scotland's defence and her education'. In the third, she denied in advance any other treaty she might sign.

The cardinal had taught her well. She sold her country, sold her oath: and then went on to take a sacred promise before the high altar, with every possible trapping of religion.

The lords of the congregation left in Scotland now asked the Queen Regent to ratify the verbal promises she had made. They were quickly disillusioned. To underline the point, at the suggestion of Bothwell's uncle, Bishop Hepburn, an aged priest called Walter Myln was arrested. He was now well over eighty and had for many years preached Reform. It was also charged against him, not only that he had married but that he had baptised his children. He defended himself ably, but would not recant. 'I am corn and not chaff. I will abide the fire.' He was found guilty and burned alive that same April in St. Andrews. He had at least his dying wish: to be the last that should so suffer.

That spring too Knox published a work that summed up all the bitterness of his frustration and despair: a work of no great importance, but of lasting notoriety: his *First Blast of the Trumpet* directed against 'this monstriferous empire of Women (which amongst all enormities that this day do abound upon the face of the whole earth, is most detestable and damnable). . . .' It was 'a trumpet that will sound in despite of the adversarie . . . may the sound . . . by the support of some wind (blow it from the south or blow it from the north, it is of no matter) come to the ears of the chief offenders. But whether it do or not, yet dare we not cease to blow as God will give strength. For we are debtors to more than to Princes, to wit, to the multitude of our brethren. . . .'

Knox had seen the misery of 'the multitude of our brethren' among the exiles in Geneva: and still more as he hid and slid across war-torn France, with the Inquisition adding its evil shadow to the landscape: and from England and Scotland there had come nothing but more and more dreadful tales of horror and persecution. Why did God allow such things? he must

D*

continually have been asked. It was the 'monstrous empire of cruel women', he answered now.

'To promote a Woman to bear rule . . . above any realm, nation or city is repugnant to Nature: contumely to God . . . and the subversion of all good order, equity and justice. . . . For who can deny but it is repugnant to nature that the blind shall be appointed to lead and conduct such as do see? That the weak, the sicke and impotent persons shall nourish the whole and strong? And finally, that the foolish, madd and phrenetic shall govern the discrete, and give counsel to such as be sober of mind? And such be all women' (says Knox rather superbly), 'compared unto man in bearing of authoritie.'

Not, however, to weaken his case by exaggeration he adds: 'I except such as God, by singular priviledge, and for certain causes known only to Himself, hath exempted from the common rank of women, and do speak of women as nature and experience do this day declare them. Nature I say, doth paint them forth to be weak, frail, impatient, feeble and foolish; and experience hath declared them to be unconstant, variable, cruell and lacking the spirit of counsel and regiment.' He has no trouble in finding confirmation of this amongst 'men of all ages', from Aristotle onwards.

To reinforce his arguments he has recourse to those early fathers whose teaching he had had so seldom regarded as final or binding in other ways. Now he quotes Tertullian, Chrysostom, Ambrose and Basillus Magnus: some of whose views on women must have caused feminine amusement throughout the centuries. 'Womankind is imprudent and soft . . . rash and foolhardy, and their covetiousness is like the gulf of Hell, that is insatiable.' Woman is 'a tender creature, flexible, soft and pitiful: . . . not apt to bear rule and forbidden to teach'. The whole curse of Eva rests upon her perpetually, she is (or should be) silent forever before Man, her lord and master (whether she be married or not): for he is ordained her superior physically, mentally, spiritually: and, where this is difficult to prove, at least by some obscure but inalienable right. 'Man is head to woman, even as Christ is head to all man.' The margins of the text are studded with Knox's ejaculations: 'God grant all women's hearts to understand and follow this!' 'Let all women take heed' etc.

When Aylmer, once schoolmaster to Jane Grey and to

Elizabeth, wrote an answer – *Ane Harbour Against the Blast*, he said expressly he did so to refute the argument, 'not to deface the man', who was so widely known and liked. It was his zeal which had carried him away, said Aylmer, seeing so many tortured and burned: 'had he not swerved from the particular to the general, he had said nothing too much'.

Why did Knox so swerve? He was happy in his marriage, he was as blessed with women friends and supporters as was St. Paul: and he was himself kindly and generous in his dealings with women. When he died he left his daughters portions, not tied to conditions or for marriage only, but to be freely theirs whenever they had reached an age of discretion. But he, and the cause of Reform which was dearer to him than life, had been defeated he thought finally by women: by Mary Tudor and Mary of Guise. And just because they were women, the crown of England might pass to Spain and the crown of Scotland to France. Most of all, he genuinely believed that man should be head of the family in State and in Church as well as at home: this last was the core of the argument.

Yet the *Blast* blew against *all* women, with an irresistible suggestion of henpecked defiance. Over and over it insists that woman in her highest state is man's humble servant, and at her best should keep silence before his superior wisdom. One cannot but remember that Knox was living with his mother-in-law: he had already in an earlier letter mentioned to Mrs. Locke 'troubles domestical, whereof being unaccustomed I am the more fearful'. He came back now to Geneva with something of the diminished status and the embittered mind of a 'stickit minister': Nathaniel was not yet a year old – 'at the worst stage' – and almost as soon as he returned Marjorie, whose health was not good, was pregnant again. Mrs. Bowes would have been less than human if she had not at this point been less the adoring follower and more just Marjorie's mother. Almost, we can see Knox hiding these furious and defiant pages behind the musty tomes of Tertullian and Chrysostom each time Mrs Bowes invaded the room with the day's disasters or a crying child.

Goodman wrote a similar treatise at the same time: 'How Superior Powers ought to be Obeyed: and wherein they may be lawfully resisted'. Elizabeth never forgave him this; but it has nothing of that personal bite which makes Knox's work so unfortunately immortal. The *Blast* is nailed as firmly to the name of Knox as Bruce to the spider, or Alfred to the cakes. Nobody knows or cares now what Knox wrote in his major work on Predestination, a huge volume published in 1560: but every man has felt an echo in his soul of his sentiments, if not on queens, at least on mothers-in-law.

Marjorie's second baby was born in November. He was christened on St. Andrew's Eve, 29 November, by Knox's colleague Goodman. He was called Eleazar, a name tinged with Knox's own despair. For you read in Numbers that Eleazar was the son born in the wilderness to Aaron the high priest, who was destined never to see the Promised Land.

'And the Lord spake unto Moses and Aaron in Mount Hor by the coast of the land of Edom, saying:

"Aaron shall be gathered unto his people: for he shall not enter into the land which I have given unto the children of Israel, because ye rebelled against my word at the water of Meribah.

"Take Aaron and Eleazar his son, and bring them up unto Mount Hor:

"And strip Aaron of his garments, and put them upon Eleazar his son: and Aaron shall be gathered unto his people, and shall die there." '

So the mantle of Aaron descended to his son, and Eleazar became priest in his stead.

That autumn Knox had had yet one more blow: he had heard that his congregations in Berwick and Newcastle had now gone wholly back to Rome. In great grief and bitterness that even that blink of light was to be swallowed up in the universal darkness he wrote to them a long exhortation, dated 10 November 1558. He begins on the general disasters and declines: and then the memory of all that they had had and had done together sweeps him away.

'How oft have ye assisted to Baptism? How oft have ye been partakers of the Lord's Table, prepared, used and ministered in all simplicity, not as man had devised, neither as The King's Proceedings did allow, but as Christ Jesus did institute, and as it is evident that Saint Paul did practise? These 2 Sacraments, seals of Christ's Evangel, ye commonly used: baptism for your children, and the Table of the Lord to your own comfort and for the open confession of your religion. . . . But O, alas! what miserable ruins hath this sudden and short storm made of that building that was begun amongst you!'

He goes on to speak of his own simplicity with them:

'I sought neither pre-eminence, glory nor riches; my honour was, that Christ Jesus should reign; my glory, that the light of his truth should shine in you; and my greatest riches, that in the same ye should be constant.

But to what purpose is this recited? . . . I fear that God hath cursed me because he hath not better blessed my labours amongst you. . . .'

He speaks of Paul's disappointments, in the falling-off of the congregations of Gallacia and Corinth:

'These and other like examples teach us how God's most true and painful servants have been frustrate of their expectation, and so humbled before God; whose fruits I have to pull, and as it were by violence to draw me from the bottom of Hell, to the which sometimes I sink for remembrance of your fall, and for my other offences against God committed.'

Then, at 'the bottom of Hell', and all unexpected, the light broke. On the seventeenth of that same November Mary Tudor died: and her country woke as from some sweating nightmare. In a great wave of thanksgiving Elizabeth was swept to the throne. She rode to London, a girl in her twenties, her red hair glinting, her laugh ringing out, Robin Dudley, handsomest of all Northumberland's sons, riding behind her on a great white charger. 'I think the Spring must be expected, the Almighty God be bound to no time,' wrote Parker, emerging from his hiding, to Bacon. In the streets the people wept with joy:

Sing up, heart, sing up, heart,
Sing no more down!
But joy in Elizabeth
Who weareth the crown!

In Geneva too there must have been tears and prayers of thanksgiving. Goodman and Knox were re-elected ministers, but already perhaps the congregation were slipping joyfully homewards. Knox still had to wait, and as he waited he wrote another letter, addressed to all England:

'For, in very deed, when in dolour of heart I wrote this former letter, I neither looked, nor could believe that the Lord Jesus would so suddenly knock at thy gate. . . .'

He conjures them to seize their opportunities, and winds up with six practical and helpful suggestions for radically reconstructing the Church of England, beginning with the abolition of archbishop and bishops and all 'pompous prelates' who have charges far too big to be effectual. He urges them to have done with the dregs of papistry and 'the glistering beauty of vain ceremonies': to consider the greater efficacy of the 'living voice above the bare letter read': and to put in hand a really comprehensive programme of education. All of which might well have done the Church of England much and lasting good: but did in fact do Knox a great deal of harm.

That November too came his third call to Scotland: and it was the first direct news he had had of the lords for nearly two years. The man who brought the letters was on his way to Rome for confirmation of the appointment of the new Bishop of Ross: but the road to Rome had taken a new bend, and he went by way of Geneva, and delivered the letters to Knox on the way. With them were letters to Calvin, urging him to send Knox back to them. It had taken the lords many months to find a sure messenger and get these letters through.

It did not take Knox long to answer. He spent one more Christmas with his little family and his beloved little flock: and then set out in January, which was still deep winter. He must have wondered when he would ever see any of them again. He wished to go home by way of England, to see his congregations in Berwick and Newcastle, so he sent off application for a pass, probably with some English exile returning at this time.

Knox had come to Geneva a penniless refugee; he left as an honorary burgess of the city – the freedom being a lasting token of its respect and admiration for him. When the congregation finally disbanded in May, Whittinghame thanked the city for their most Christian hospitality and handed over their records, the *Livre des Anglais,* as a memento of their stay: it is still there.

It took Knox till March to reach Dieppe. There he found a letter from Mrs. Locke, dated the previous February in Geneva: and as she had waited so long for an answer he wrote her an unusually friendly one. There also, where he had had so many disappointments, he had yet another. For he heard that not only had his request for a pass been flatly refused, but that the bearers of it had almost been flung into prison.

Nothing is more astonishing in Elizabeth than the instancy and certainty with which she gathered up the reins of government in her slim, beautiful hands. She knew all about the *Blast,* and she had her own views on the fitness of feeble-minded females to rule. She had views too on the fitness of low-born subjects to advise rulers. Knox daren't set foot in England.

'England hath refused me" he wrote to Mrs. Locke, on 6 April: 'And yet have I been a secret and assured friend to thee, O England. . . . No man will I salute in commendation specially, although I bear good will to all that unfeignedly profess Christ Jesus: for to me it is written that my *First Blast* hath blown from me all my friends in England.'

As to Mrs. Locke's anxious queries on the English Prayer Book, 'Mr. Parson's pattering of constrained prayers' are neither here nor there: 'But consider, Sister, what I have affirmed, that where Christ Jesus is not preached (mark well that I say, preached), that here hath the Sacrament neither life nor soul.'

Once again Knox cooled his heels at Dieppe, craving with all his heart to be gone. On 22 April he wrote to Cecil. He would not, he said, labour 'to conciliate your favours'. In an age when Court flattery was a high art Knox did not compete.

'This your horrible defection from the truth known and professed, hath God unto this day mercifully spared . . . seeing that his mercy hath spared you, being traitor to his Majestie: seeing further, that you, worthy of Hell, he hath promoted to honours and dignity: of you must he require earnest repentance for your former defection ... to the performance where of carnal wisdom and worldly policy (to which both, ye are bruited to be much inclined) give place to God's simple and naked truth. Very love compelleth me to say, that except the spirit of God purge your heart from that venom ... you shall not long escape the reward of dissemblers.'

Knox was writing in hot defence of his returned flock, who were not getting too good a welcome. He asked, for the third time 'and by diverse messengers, such privileges as Turks do commonly grant to men of every nation: ... to wit, that freedom should be granted me peaceably to pass through England'. As for the *Blast*: 'If Queen Elizabeth shall confess, so that the extraordinary dispensation of God's great mercy maketh that lawful unto her, which both nature and God's law deny ... then shall none in England be more willing to maintain her lawful authority than I shall be.'

Fortunately, he had not to wait for the answer to this singular approach. The very next day he found a boat which would take him to Leith – was it brother William, or some stray craft he found in the harbour? He embarked at once, and eight days later landed on Scots soil.

PART FOUR

12

'John Knox Is Come!'

'THE *Blast*' was not only 'blown out of season', as Aylmer said: it wasn't even necessary. For all this time 'the Lords and Others' had held doggedly to their purpose of Reform.

After Knox had left in 1556 the Romans had made some effort at reform themselves. Priests' bastards were not to be raised in their fathers' house, nor presented to their fathers' livings: and there was 'much ado for caps, shaven crowns, tippets, long gowns and such other trifles'. They also published *The Tuppenny Faith*. If their efforts were not great, they had the merit of independence: repeated appeals to Rome in the years past had resulted in nothing. Rome was absorbed in the gorgeous, gifted, corrupt Italy of the Medicis; she had international wars and power politics on her hands: there was no moment to spare for the spiritual anxieties of a small, cold, poverty-stricken peninsula on the outermost fringe of the world.

The richer Roman prelates were not concerned even for these minor reforms. Knox wrote sarcastically that Dury, Bishop of Galloway – 'Abbot Stottikin, for filthiness' – 'departed this life even as he lived: for the articles of his belief were: I refer: décarte you: ha, ha, the 4 kings and all made: the devil go with it, it is but a varlet'.

'After him followed that belly-god, David Panter, Bishop of Ross, with the like documentis, except that he departed eating and drinking which, together with the rest that thereupon depends, was the whole pastime of his life.'

Meanwhile in secret the 'Privy Kirk' of the Protestants

continued to meet in each others houses. 'God so did bless our weak beginnings' that some elders were elected to lead these meetings in prayer and Bible-reading. Paul Methven preached in Dundee, and right through Fife: and late that autumn Willock arrived back in Scotland from Friesland, this time for good. He landed in Dundee, then made his way to Edinburgh where he fell dangerously ill: but he continued to teach and preach from his bed, and eventually recovered.

By spring, 1557, the call to Knox had been planned; and it was signed in Stirling on the 10 March, and smuggled off with Barron and Sym. During the summer war broke out between France and Spain, with England dragged in on the side of Spain. To support France, Mary of Guise summoned the Scots troops and marched them to the Border to make the traditional raid of diversion. As Shakespeare was later to write in *Henry V:*

> For you shall read that my great-grandfather
> Never went with all his forces into France
> But that the Scot, on his unfurnished kingdom,
> Came pouring like the tide into a breach
> With ample and brim-fulness of his force;

Once on the Borders, however, the nobles halted: and so far from pouring like the tide into a breach, refused to go a yard farther. The Regent was obliged to retire and consider policy.

Meanwhile news came through of the Cardinal's cruelties in Paris during that August. No one knew if Knox himself might not be among the captured Protestants – there were nearly two hundred of them. Feeling ran high along the Royal Mile of Edinburgh, which stretched from the castle on the hilltop to Holyrood Palace in the valley, with the great kirk of St. Giles' Edinburgh, which stretched from the castle on the hilltop to half-way down. On 1 September, St. Giles' Day, the traditional procession started out from the church, with monks and friars, 'tabors and trumpets, banners and bagpipes', and bearing the arm-bone of St. Giles', mounted in gold with a diamond ring on its skeleton finger, which had been donated at high cost by one

Preston. It also carried the big wooden image of St. Giles, freshly
gilded by the town at a cost of five shillings each time. The Queen
Regent led the procession, while the people looked on, and jeering
grew. Then she went in to dinner, and the tide of resentment burst
its banks. The mob set on the monks, upset the relics and images,
and flung St. Giles into the Nor' Loch – that is, the deep ditch
that once ran between the castle and what is now Princes Street.
Later, they fished it out and burnt it.

'The friars, rowping like ravens, ran upon the Bishops: and the
Bishops ran to the Queen.' She summoned the preachers to stand
their trial in Edinburgh. They came: and the Ayrshire lairds,
well-armed and with a good 'tail' of followers, came with them.
The Regent ordered them to march to the Borders: but they
'made passage for themselves to the Queen's privy chamber where
she was with her Bishops'. Chalmers of Gadgirth spoke for them,
his eye on the rich churchmen.

'Madam, we know that this is the malice and device of these
jeffwellis . . . we vow to God we shall make a day of it. They
oppress us and our tenants that they may feed their idle bellies.
They trouble our preachers, and would murder them and us: shall
we suffer this any longer? Nay, Madam, it shall not be.'

'And therewith every man put on his steel bonnet.'

Then was heard nothing on the Queen's part but: 'My joys, my
hearts, what ails you? Me means no evils to you nor to your
preachers.' . . . And with 'these and the like fair words' she
managed to keep the peace for the time.

Meanwhile, Knox had reached Dieppe, and found the letters of
discouragement waiting for him: and had written off his heart-cry
of reproach and exhortation. When that was received by the lords
of the congregation, they met in Edinburgh and on 3 December
drew up and signed a common bond. In it they swore they would:

'. . . strive in our Master's cause, even unto the death, being
certain of victory in Him. The which our duty well considered,
we do promise before the Majesty of God and His Congregation, that by His grace, shall with all diligence continually
apply our whole power, substance and our very lives to maintain, set forward and establish the most blessed Word of God
and His Congregation; and shall labour at our possibility to

have faithful ministers purely and truly to minister Christ's Evangel and Sacraments to his people. . . .'

God called to witness, Archibald, Earl of Argyle
Glencairn
Morton
Archibald, Lord of Lorne
John Erskine of Dun.

But no news of this reached Knox, waiting wearily at Dieppe. All he heard that winter was the evil news from England, and discouragement from Scotland, finishing up with the Royal Commissioners riding through to arrange the French marriage.

Yet in spring, as he arrived back despairingly in Geneva, old Lord Sandilands of Calder House, where Knox had stayed and had given communion, was presenting to the Queen Regent a petition on behalf of the Protestants; this was really a request to her to ratify those verbal promises she had made so freely when she sought the Crown Matrimonial. The petition asked for freedom to have the Bible read 'in our common vulgar tongue' at conventions public or private of common prayers: that some 'qualifyed person' being present might open up and interpret the hard places: that Baptism be in the vulgar tongue that parents and godparents might understand the contract: that the Sacrament of the Lord's Supper be likewise administered and in both kinds 'according to the plain institution of our Saviour Christ Jesus': and lastly, 'that the lives of the clergy be reformed, that they be no longer a slander to God's word'.

They were told they might pray and baptize in their own tongue, if it were done secretly, and public reverence still be given to the Mass: which 'with one voice' they refused. The Queen Regent said she would give them greater freedom, so long as there were no public assemblies in Edinburgh or Leith: so John Douglas, a preacher, cancelled a public preaching in the port. They were, in short, bought off. But it is easy to read clerical vengeance in the seizing almost immediately of old Walter Myln, and his burning in St. Andrews.

The Regent received their protests over this with every appearance of sympathy – 'buying time with fair words', as Knox put it.

There was a second appeal to her that summer. She promised 'me will remember what is protested: and me shall put good order after this to all things that now be in controversy'. She 'spared not amiable looks, and good words in abundance; but she kept our bill in her pocket'.

September was coming round again, so the friars asked the town to replace their wooden image of St. Giles. But the town had profited by its Bible reading, and replied firmly that 'to them the charge appeared verra unjust; for they understood that God in some places had commanded idols and images to be destroyed: but where he had commanded images to be set up, they had not read'. The bishops threatened a Great Cursing: and had recourse to borrowing 'a marmoset idol' from the Grey Friars, which they thoughtfully nailed down to its 'fertour'. That did not save it in the ensuing riot, which was much enjoyed by one 'a merrie Englishman', who leaned over the fore-stair of a house in the Royal Mile and cheered on both sides impartially. This was the last St. Giles' Day procession.

With genuine courage and infinite determination Mary of Guise had fought to bring Scotland under France, and back to the fold of Rome. That autumn the game was almost in her hands: she had only to wait. And then, in November, Mary Tudor died; on the face of it, that made Mary Stewart heir to three crowns: but in the way stood Elizabeth. Winter wore round to spring again, with Knox once more waiting in frustration and desperation at Dieppe. On 2 April peace was signed in the Treaty of Cateau Cambresis: and Mary signed that Treaty for Scotland, France and England. Knox heard that the de Guise brothers said, 'This will breed business ere long!'

The last call had been sent off to Knox, with the envoy to the Pope, and now, in Scotland, the situation was growing desperate. Now that the war was over, a French expedition to Scotland was being planned.

French troops were increased, and Frenchmen filled all the high offices of State; d'Oysel was chancellor, de Rubay and others held the most important posts. When the Protestant lords pressed once again for freedom of worship, the Regent snapped her fingers at them. She would, she said, have them all banished 'albeit they preached as truly as Saint Paul'. Glencairn and Campbell of

Loudoun, Sheriff of Ayr, went to reason with her, and she 'somewhat astonished, said she would advise'.

But she felt sure of herself now. She made a bold drive to have Easter celebrated with Roman rites throughout her household, and as far as possible throughout the land, she herself attending High Mass in public. Perth had gone over wholly to Reformed faith: so she sent an order to Ruthven the Provost demanding the full suppression of heresy there. He replied that he could make their bodies obedient, but scarcely their consciences. Then she demanded of Haliburton, Provost of Dundee, that he should arrest Paul Methven: 'but he, fearing God, gave secret warning to the man to leave the town for a time'. Men were also sent to try to enforce the Mass that Easter of 1559 at Montrose, Dundee and Perth: 'but they had no success'.

She was then provoked to go that one step further than was wise. She summoned the preachers to answer charges at Stirling on the 10 May. 'The whole brethren agreed that the gentlemen of every county should accompany their preachers on the day appointed. All men were most willing, for that purpose the town of Dundee and the gentlemen and of Angus and the Mearns proceeded with their preachers to Perth, without armour, as peaceable men, desiring only to give confession with their preachers.'

But lest so huge a multitude should give excuse to a cry of rebellion, Erskine of Dun, trusted by both sides all the time, went on to Perth to interview the Regent. She once more was all amiability: and begged him to stay the preachers and their supporters while she made 'better arrangements'.

Once again, the whole thing might have blown over, while the Regent increased her French support, and played for time. But in a flash the situation changed: John Knox had landed at Leith.

He spent two nights in Edinburgh, getting his breath and his bearings. The second evening he found time for a short note to Mrs. Locke:

'The perpetual comfort of the Holy Ghost for salutation.
    These few lines are to signify unto you, dear Sister, that it hath pleased the merciful providence of my Heavenly Father to conduct me to Edinburgh, where I arrived the 2 of May;

uncertain as yet, what God shall further work in this country, except that I see the battle shall be great, for Sathan rageth even to the uttermost: and I am come (I praise my God), even in the brunt of the battle: for my fellow-preachers have a day appointed to answer before the Queen Regent, the 10th of this instant, where I intend, (if God impede not) also to be present, by life, by death, or else by both to glorify His godly name, who thus mercifully hath heard my long cries. Assist me, Sister, with your prayers, that now I shrink not when the battle approacheth. Other things I have to communicate with you, but travail after travail doth so occupy me, that no time is granted me to write.'

Knox probably stayed with James Barron, in the High Street. And now, when the rumour of his landing ran along the Royal Mile it was not whispered but shouted. The Black Friars were sitting in convocation in their great hall in the Lawnmarket – possibly under the same roof that today covers a junk store: when the cry reached them: 'John Knox is come!' they rose up without word and 'passed forth to the yard, altogether abashed'.

John Galt, in a novel gives an account based on oral tradition of how that cry travelled across Scotland: of horsemen checking to shout it at each clachan, of fishing-boats about to call it to each other, of shepherds crossing mountains to pass it on.' John Knox is come!' The word rang through all Scotland: and the people took heart.

He had landed on the 2 May: and had set his heart on joining those who had been summonsed for the 10th. On the 4th he set out, going first to Dundee to seek acceptance and permission to preach. On Saturday the 6th he had been denounced as an outlaw at the Town Cross in Glasgow: but by the day appointed the great gathering, preachers and supporters and John Knox among them, were all in Perth, waiting for the outcome of Erskine of Dun's embassy to the Queen Regent. They had not to wait long. He came back in haste, and distressed. After telling them to halt at Perth, the Regent had then outlawed them for non-compearance!

Knox preached a rousing sermon against broken faith, lies,

deceit and the senseless idolatry of Rome. Then the congregation went home to dinner, and a priest spread a gaudy triptych on the altar, and began to say Mass. A lad cried out against it, and a priest boxed his ear. That was the match set to tinder. The whole mob rose as one man, stones flew like hail, images melted like snowflakes. Before a tenth of the populace knew of it, the place was purged of the symbols of Rome. Then what Knox calls 'the rascal multitude' ran to join in: they went to the Grey and the Black Friars, first to remove images and then the common people began to seek some spoil. The Grey Friars (Franciscans) had 'sheets, blankets, beds and covertours such as no Earl in Scotland had better. They were but eight persons in the convent, yet they had eight puncheons of salt beef (consider the time of year, the 11th May), wine, beer and ale, besides stores. . . .' The poor had a great day of it. The Prior of the Charterhouse was allowed to take with him all he could carry: there was no opposition, no bloodshed. But the strongholds of property became bare walls.

It is a complete error to see Knox delighting in the destruction. He opposed it, except for the removal of images, with all his strength: for it was discreditable to his Church. But nothing could check the fury of the poor and needy, who had grudged the wealth of Rome for so long.

When the Queen Regent heard it, she swore to destroy Perth and 'sow it with salt'. She called out the levies of Clydesdale, Stirlingshire and the Lothians, and put about 18,000 men in the field, well-armed and equipped, stiffened with trained French soldiers and under the command of d'Oysel. She would, she vowed, make an end of the heretics.

By the time this news had reached Perth, many of the lairds had gone home. Knox had written triumphantly to Mrs. Locke that the Church was taking the field against the might of Satan 'with trumpet and banners'. But now the moment had come, and he had no banners and no trumpet: he had no soldiers, trained or raw, no arms, no army: and no money or resources wherewith he could raise them. The congregation, however devoted, must have numbered as many old women, children and cripples as men. It looked quite clearly like the end.

Even Ruthven the Provost thought so. He fled by night, leaving a wave of panic behind him.

But Knox still had something: he had his faith and the power of his word. After the Provost fled, he collected the people and preached them back into good heart and 'reasonable esperance' – when esperance seemed madly unreasonable. He had already drawn up letters, and these were copied ceaselessly and broadcast to the people wherever they could be carried. He was the first man in Scotland, possibly in Europe, to fight a war by words, and to win. Copies of his letters went at top speed to Kyle, and elsewhere: asking the Roman Catholics to hear their case before they joined in the attack, rallying all those who had once leaned to the Reformed faith, begging them no longer to 'look through their fingers' but to come out and fight.

When the Queen Regent went to Mass, there was a letter pinned to her cushion telling her that to fight against the Kirk was to fight against God. French soldiers themselves, of Huguenot leanings, smuggled to the hands of d'Oysel and the other French leaders letters written in French, telling them to go home and not to meddle in Scots wars, when Scots had for so long been their allies.

When the brethren of Cunningham and Kyle convened in the church of Craigie to discuss Knox's letter, there was apparently some doubt as to whether it was worth trying to reach Perth in time. It looked as if the story of George Wishart was going to be repeated, and Knox in his turn abandoned. Then Glencairn 'burst forth in these words: Let every man serve his conscience. I will, by God's grace, see my brethren in St. Johnston: yea, albeit never man should accompany me, I will go, and if it were but with a pike upon my shoulder: for I had rather die with that company than live after them'.

So they all went, and Willock with them, and the whole congregation of 'Carrick, Kyle and Cunningham'. Two of the lairds, Campbell of Cessnock and Chalmers of Gadgirth, were direct descendants of Lollards accused before James IV in 1494. When they came to the little cathedral city of Glasgow, Lyon Herald, with trumpet and coat-armour, commanded every man 'under the pain of treason to return' but 'never man obeyed that charge, but all went forward'. The bridges over the water of Forth had been cut by the Regent's forces, but the Ayrshire men struck into the hills and made forced marches 'by desert and mountain' with such speed that they were within a few miles of Perth before any knowledge of it reached the congregation.

It was 22 May when the Regent collected her forces, 23 May when the Provost fled: and on the 24th Argyle and James Stewart – 'the Lord James' – came on embassy from the Regent to see Knox. Knox claimed they were raising no rebellion, only claiming the right of freedom of worship. He was now testing in practice the rights of subjects to resist their rulers. To the Regent's assertion that he was raising a revolt, the people cried with one voice: 'Cursed be they that seek effusion of blood, war or dissention. Let us possess Christ Jesus, and the benefit of his Evangel, and none within Scotland shall be more obedient subjects than we shall be.'

Although nothing was known then of the Ayrshiremen's approach, Knox laid down courageous terms: and these he made fully known to all the congregation on Sunday, 28 May. They would give up Perth on condition the Queen did not garrison it with French troops or use any retaliation but 'suffer the religion begun to go forward'.

Then Glencairn marched in, with 2,500 men, including cavalry: and Lords Ochiltree, and Boyd, the lairds of Cessnock, Barr, Craigie-Wallace and Gadgirth and the Sheriff of Ayr. 'And then began all men to praise God, for that He had so mercifully heard them in their maist extreme necessity.'

Now they were ready to take the field: but Argyle and the Lord James came back to plead the terms drawn up, which d'Oysel was eager to sign. Knox and Willock together went to these two, 'accusing them of infidelity' to the cause of the Kirk. This they denied, saying they worked only for peace and the defence of the throne: and promising, if the treaty was signed and the Regent broke it, to abandon her. With 'great labours' then the people were persuaded to agree to the terms of truce – it was a feat indeed to get them quietly and peacefully to disperse.

Knox preached a final sermon, at which many of the Regent's advance party were present. A new bond was signed by Glencairn, Ochiltree and Boyd, and by Argyle, Lord James and Campbell of Tringland, the Sheriff of Ayr, promising mutual support.

On 29 May the Regent marched in with French soldiers, and immediately broke all the terms of the truce, as Knox had known she would. On the 1 June Argyle and the Lord James kept their word and marched out, taking with them the Earl of Menteith, the laird of Tullibardine and Provost Lord Ruthven who, like them, was changing sides for the last time. When the Queen sent after them they defied her: and sent word to all the congregations to rally to St. Andrews on the first Sunday of that month, in three days time.

It was the first great victory.

13

St. Andrews at Last

THE day after Knox left Perth with the lords of the congregation he preached in Crail, and the day following in Anstruther: and in both places the people rose and purged chapels of Rome into kirks of Scotland. The third day – 4 June – he trysted with the congregations in St. Andrews, a place of special meaning to him: and he had intended to preach there that day, being Sunday.

But he had been forestalled. The bishop 'hearing of Reformation to be made in his cathedral church, thought time to stir, or else never'. So he 'came to the town upon the Saturday at night, accompanied with a hundred spears'. The Regent too had left Perth, and was at Falkland, within twelve miles of St. Andrews, with all her Frenchmen: whereas at that time the lords had only small bands of personal retainers. No one yet knew which side St. Andrews itself would take, for it had given no sign; so the position was critical, threatening acute danger if Knox was to preach. The bishop himself sent word that, if he did, 'he would be saluted with a dozen of culverins, whereof the most part should light upon his nose'.

For a whole week the lords debated, most of them thinking the risk too great. Then they sent for Knox, to hear his own opinion.

'God is witness,' said he, 'that I never preached Christ Jesus in contempt of any man ... but to delay to preach the morrow (unless the body be violently with-holden) I can nocht of conscience. For in this town and church began God first to call me to the dignity of a preacher, from the which I was reft by the tyranny of France, by procurement of the bishops, as ye all well enough know. How long I continued prisoner, what torment I sustained in the galleys, and what were the sobs of my heart, is now no time to recite: this only I can nocht conceal, which more than one have heard me say, when the body was far absent from Scotland, that my assured hope was, in open audience, to preach in St. Andrews before I departed this life. And therefore,' said he, 'my lords, seeing that God, above the expectation of many, hath brought the body to the same place where first I was called to the office of a preacher, and from the which most unjustly I was removed, I beseech your honours not to stop me to present myself unto my brethren. . . . I desire the hand nor weapon of no man to defend me: only do I crave audience.'

So, on the 11 June he preached below that steeple he had last seen through the port-hole of the French galley, from a pulpit still in use. He preached on the cleansing of the temple: with such effect that the provost and bailies as well as the magistrates and most part of the common folk rose up and removed for ever the gilded dolls of saints and simpering madonnas. One account says they were carried to the cairn where the living body of old Walter Myln had been burned, and there made into a bonfire.

The bishop fled to the Regent, and together they decided to take St. Andrews before reinforcements could reach the lords. She at once sent forward posts, to secure the little village of Cupar six miles from St. Andrews, and to arrange billets there for her staff. Word of this was carried straight to the lords: and with less than a hundred horse and a few foot-soldiers they stole a march on her, and occupied Cupar.

Next day she was on the move, with a heavy force and every confidence. Once again it looked as if nothing could save the congregation; and yet once again the miracle happened. Before noon next day 'their number passed three thousand men, which by God's providence came unto the lords. From Lothian, the lairds of Ormiston, Calder, Halton, Restalrig and Colston'. Ruthven came from Perth, with horsemen. 'The Earl of Rothes, Sheriff of Fife, came with an honest company'. The towns of Dundee and St. Andrews, and the little town of Cupar 'declared themselves both stout and faithful'. Finally, 'God did so multiply our number that it appeared as men had rained from the clouds'.

Before midnight on that Tuesday, 13 June, the French guns were advanced: and they themselves followed in the small hours. Before dawn, the lords moved out. Halliburton, Provost of Dundee, who had refused to surrender Paul Methven, was captain of his own townsfolk: it was he who advised the choice of Cupar

Muir for a stand. Ruthven had the cavalry: and managed them so that the enemy could never get a true estimate of their number.

The day broke misty: the enemy, fearing no opposition, marched briskly forward to within a mile of the congregations, and then moved off as if to St. Andrews. A small body of troops kept skirmishing in front of them; but when the mist lifted, horsemen reconnoitring on a hill-top saw body after body of troops come into view: here the lords with 1,000 spears, there the two chief towns under their provosts, farther back the guns and the cavalry. Posts ran to the Duke (Chatelherault) and to d'Oysel, and messengers were sent under a white flag to offer truce: which was finally concluded for eight days, with many assurances given by the Regent. 'And so we returned to Cupar, lauding and praising God for his mercy showed.'

At this moment James Melville, the Scots lad who had gone to seek his fortune at the French Court, rides into the story again. Henri II of France wished to know exactly how critical the Scots situation was: and his Constable, de Montmorenci, produced Melville, a born Scot of inconspicuous rank, as a suitable observer. The report in France ran that it was an armed rebellion that was taking place, with the aim of placing the Lord James Stewart on the throne. Melville had an audience with the King who remarked that: 'if it be only religion which moves them, we must commit Scotsmen's souls unto God: for we have difficulty enough to rule the consciences of Frenchmen'. The Constable clapped him on the shoulder and told him: 'The King will stay or send his army according to your report.'

It was Melville's great chance: the chance for which every page and hanger-on at Court longed and prayed. He made good speed to Scotland, and reached Falkland on the eve of Cupar Muir: so he had a grandstand seat for the action. In spite of the complaints of the Regent, he concluded definitely that no revolution was intended. He accepted the assurances of Sir Henry Balnaves, the old Reformer he had once helped in exile, and who had come to love him 'as I had been his own son'.

Long after, a middle-aged Melville sat down to write his *Memoirs:* and recollected the romantic dreams of his youth, when he thought that to gain advancement by flattery 'might be easily done by the dullest sort of men. But my daft opinion was, that I might stand by honesty and virtue: which I now find to be but a vain imagination'. Yet it was his kindness to the banished Balnaves which was to bring him a heritage at the end of the day: and not the romantic great chance.

For that ended in nothing. When he got back to France at the end of June with a full report to deliver, he found the King dying and the Constable permanently disgraced. On 29 June the marriage had been celebrated of two of the royal princesses and during the jousting Henri and the Constable rode a course against each other: the sort of exhibition bout they must often have done. As they galloped towards each other for the third time the Constable aimed his lance for the difficult head-stroke – which generally either missed or glanced off the convex helm. But this time the tip of his lance caught in the barred visor of the shining gilt tilting-helm: the wood splintered, entering the King's eye and bearing him off his horse.

The news of this tragedy did not reach Scotland till mid-July.

Meanwhile, Balnaves was not the only Reformer of Wishart's day who came forward now to support Knox. Kirkcaldy of Grange, who had also been at the siege of St. Andrews' Castle, indeed who had been one of Norman Leslie's party at its taking, now joined Knox at St. Andrews. There the lords waited for the Regent's peace envoys, who of course never came. But while they waited Knox and Kirkcaldy wrote to Cecil, to clear the congregation of the charge of treason. Kirkcaldy had been for the past two years serving the Regent on the Borders, and knew the English officials there: including Knox's brother-in-law, George Bowes, who was now a marshall. He had also been an agent for Cecil in France. In these letters to England they asked for understanding and co-operation, and a chance to meet and talk things over.

Norman Leslie was no longer alive to join them. During the Franco-Spanish war he had ridden against a Spanish culverin 'on a fair grey gelding', wearing mail over black velvet, with conspicuous white crosses back and breast and a red cocked bonnet. He unhorsed five men, breaking his spear; drew his sword and fought on, till a fresh troop approached: then galloped back and dropped, mortally wounded, at the Constable's feet. He was carried to the King's own tent; and died a fortnight later.

'No man made more lamentation than the Laird of Grange who came to the camp the next day after.' Moved by this gallantry, the French King had interceded with the Regent for the men who had killed the Cardinal and taken St. Andrews' Castle: and that was how Kirkcaldy had come back to Scotland.

The fruitless truce over, the congregation decided to relieve Perth from its French garrison. Argyle and the Lord James addressed a letter of protest to the Regent for her breach of the agreement, and then the Lords convened at Perth on Saturday, 24 June. They summoned the town to surrender, and when the garrison refused, Ruthven fired a salvo on the west side, and Dundee on the east. It was now ten o'clock at night, but still clear daylight. The captain of the garrison sent a deputation to say that if he were not relieved by the next day at noon, he would be prepared to surrender, provided they might leave unmolested and with ensigns flying. This was agreed. And as no help did come, the agreement was carried out. Next afternoon, Sunday the 25th, the whole congregation entered Perth once more: and once more met to hear Knox preach. The kirks were again cleared of the improvized altars the Regent had set up, one of them being a dicing-table: and thanks were again given for another bloodless victory.

On the way to Perth, the abbey of Lindores had been purged: and now some of the congregation, mainly Dundee, determined to slip over to Scone to settle scores with Hepburn, Bishop of Moray, Bothwell's uncle, who had been blamed for Myln's death. Both to save the building and possibly to gain an ally, the lords were against this. Argyle and Stewart hastened off to stop them: but on the way word came that the Regent was moving to occupy Stirling with its bridge, and so cut off the way to Edinburgh. Again Stewart made a swift dash by night with a small force, and forestalled her. Meanwhile Knox himself went to stay the mob at Scone. For a little he was successful: then one of the bishop's sons drew a rapier and ran through a looter; and after that nothing would hold them. It was an odd paradox that made Protestant leaders try to save buildings that for years the Romans had allowed to crumble with neglect.

Now that they held Stirling, the way to Edinburgh was clear. The Regent and d'Oysel retired in complete dismay to Dunbar,

E

leaving the town open. Purging Linlithgow on the way, the congregation marched into the capital 6,000 strong, with a King's son and five earls at their head.

It was not eight weeks since Knox had landed at Leith, alone and empty-handed. Now they came as conquerors, but of the strangest sort: they had taken a whole country almost without firing a shot or losing a life.

As they entered Edinburgh the Provost, Lord Seton, fled: he was, comments Knox, 'a man without God, without honesty and often-times without reason'. The people made swift Reformation of the friars and kirks. St. Giles' with its seventeen chapels was cleansed of images and *bon Dieuserie*. The tradeshouse took from St. Eloi's chapel, which they regarded as their own, the 'Blue Blanket' – an old saltire flag said to have been carried on crusades and to be the only banner to return from Flodden. This they kept as sacred: and they keep it to this day.

On Sunday 1 July the congregation went up to St. Giles' to hear Knox preach. It was a wonderful moment, for St. Giles' was and is the very heart of Scotland. They had attained their Jerusalem.

When a man lives for a dream and by a dream, through exile, fear and despair, its sudden miraculous fulfilment must bring almost a stupefaction. Knox's wildest dreams had come true: and now he feared lest, like dreams, they might vanish again. He had sought only a Kirk: and had been handed a country. Scotland had had no national policy since Flodden: but the congregation was utterly unprepared to give her one. They had intended only passive resistance, and now found themselves in full power: and worse still, if they could not make good their position they would lose all.

During the truce, Knox had written to Mrs. Locke from St. Andrews.

'O that my heart could be thankful for the super-excellent benefit of my God! The long thirst of my wretched heart is satisfied in abundance . . . for lo, forty days and more, hath my God used my tongue in my native country, to the manifestation of His glory. . . . The thirst of the poor people, as well as the nobility here, is wondrous great, which putteth

me in comfort, that Christ Jesus shall triumph for a space
here. . . .'

But he dreads the coming French invasion. He begs her to tell
his dispersed flock the true facts of the Scottish struggle: and asks
above all for his colleague Goodman. 'Will him therefore in the
name of the Lord Jesus (all delay and excuse set apart) to visit
me, for the necessity is great here.' Then there is a message
to 'my Mother and my Wife': and he commends the bearer 'a
poor man'.

He wrote to her again from Edinburgh, asking for Goodman.
'More trouble than ye see lyeth upon me.' He had written to Cecil
from Perth: 'My eye hath long looked to a perpetual concord
betwixt these two Realms, the occasion whereof is now most
present. . . .' On that same Sunday 1 July that he preached in St.
Giles', he and Kirkcaldy both wrote to Henry Percy, warden
depute of the Marches, pressing for a meeting there. Cecil wrote
back by Percy, eager himself to end the futile and wasteful wars
with the 'perpetuity of a brotherly and national friendship
betwixt the two Realms'. But Percy was not to say so much, nor
promise open help. Elizabeth was an expert in not letting her right
hand know what her left hand was doing: and in denying
it on oath if it were pointed out to her. Moreover, she would
bring Knox to his knees for the *Blast* before she parted with a
penny.

She had other reasons. With inspired meanness this 'feeble,
fickle' woman had solved the first, worst problem of every ruler:
she had made the hitherto debased English money acceptable for
value even by the money-lenders of Amsterdam: whereas Scotland
still floundered with inflation. The Regent had helped to maintain
her French forces by churning out money: and had let the soldiers
use sous that were no longer legal tender in France. As a result,
prices had shot up. Scotland was flooded with 'hardheads' and
'non-solus's' which were worth very little. The 'non-solus' was the
attractive but uneconomic little coin that shows Mary and Francis
the Dauphin, struck on the occasion of their marriage: '*Non.
solus, duo. sed. una. caro*'.

To prevent further inflation, the lords seized the coining-house
and the dies. This gave the Regent a real grievance, for it infringed

sovereign rights. It gave her an excellent chance too to spread the rumour that with the dies the lords had seized great sums of treasure for their own use: treasure that rightly belonged to the people. Nothing grows faster than such a tale, and the congregation lost support over it: though Knox says they handed over all precious metal to the treasurer, Richardson, and kept not so much as 'the value of a bawbee'. The end of their dream of a bloodless victory came sooner than even Knox could have expected. On 19 July he wrote to Cecil once more on the subject of amity and concord between the nations: he included a letter to Queen Elizabeth that Cecil was to present 'if he thought it meet'. Probably Cecil didn't: it was a dogged defence of the principles of the *Blast* – 'of an almost sublime offensiveness', as Lord Eustace Percy, the modern historian puts it. The Queen's letter is dated the 20th: and on Sunday 23 July, the Regent marched again. She had learned that most of the congregation had scattered to their own homes, and that there was now no real force in Edinburgh. As she put it: 'The congregation has reigned these two months bypast: me myself would now reign other two.'

She had gathered forces steadily under d'Oysel, the duke and Bothwell. Now she demanded the surrender of Leith, and it yielded without a shot fired. All Monday, the supporters of the congregation watched from the Crags, while their leaders debated. Then Lord Erskine in the castle declared for the Regent, and so they were caught between the two. Their own supporters could not come in time: they had to accept unfavourable terms, signed on the Tuesday. Next day 'after sermon, dinner and a proclamation made at the Mercat Cross, we departed.'

Knox, a proscribed outlaw and a ringleader, who could be legally seized and burned alive at any time, went with them. Willock, who was in a much safer position, although it was dangerous enough, volunteered to stay and hold the pulpit of St. Giles'. Knox pays a characteristically generous tribute to him over this: 'For comfort of the brethren, and continuance of the Kirk in Edinburgh, was left there our dear brother John Willock, who, for his faithful labours and bold courage in that battle, deserves immortal praise. . . .' He so gladly consented to stay 'that it might evidently appear, that he preferred the comfort of his brethren, and the continuance of the Kirk there, to his own life'.

Some effort was made to put him out: but the congregation claimed they had 'peaceably possessed' St. Giles', and therefore under the terms of truce could retain it. So here, in the very face of the enemy, they met for prayer and preaching and public baptism, and spread the Lord's Table in sight of all.

14

'Dark and Dolorous Night'

THE last letters Knox had written from Edinburgh to Cecil and Queen Elizabeth had been sent south with Whitelaw, an old Reformer who had just come home from France. He was presumably a prim figure, as Throckmorton, English ambassador in France, once hoped he would see 'as little Sin in England as possible'. He was not long gone when another messenger brought letters to Knox from Henry Percy suggesting a meeting at Alnwick.

So as soon as the defeated congregation had reached Stirling and the lords held council, Knox with another minister called Hamilton of St. Andrews set out on this dangerous journey. They sailed from the little harbour of Pittenweem, and reached Holy Isle about the 2nd August, or possibly a little before. There Knox had probably preached, long before, when he was at Newcastle, and there he was no doubt both recognized and welcomed.

Nothing, from the official English point of view, could have been more disastrously unwelcome than the news of his arrival. The Regent had just been accusing England of aiding the rebels, and Elizabeth and Cecil were covering pages with sworn denials. Henry Percy was careful not to keep the rendezvous: but Knox by now was so famous that the news of his arrival ran like wildfire. Worst of all, a French envoy at that very time was passing north through the Borders, bearing threatening letters from Francis II and Marie, King and Queen of France and Scotland. Sir James Croft, Captain of Berwick, and also a liaison official, took the ministers into Berwick Castle where he took note of all their pleas and suggestions.

While Knox was staying 'very secretly' in Berwick Castle, Whitelaw brought a letter from Cecil, dated at Oxford the week before. It was presumably an answer to Knox's last letters to him and to the Queen: and carries a dry reproof in the text which prefaces it:

'*Non est masculus neque femina, omnes enim, ut ait Paulus, unum sumus in Christo Jesu.*' (In Christ, says Paul, there is neither male nor female, for all are one). He adds: 'Blessed is the man who trusteth in the Lord; and the Lord will be his confidence.'

It was about all the comfort he gave Knox in a very brief and non-committal letter: and Knox would not answer it without consulting the lords. He made a dash for home that same night, with the Regent's forces on the look-out for him. Poor Whitelaw took ill on the way back, and had to come on later with William Knox: and Provost Lord Seton, believing him to be Knox, chased him three miles to Ormiston, where he 'brake a chaise over his head'.

On 4 August, the day after Knox departed secretly from Berwick, Percy wrote peevishly to Cecil: 'since my departure from Norham, there hath arrived at the Holy Island Mr. Knox, in such unsecret sort, that it is openly known both unto England and Scotland; wherefore I think he hath not discreetly used his coming, for the Dowager of Scotland hath so burthened me, both by letters to my Lord of Northumberland, as by message yesterday with the Lord Bothwell and Sir James MacGill' . . . He suggests instead communicating in cipher with 'L.P.' – James Stewart, the lord prior. Knox had already realized what a blunder it all was, and that he was out of his depth in politics: Croft reported that he no longer thought of trying to meet Cecil: he 'sayth that in no wise can he be long from his flock: and besides, he is not himself meet to treat of so great matters, but thinks rather to devise that Master Henry Balnaves, or some other wise men, may be sent to you.' But Croft had at least caught some of Knox's sense of urgency, for he adds: 'It is now then time to determine what to do, for I see great peril to both the Realms by wasting of time.'

Thanks to the good horses he had been lent, Knox was back in Stirling with his report on 5 August. The lords were not taken with it, or with Cecil's chilly letter: they wrote forthwith a reply as chilly. Knox added an appeal: 'unless the council be more forward in this common action, ye will utterly discourage the hearts of all here, for they cannot abide the crime of suspicion . . . if they cannot have present support of them, they will seek the next remedy . . . to preserve their own bodies. . . .'

Either Knox's mission or his letter had some effect: for at

Nonsuch on 8 August Elizabeth dictated to Cecil the commission to Sir Ralph Sadler, the former envoy:

'Trusty and well-beloved, We greet you well . . . we do authorise you to confer, treat or practise with any manner of person of Scotland, either in Scotland or England, for those purposes and for the furtherance of our service and of any other thing that may tend to make a perpetual concord betwixt the nation of Scotland and ours.

We do also authorise you to reward any manner of person of Scotland, with such sums of money as ye shall think meet, to be taken of the sum of three thousand pounds, which we have ordered should be delivered unto you in gold. Wherein such discretion and secrecy is to be used, as no part of your doings may impair the treaties of peace lately concluded betwixt us and Scotland.'

This was 'given under our signet, the first year of our reign.'

The lords, knowing nothing of this, had decided not to look any further for English support. Knox pled with them in vain. The most he could win from them was leave to continue the appeals on his own. Argyle had had to go home to settle some trouble 'in his own country', and the next tryst was at Glasgow on 10 August. Knox had done with politics. He went back instead to his own job, to preaching the word and planting the Kirk. Since the disastrous dash to Berwick and back, fevers had racked and shaken him: and he appealed to Cecil to speed the passage of his wife and children. 'Notwithstanding . . . yet have I travelled through the most part of this realm, where (all praise be to his blessed Majesty) men of all sort and conditions embrace the truth.'

This was to Mrs. Locke on 2 September, and it is a grand letter. Things may not look any better, but Knox has got back to his people and his Gospel: and the right note rings through.

'We do nothing but go about Jericho, blowing trumpets, as God giveth strength, hoping victory by His power alone. Christ Jesus is preached even in Edinburgh, and His blessed sacraments rightly ministered in all congregations where the ministry is established: and they be these: Edinburgh, St. Andrews,

E*

Dundee, St. Johnston' (i.e. Perth) 'Brechin, Montrose, Stirling, Ayr. And now, Christ Jesus is begun to be preached upon the South Borders next unto you, in Jedburgh and Kelso, so that the trumpet soundeth over all, blessed be our God. We lack labourers, alas! and you and Mr. Wood have deceived me, who, according to my request and expectation, hath not advertised my brother, Mr. Goodman.

He (Mr. Goodman) came to the Border, but for lack of advertisement is returned. Mr. Smith came from him, and is presently with me: but I cannot understand whether my brother is repaired. I beseech you to inquire, and to cause him to repair to me with all diligence that is possible. . . . If he can come by sea, it shall be most sure to address him to Dundee, Montrose, St. Andrews or to any part in Fife: and let him enquire for me, and desire to be conducted to me, and he cannot lack friends.' This last was almost a boast for Knox. 'If my brother be not with my wife, I fear he cannot come to me before I shall have more than need of him.

Now, to the complaint and prayer of your letter written ye say, at midnight. Be of comfort, sister, knowing that ye fight not the battle alone. . . .'

In the middle of his travelling, preaching, teaching and sickness, Knox continued to beg Cecil for help. He knew, better than the lords, that they could not hope to beat the French without England's help: and this was still not forthcoming. Cecil had been irritated by Kirkcaldy's assurances that they meant no rebellion: and still more that they had not touched 'a pennyworth' of the old Church's revenues. He wrote back in pointed praise of the popish kirkmen 'wise in their generation', and of Henry VIII's way of dealing with the monasteries: 'I like no spoil, but I allow to have good things put to good uses, as to the enriching of the Crown', and so on. Neither he nor Elizabeth indulged themselves in the luxury of scruples: and they found them exacerbating in beggars.

On 15 August Knox sat down to write one more appeal to Cecil. He wastes no words:

'The case of these gentlemen standest thus: That unless without delay money be furnished to pay their soldiers (who in number are now but 500) for their service by-past, and to retain another thousand footmen, with 300 horsemen for a time, they will be compelled every man to seek the next way for his own safety. I am assured (as flesh may be of flesh) that some will take a very hard life, before that ever they compone, either with the Queen Regent, either yet with France. But this I dare not promise of all, unless in you they see greater forwardness to their support. To aid us so liberally as we require, to some of you will appear excessive, and to displease France to many will appear dangerous. But Sir, I hope that ye consider that our destruction were your greatest loss, and that when France shall be our full masters (which God avert) they will be but slender friends to you. I heard Bethencourt brag in his credit, after he had delivered his menacing letters to the Prior' – Lord James – 'that the King and his Council would spend the Crown of France unless they had our full obedience: I am assured, that unless they had a farther respect, they would not buy our poverty at that price. . . . in the bowels of Jesus Christ I require you, Sir, to make plain answer what they may lippen to, and at what time their support shall be in readiness (how dangerous is the drift of time, in such matters, ye are not ignorant). . . .'

The Queen Regent was making good use of 'the drift of time'. She wrote to the Duke, who was beginning to waver, and to other great nobles, assuring them of her peaceful intentions towards the congregation: and all the time, steadily, she increased the French forces in the country. She also took a leaf almost literally from Knox's book in producing broadsheets to convince and soothe down the common people. But here he was more than her match: and the counter-sheet, full of Knox's unmistakeable fire, would have roused the feeblest. It was a tremendous attack, both on the Regent's policy and on her Frenchmen: it was a national call to arms.

The Regent's luck had changed. The Duke, old Chatelherault, had heard that his son, the young Earl of Arran, had escaped out of France to Geneva and was on his way home by Germany and England. Some saw this as a blessing of Providence: but Elizabeth's agents had had a hand in it: for Arran was a Huguenot Now the Duke made cautious overtures to the Lord James and Argyle, and was received with open arms. With him, next heir to

the crown, and his son joining the congregation, the whole movement took on a different standing. The Lord James replied coolly
enough to the menacing letters from the French Court.

On 19 August Sadler and Croft got Knox's appeal at Berwick,
from 'a secret messenger'. They agreed with all of it: and sent the
information on to Cecil with a great deal of '(as Knox sayeth)'.
'And to say our poor minds unto you, we see not but her Highness
must be at some charge with them, for of bare words only . . . yet
can they receive no comfort. The bestowing of 2,000 or 3,000
crowns to relieve them, which have sustained great losses, and
spent, as we understand, in manner all they had in this matter,'
would be, they hinted, both a bargain and a necessity. The same
day, they wrote to Knox to suggest that Balnaves, or some other
'discreet and trusty man' should come secretly to Holy Island,
and lodge with one Captain Reid, till he could get in touch with
Croft.

Knox handed over the letter to the lords. Elizabeth at long last
unloosened the purse-strings, and gave Sadler permission to hand
over the gold. Balnaves reached Holy Isle on 2 September and was
back in Stirling for the next meeting of the lords, convened for
10 September, with the £3,000. Arran came to the meeting, that
lad from whom so much was hoped; and they all adjourned to
Hamilton, the Duke's principal seat, where a declaration was
drawn up against the Regent on 19 September. This called on her
to stop the French fortifying Leith, as that was 'prejudicial to the
Commonweal and plain contrar to our ancient laws and liberties'.
They also called upon Erskine of Mar, captain of Edinburgh
Castle, to join them.

The Regent also addressed letters, first pleading and offering
rewards and then threatening, to those lords she thought she
might detach, including Lord James: who answered briefly: 'I will
not conceal from your Grace, that amongst us there is ane solemn
oath, that none of us shall traffic with your Grace secretly:
neither yet that any of us shall make ane address for himself
particularly: which oath, for my part, I purpose to keep inviolate
to the end.' She then made a declaration against them, they in turn
denying her charges. Lockhart of Barr turned pacifist, and got in
everyone's road, insisting that there might yet be compromise.
But when Knox gave in to him and wrote again to the Regent –

in his own terms – he was 'offendit', and 'would not deliver that letter'.

The whole congregation met in Stirling on 15 October and on the 16th they marched once more into Edinburgh. There, having met in council, they once more asked the Regent to 'cause your strangers and soldiers whatsumever to depart of the said town of Leith, and make the same patent'. Because the rumour was strong that the Duke would make himself king, he went with a trumpeter to the Mercat Cross and 'purged himself' of that charge.

A week later 21 October, Lyon King came with the Regent's reply. 'She wondered how any durst presume to command her in that realm, which needed not to be conquest by any force, considering that it was already conquist by marriage; that French men could not be justly called strangers, seeing that they war naturalized; and therefore that she would neither mak the town patent neither yet send any man away, but as she thought expedient.'

A council was called for the same day, with Lord Ruthven in the chair, to decide whether they would depose the Regent. They asked the preachers if they had the moral right: and Willock spoke first, as Edinburgh was at that time his parish. He, after a long argument about the divine sanctions of authority and her defections concluded that 'he could see no reason why they . . . might not justly deprive her from all regiment and authority amongst them'.

Knox was then called: and did not produce another *Blast*, but instead suggested they should but suspend her rule, till they were satisfied of her good faith. On a vote, the whole council were unanimous to deprive her: and an Act of Suspension was thereupon written signed and read at the Mercat Cross.

Leith was called to surrender, but 'defiance given'. Now the congregation had really bitten off far more than they could chew. They used St. Giles' to make scaling-ladders to attack Leith, 'which did not a little grieve the preachers' who 'spared not openly to say that they feared the success of that enterprise would not be prosperous, because the beginning appeared to bring with it sole contempt of God and his word'.

There were other reasons to fear the same. The Regent had her spies everywhere, and knew how inadequate and incapable were their real forces. 'The Duke's friends gave unto him such terrors, that he was greatly troubled; and by his fear were troubled many others. The men of war' – mercenaries – 'made a mutiny, because they lacked a part of their wages'. They also 'made a fray upon the Earl of Argyle's Hieland men, and slew one. . . .'

'To pacify the men of war, a collection was devised. But . . . some were poor, and some were niggards. . . .' Then they called on the nobles for their silver work, to be melted down: but the coiners stole off, to join the Regent, presumably. Only one material aid could save them now: and Sandy Cockburn of Ormiston, once Knox's pupil in the quiet Haddington days, was sent to collect a bag of gold from Sadler and Croft on the Borders, to pay the troops.

But the Regent got word of that too: and passed it on to Bothwell, who had been pretending sympathy to the congregation. He departed secretly and collected his Border cut-throats: and on Hallowe'en, the night of witches and warlocks, bogies and unco' ferlies, he caught Sandy Cockburn, stunned him with a shattering blow on the head, and stole 4,000 crowns-of-the-sun, the life blood of the congregation's army.

Arran, Lord James and the Master of Maxwell made a dash with the cavalry to try to catch him: but he was too well used to such business to be caught. And while the Duke and other nobles had gone to the preaching, presumably in St. Giles', the provost and men of Dundee dragged ordnance out on the Crags, to shoot down into Leith. They had better have gone to the service. The French knew by their spies that the cavalry were away, and the rest gone, after preaching to 'denner': and making a sudden sortie, they beat back the Dundonians, captured their guns and pursued them right up the Canongate to the foot of Leith Wynd. Even then, grieves Knox, much might have been saved: but someone raised a cry that the whole of the French had entered the town: 'What clamour and misordour did then suddenly arise, we list not to express with multiplication of words.'

The French slew a number of innocent people, and collected all the booty they could, which did not increase the congregation's popularity in the town.

Worst of all, morale was quite gone. 'Many fled away secretly, and those that did abide (a very few excepted) appeared destitute of counsel and manhood'. The Master of Maxwell wished either to have order taken within the town, or an organized withdrawal, with ordinance and 'banners displayed': but the confusion was complete. 'Never two or three abiding firm in one opinion the space of twenty-four hours.'

Yet another blow fell. The French 'ished' from Leith to intercept food supplies coming to the congregation. Arran and Lord, James rode against them, and venturing too far, were trapped by bodies of French soldiers between the sea and the marshes of Restalrig. They might have been wholly cut off, if it had not been for Kirkcaldy and the redoubtable messenger Alexander Whitelaw, now soldiering. Some thirty men were lost, many wounded, and several of the lairds taken prisoner, including Pitmillie. A Halliburton, brother of the Provost of Dundee, fought a very gallant rearguard action to let others escape: and was carried in hacked to death, Knox being at his death-bed.

It was the end. 'Fear and dolour had so seized the hearts of all that they could admit no consolation. The Earl of Arran and Lord James offered to abide, if any reasonable company would abide with them. But men did so steal away, that the wit of man could not stay them.' Nor would the castle assist. Erskine 'must needs declare himself friend to those that were able to support and defend him'. Impossible now to take the advice of Maitland of Lethington, and stay. He was the son of the laird who had once dined George Wishart: and like his father was worldly-wise rather than enthusiast. But partly because he was suspect to devout Catholics for his worldly wit, and partly for 'liberty of tongue' he had slipped out of Leith and joined the Reformers in these days of defeat. His advice was good, and 'prudently' given: but they were beyond advice. Their whole thought was, how to get out.

The last defeat had been on Monday 6 November. Shortly after midnight that very night they began to steal out of Edinburgh like thieves in the dark. And at that cringing departure the malice of the mob woke: they saw themselves abandoned to the French, and ran after them jeering: 'every one provoked others to cast stones at us'. And thus, says Knox, 'the sword of dolour passed through our hearts'.

In fear, in shame, in black defeat they hastened all day back down the road to Stirling.

15

'One Voice'

A ND in very deed, dear Sister,' wrote Knox to Mrs. Locke, 'I
have no less need of comfort . . . than the living man hath to
be fed, albeit in store he hath great abundance. I have read the
cares and temptation of Moses, and sometimes I supposed myself
to be well practised in such dangerous battles. But, alas! I now
perceive that all my practise before was but mere speculation: for
one day of troubles, since my last arrival in Scotland, hath more
pierced my heart than all the torments of the galleys did the space
of nineteen months; for that torment for the most part, did touch
the body, but this pierces the soul and inward affections.'

And like Moses' rebellious people in the desert, the congregation had lost all heart and hope to go on. They limped into Stirling,
a disorganized rabble, the reproaches of Edinburgh still ringing in
their ears. They were ready and willing to abandon the whole
enterprise.

But on the next day, Wednesday, they gathered in Greyfriars
Church: and there Knox breathed back into them heart, hope,
faith, and purpose. He had been preaching in St. Giles' on the
80th Psalm: first, on its invocation: 'Give ear, O Shepherd of
Israel, thou that leadest Joseph like a flock'; now he had arrived
aptly at the fourth verse,

'O Lord God of Hosts how long wilt thou be angry against
the prayer of thy people?
Thou feedest them with the bread of tears, and givest them
tears to drink in great measure.
Thou makest us a strife unto our neighbours, and our
enemies laugh among themselves.'

'How dolorous and fearful it was,' warned Knox, 'to fight
against that temptation, that God turns away His face from our

prayers.' But they must fight on in the battle of faith, 'as Jacob did in wrestling with his angel'. 'I doubt not that some of us have ofter than once read this psalm, as also that we have read and heard the travail and troubles of our ancient fathers. But which of us, either in reading or hearing, did so descend into ourselves that we felt the bitterness of their passions? I think none. And therefore has God brought us to some experience in our own persons.'

There follow the lovely verses, surely to Knox like a vision of his kirk:

'Thou hast brought a vine out of Egypt: thou hast cast out the heathen and planted it.

Thou preparedst room before it and didst cause it to take deep root, and it filled the land.

The hills were covered with the shadow of it, and the boughs thereof were like the goodly cedars.

She sent out her boughs unto the sea, and her branches unto the river.'

But affliction had come. Why?

'Why hast thou then broken down her hedges, so that all they which pass by the way do pluck her?

The boar out of the wood doth waste it; and the wild beast of the field doth devour it.

Return, we beseech thee, O God of Hosts; look down from Heaven, and behold and visit this vine;

And the vineyard that thy right hand hath planted, and the branch that thou madest strong for thyself.'

Why this affliction? echoed Knox, looking round on the great Duke, and on the lords and the others: 'Let us begin at ourselves, who has longest continued in this battle. When we were a few number . . . when we had neither Earl nor Lord to comfort us, we called upon God: we took him for our protector, defence and only refuge. Amongst us was heard no bragging of multitude, of our strength nor policy: we did only sob to God . . . But . . . chiefly since my Lord Duke his Grace with his friends have been joined with us, there was nothing heard but, "This Lord will bring these many hundred spears: that man hath the credit to persuade that country: if this earl be ours, no man in such a bounds will trouble us." And thus the best of all hath ... put flesh to be our arm.'

'But wherein ye hath my Lord Duke his Grace, and his friends, offended? Knox was coming to that: if his sermons were long, there was little fear of anyone going to sleep in them.

'I have not yet forgotten what was the dolour and anguish of my own heart, when at Perth, Cupar Muir and Edinburgh Crags these cruel murderers, that now hath put us to this dishonour, threatened our present destruction: my Lord Duke his Grace and his friends at all three Journeys was to them a great comfort, and unto us a great discourage: for his name and authority did more affray and astonish us, than did the force of the other; yea, without his assistance they could not have compelled us to appoint with the Queen upon so unequal conditions. I am certain if my Lords Grace hath unfainedly repented of that his assistance to these murderers ... or of that innocent blood ... shed in his default. But let it be so that he hath done (as I hear that he hath confessed his offence before the Lords and Brethren of the Congregation) yet am I assured that neither he, nor yet his friends, did feel before this time the anguish and grief of heart which we felt, when in their blind fury they pursued us: and therefore hath God justly permitted both them and us to fall in this confusion at once.'

Only a man completely certain God was in command could have dealt so firmly with the Duke: and the certainty made itself felt throughout the congregation. Forthwith they believed with Knox 'that this cause (in despite of Satan) shall prevail in the realm of Scotland. ... In the end it shall triumph'.

'Turn us again, O Lord God of Hosts; cause they face to shine, and we shall be saved.'

Randolph, the English envoy, spoke the simple truth when he wrote to Elizabeth later in a dispatch that 'the voice of one man is able in one hour to put more life in us than 500 trumpets continually blustering in our ears.'

They passed from sermon to dinner, and thence to council, opened with prayer by Knox, on invitation. It was decided to send Maitland south to persuade both the Queen and her council to aid them openly: and the rest dispersed quietly for a month.

Knox had been pressing for this expedition south through all the last hectic days in Edinburgh. On the 29th October he had written to Croft: 'I hope that God hath delivered me from the most part of these civil affairs, for now are men of better judgement and greater experience occupied in these matters. Young Lethington, secretary, is delivered from the fearful thraldom of the Frenchmen, and is now with us in Edinburgh, who I trust shall relieve me of the presupposed journey.'

If one man could alone have saved the congregation, then Knox's merciless driving of himself would have done it. He wrote to Croft, too, to beg for those who had spent all they had in the cause, who were 'so super-expended already, they are not able to bear out their train', i.e., pay their men: 'If I did not perfectly understand their necessity, I would not write so precisely'. The Regent on the other hand continually offered large bribes: 'I have done what in me lieth, that corruption enter not amongst them'. All he ever begged for himself was a pass for his mother, Mrs. Bowes, 'to remain with me for a season'. Goodman had brought Marjorie and the two little boys north at the end of September, and they had set up house in St. Andrews. Mrs. Bowes's conscience, 'which cannot be quiet without God's word truly preached and His sacraments rightly ministered, is the cause of her request, and of my care'.

Some of his letters show, without words, how he strained himself to the uttermost. One letter tails off, after efforts at a signature, and a note of explanation is added: the rigors of an ague were so shaking him that he could not steady the pen. Again, he writes to England: 'They brag, and the Queen especially, that ye will leave us in the midst of the trouble. . . . My battle to this day hath been very bitter, but if ye frustrate my expectation, and the promises that I have made in your name, I regard not how few my dolorous days shall be.' The French held the Forth, and many of the Scots ships had been 'stayed' in France: 'Make ye advertisement as ye think good, for I cannot write to any especial for lack of opportunity: for in twenty-four hours, I have not had four free to natural rest, and ease of this wicked carcase. Remember my last request for my Mother, and say to Mr. George' – (his brother-in-law) – 'that I have need of a good and an assured horse; for great watch is laid for my apprehension, and large money promised to any that shall kill me.'

'And yet,' he goes on, thinking apparently of Berwick, 'would I hazard to come unto you, if I were assured that I might be permitted to open my mouth, to call again to Christ Jesus those unthankful children, who alas! have appeared utterly to have forgotten his loving mercies. . . . And this part of my care now poured into your bosom, I cease farther to trouble you, being troubled myself in body and in spirit, for the troubles that be present, appear to grow.' This is subscribed: 'At midnight', and trails off into incoherence: with a final line, 'I write with sleepand eyes'.

Marjorie most gallantly helped him every way she could. 'The rest of my wife hath been so unrestful since she came here,' he tells Mrs. Locke, 'that scarce could she tell upon the morrow, what she wrote at night.' That was from St. Andrews, where he had gone from Stirling. There he found letters from Mrs. Locke, and he shows a true parish minister's patience in dealing with them: she had been in *dreadful* danger from 'a fire in a lodging nearby'. She hoped he would keep out of danger behind the lines: and she was suffering from 'Dowbts' again – good Anglican 'Dowbts' about the propriety – or otherwise – of surplices.

In return he begs her for books – 'Calvin upon Isaiah and his Institutes revised . . . or any other that be new and profitable'. He also suggests a collection for their fighting fund: but that does not seem to have been a success: 'it was supposed, that the Highest would support us'.

He had written once or twice to Calvin, in Latin, on the problem of indiscriminate baptism without discipline: and got enthusiastic letters back praising his efforts and calling him 'excellent Sir, and brother most dear to us'. He had also worked hard at the lords' request on a *History of the Reformation* to date: which is now Bk. II of that fascinating work.

He was able, too, to give Cecil one more good excuse for intervention. He sent confirmation to Gregory Railton, official at Berwick and once in his congregation there, of the rumour that Mary had quartered the arms of England with those of France and Scotland on her seal. Knox had seen this 'most secretly' on the very boat that had brought him from France that May: though the Regent was far too wise to disclose it. He wrote in a kind of code: and signed all his letters at this time: 'John Sinclair'.

The lords met again at Stirling on 16 December and Maitland brought a draft treaty from London, promising England's complete and open support. Rejoicing was tempered with fear: would it be in time? Or would it be a case of Somerset and the Castle of St. Andrews all over again?

The Regent, getting wind of it, was urging on France to send their great expedition with every possible speed. d'Oysel gathered a large force, and swooped on Stirling at Christmas: he was just too late. They had all scattered for safety, sending Knox back to St. Andrews to speed off an urgent plea to Cecil for ships: to blockade the Forth from French supplies, to keep out d'Elboef, Mary's uncle, with the main expedition: above all, to save St. Andrews, which was the next objective. Would they be in time?

In the last desperate days in Edinburgh, Knox had written to Croft suggesting that English soldiers should slip across the Border: and then 'ye may declare them Rebels . . . when ye shall be assured they be in our company'. Croft had pretended to be shocked: but Elizabeth did this often enough, as Knox knew: and she and Cecil did it now, sending Admiral Winter, who was half a pirate, quite unofficially to the Forth. But would he be in time?

For d'Elboef had sailed with a great force: and d'Oysel was marching through Fife to St. Andrews, keeping to the coast so as to watch for d'Elboef's sails: and giving his soldiers freedom to loot, slay, pillage as they went.

They marched on Kinghorn: and there the uncontrollable 'rascal multitude' element of the congregation foolishly attacked. Only Lord Ruthven, riding in with his force, saved them from total annihilation. Losses were heavy, discouragement complete. The French spoiled Kinghorn and laid waste all the country round, driving off sheep, cattle, horses. The lords retired in despair to Cupar.

There Knox came to them, 'and in our greatest desperation, preached unto us a most comfortable sermon. His text was, "The danger in which the disciples of Christ Jesus stood when they were in the midst of the sea, and Jesus was upon the mountain". His exhortation was, "That we should not faint, but that we should still row against these contrarious blasts, till that Jesus Christ should come. For (said he), I am as assuredly persuaded that God shall deliver us from the extreme trouble, as that I am assured that this is the Evangel of Jesus Christ which I preach unto you this day. The fourth watch is not yet come; abide a little; the boat shall be saved and Peter, which has left the boat, shall not drown. I am assured, albeit I cannot assure you, by reason of this present rage; God grant that ye may acknowledge his hand, after that your eyes has seen his deliverance".'

He comforted many: but not all. He took occasion, by means of the story of the leader Jehoshaphat, who comforted his people by his continual cheerful presence, to infer a rebuke to the Earl of Arran, who was moody and solitary. But after this Arran rode with the Lord James to the coast to harry and hamper the French, at all costs to delay them. 'They did so valiantly, that it passed all credibility: for twenty and one days they lay in their clothes: their boots never came off: they had skirmishing almost every day: yea some days from morn to even.' This in a January of bitter storm, sleet, snow, and savage wind: and they were enormously out-numbered.

Kirkcaldy of Grange, whose house had been razed to the ground, joined with the Master of Lyndsay in the same guerilla warfare. 'They escaped many dangers. The Master had his horse slain under him; the said William was almost betrayed in his house at Hallyards. But yet they never ceased, but day and night they waited upon the French.' Lyndsay slew Captain Battu in a hand-to-hand fight. Kirkcaldy got a bullet 'right under the left pap, through the jack, doublet and sark, and the bullet did stick in one of his ribs.' Courageous old Alexander Whitelaw, the messenger, got a fall 'by the which he is unable to bear armour'. The paid soldiers had given up after two days – they were worse than useless, said Knox – but the men of his congregations throughout Fife 'never came in bed, neither yet did they ever sleep but in their jacks and armour: for they only assisted Mr. Kirkcaldy to annoy the enemy'.

Yet still the French came on. The Regent was jubilant, saying 'Where is now John Knox his God? My God is stronger than his, yea, even in Fife!' d'Elboef's great fleet had been sighted, running before the storm. Men watched the sea for its sails every day.

To Knox in St. Andrews it must have seemed almost like the old nightmare back again. But now it was not the galleys that awaited him, but the devouring fire that had eaten the living bodies of Patrick Hamilton, George Wishart, old Walter Myln and so many more: that fire that must have flickered in his subconscious fears ever since the night of Wishart's taking, when he had known himself committed.

It was very near now. The French army was eight miles from St. Andrews: and sails had been seen standing in from the grey and stormy North Sea. This was on Monday 22 January at noon.

d'Oysel believed them to be French: and to the utter despair of the people of St. Andrews, they let off a volley for salutation, and rushed forward within six miles of the town. Then came sudden and definite tidings that they were wrong – they were English!

Next day the French retired more in one day 'than they did in two marching forward'. The storm lifted: and hoping to catch them Kirkcaldy cut the Brig o' Tullibody: but they took the roof off the parish kirk to bridge the Devon, and so got back to Stirling 'and syne to Leith'. Best of all, word came through that many of d'Elboef's fleet had been wrecked on the Dutch coast, and the rest driven back to Dieppe. They were saved.

'The parts of Fife set at freedom from those bloody worms, solemn thanks were given, in St. Andrews, unto God for His mighty deliverance.' It must have been a tremendous heart-stirring occasion.

The French, falling back on Leith, collected all the provisions they might for a siege. Cruelty called forth cruelty. One, 'in red cloak and gilt morion', entered a poor woman's hut, and not content with her bread, would empty her meal and salt mutton barrels to the uttermost: although it was all that stood between her children and starvation until winter passed. 'Neither could tears, nor pitiful words, mitigate the merciless man.' However, as he scraped into the bottom of the barrel, the resourceful wife 'cowpit his heels' and drowned him. One hopes the pickle tasted none the worse.

Now that the politicians were in command, Knox asked only to get back to his people and his preaching. He wrote a farewell letter to Gregory Railton on 29 January pleading for full confidence between the leaders of the nations, asking for some trained and tough captains to knock discipline into the paid – and unprofitable – foot-soldiers: and recommending generously both for praise and any possible compensation those who had borne the brunt of the fighting in Fife. In it he also says: 'I am judged among ourselves too extreme: and by reason thereof I have extracted myself from all public assemblies to my private study.'

But his seclusion never lasted long. The Duke of Norfolk had been sent to Berwick with full instructions, power and commission to conclude a treaty with the lords for England's open and complete support. The 'advertisement' of this first reached the Duke's Grace at Glasgow, where he was with the Ayrshire and west-land lords: they decided Berwick was too far to the east, and they would rather meet at Carlisle! It looked for a moment as if all the pleading and planning of the year would come to nothing: that England might easily be offended and march away again. In distress the eastward lords asked Knox to answer the Duke his Grace – to 'sort' him, in a comprehensive Scots word. Knox sorted him for four pages with a savage pen: for all the world like the schoolmaster he once was with the worst member of the lower fourth.

'Albeit ,(I say), that of those things I have before complained. ... Now I can not cease both to wonder and lament, that your whole Council was so destitute of wisdom and discretion as to charge this poor man the Prior' (Lord James) 'to come to you to Glasgow and thereafter to go to Carlyle ... if none of these former causes should have moved you to consider that such a journey at such a time was not meet for him . . . yet discreet men would have considered, that the men that have lain in the jacks and travailled their horse continually the space of a month, requireth some rest, both to themselves, but especially to their horses. ... Wonder it is ye did not consider to what pain and fasherie shall ye put your friends of England ... whom ye shall cause travel the most wearisome and faschious gate that is in England. In my opinion, whosoever gave you that counsel either lacked right judgement ... or else had too much respect to his own ease and too small regard to the travail and danger of their brethren. A common cause requireth a common concurrence, and that every man bear his burden proportionably. ... To speak the matter plainly, wise men do wonder what my Lords Duke's friends do mean, that they are so slack and backward in this cause. . . .'

They went to Berwick. And there, on the 27th February, 1560, treaty was signed on behalf of England by Norfolk, and of Scotland by the Great Duke: 'James, Duke of Chatelherault, Earl of Arran, Lord Hamilton, second person of the realm of Scotland, and heir-apparent to the Crown'. Knox had sorted him.

At the end of March a great English Army crossed the Borders and made history by meeting the Scottish forces at Preston in friendship and amity. The faith and perseverance of one man had made this possible.

The Queen Regent knew it was the end. A dying woman, she asked sanctuary in Edinburgh Castle on 1 April. Yet she was able to watch with pleasure the joint forces being repulsed from besieging Leith. Earl Bothwell, who remained with d'Oysel and Seton (once Provost), made a fairly successful sortie. The Scots lost only two men of note: a brother of Lockhart of Barr who 'rashly discovered himselfe in the trenches', and Campbell of Cleish – the 'Squire Meldrum' of Lyndesay's poem – who was shot in the thigh and died later. Bothwell went overseas, by way of Denmark, to the French Court to ask for help: the English forces sent word to Berwick, and received 2,000 fresh men who came with 'pavilions' to camp in the field – a novelty to Scotland.

The Regent tried to slip out a last message to d'Oysel, written possibly in milk, for it was discovered on heating her list of drugs required. She refused Willock's prayers, and died on 10 June.

Six days later there arrived the Bishop of Valance and Charles de la Rochefoucauld, Seigneur de Randan, in commission from France to sign terms of peace. Cecil himself came north from the English Court with Dr. Wotton, Dean of Canterbury and York. They signed the Treaty of Edinburgh in that city on 6 July, 1560. By it the Estates – the Scottish Parliament – was restored to power: and all foreign troops, both French and English, were to evacuate the country. Nothing was concluded on religion, for the English would have liked to see uniformity with their own Church: the Scots thought their Genevan doctrine 'more pure': and the French would admit 'nane of the twa'.

On 15 July 10,000 French troops set sail, mostly in English ships. So ended the Auld Alliance, which had brought nothing to Scotland but sorrow and loss.

On Sunday, 19 July, there was a great public thanksgiving service in St. Giles', the Kirk of Edinburgh. Knox had been preaching there since the end of April: but this was a statutory occasion, when the 'whole nobility and the greatest part of the congregations gathered together'. and special prayers were offered. Knox gives us no hint of his sermon: but surely it was on the promises of God. Six years later he wrote: 'For what was our force? What was our number? Yea, what wisdom or worldly policy was into us, to have brought to an good end so great an enterprise?' Then he quoted the prophet Isaiah, with triumphant faith: 'They that wait upon the Lord shall renew their strength; they shall lift up their wings as the eagles; they shall run, and not be weary; they shall walk, and not faint'.

16

The Kirk of Scotland

At the beginning of August the Three Estates – the Scottish Parliament – met briefly and then adjourned. They asked Knox for a plain statement of faith, and a constitution for his Kirk. The Confession of Faith was produced in incredibly short space and immediately adopted. The large Book of Discipline was also produced in four days, and was approved: but as it asked for one third of the confiscated Church wealth to support the schools, the clergy and the poor, its promises were constantly 'eluded'.

It is given to few men to shape the minds of future generations: but Knox did, in Carlyle's phrase, 'make Scotland over again in his own image'. He did not create the Kirk of Scotland out of his own dreams only: he bodied forth the desire and will in the people. But the most part of the people at that date were ignorant, leaderless starvelings: the body he gave it was his own shaping, and that shaping moulded the Scotland of succeeding centuries. It moulds the minds of Scots and their descendants overseas, to this day.

Knox's Kirk was the Kirk of Everyman. Erskine of Dun, a layman, was moderator of many of the first general assemblies: where still today lay elders of the Kirk have equal voting power with the clergy. In the Sessions, in the Presbyteries which came twenty years after the Reformation and after Knox's death, that still held good. How right were the de Guises to crush and butcher Reformers where they could! There is a sense in which every new Day of the Common Man is a coming with power of the Lord: that Risen Lord, who was once himself mistaken for a gardener.

There were to be frequent meetings, Knox planned, not only for Bible reading and study, but for discussion: with one day in the week kept 'for answering of questions' and reasoning with doubters. Without 'right understanding, and teaching and worship', said Knox: 'there cannot be the face of ane visible Kirk'.

The whole world knows now 'the face' of the Kirk of Scotland: but only Knox could see it clearly then, four hundred years ago and more, hidden by the mists of the future and the black darkness of his own times.

And what madness that vision must have seemed! To call a whole nation to reject, by its own will, the conditions of its own Age: to deny the mountainous and accepted ignorance and superstition, the illiteracy and apathy. To ask the leaders to trust that the rabble would show wisdom and responsibility: to ask the commoners to trust their souls outside the golden railings of Rome, which ringed with restrictive safety all 'Christendom : – and had done for so long! – to expect a whole realm, poor, powerless and disarmed, to trust like Israel of old in the promises of the Lord of Hosts, that His arm only would be their defence.

When Knox presented the Book of Discipline to the Great Council in 1560, he did so with this appeal:

'If God shall grant quietness, and give your Wisdoms grace to set forward letters in the sort prescribed, ye shall leave wisdom to your posterity: a treasure more to be esteemed than any earthly treasure ye are able to provide for them, which without wisdom are more apt to be their ruin and confusion than help and comfort.'

At the end of his appeal, as if realising how mad his vision must still seem to many sensible people, he adds the prayer:

'and yet shall this our judgement abide to the generations following for a monument and witness, how lovingly God called you and this Realm to repentance, what counsellors God sent unto you, and how ye have used the same.'

Judgement does abide, for Knox's 'monument and witness' is the whole Scots people. The frugal Scottish home, the passionate belief in democracy and education, the love of religious discussion, the father the head and priest in his own house, are all latent in Knox's Book of Order and later and fully expressed in his Confession of Faith and Book of Discipline. From these writings grew Knox's Kirk, the Kirk of Scotland: and all the traditions that we think of as particularly Scots. The incorrigible independence, the hunger for learning, the brilliant 'lad o' pairts' from a poor home, given – and making – his chance in the world: the peasantry who broke a dynasty sooner than accept the Anglican creed: the men who left stony furrows to control giant powers and become the chief engineers of the new Industrial Age.

When, hundreds of years after Knox, a national poet was born to Scotland, it was in 'that receptacle of God's servants of old':

> There was a lad was born in Kyle,
> But whatna day nor whatna style
> I trow it isna worth your while
> To be so nice with Robin!

Rantin' rovin' Rabbie Burns was no admirer of a Kirk that in his day had lost its vision: yet its belief was at the very core of his singing, as it is still at the heart's core of the common man's life. Knox wrote to the Commons: 'Ye are in your own houses Bishops and Kings . . . let there be worship of God morning and evening . . . and let no day slip over without some comfort received of the Word of God'. Even a hundred years ago the sound of the evening psalm would rise from every weaver's cottage at dusk. In Burns's time it was accepted custom. In one of his best-loved if not his greatest poems, *The Cottar's Saturday Night*, he describes the labourer coming home from the fields to his crowded cabin, and the supper of porridge, bringing with him as guest the lad who courts his daughter. After the psalm, 'The priest-like father reads the sacred page'.

> From scenes like these auld Scotia's grandeur springs,
> That makes her lov'd at home, rever'd abroad:
> Princes and lords are but the breath of Kings,
> An honest man's the noblest work of God.

There is one poem of Burns that is quoted by Russians, Indians, and Chinese. It is a poem of the future, although written more than a hundred and fifty years ago. It is a kind of setting in metre of Knox's belief in the common man:

> For a' that and a' that,
> Our toils obscure, and a' that,
> The rank is but the guinea-stamp,
> The Man's the gold for a' that.

> Then let us pray that come it may
>   (As come it will, for a' that),
> That sense and worth o'er a' the earth
> Shall bear the gree, and a' that.
> For a' that and a' that,
> It's coming yet for a' that,
>   That man to man the world o'er
>   Shall brithers be for a' that!

Thanks to the Kirk that taught them to think and reason, the Scots were ready both in mind and in heart for the Industrial Revolution: in which their tiny country took and still takes so great a part. Only men with alert, thinking brains could have first made a river to sail great ships, and then ever greater ships to sail the world's seas. It was the English poet Kipling who wrote their 'Hymn' – for 'MacAndrew', the engineer from the Clyde:

> Lord, Thou has made this world below the shadow
>   of a dream,
> An taught by time, I tak' it so – exceptin' always Steam.
> From coupler-flange to spindle guide I see Thy Hand,
>   O God –
> Predestination in the stride o' yon connectin'-rod.
> John Calvin might hae forged the same – enorrmous,
>   certain, slow
> Ay, wrought it in the furnace-flame – *my* 'Institutio'. . . .

Knox's Book of Order, which outlined the worship of the new Kirk had been first published in Geneva early in 1556, while Knox himself was still in Scotland. It was based on that draft he and Whittinghame had drawn up in Frankfort: and Goodman and probably others also collaborated in it. Knox soon put its reprinting in hand in Scotland, and this was achieved, with Calvin's Catechism and the Psalms in English Metre, by 1562. 'Our book', as Knox proudly calls this Book of Order in a letter to Mrs. Locke, then permanently took the place of Edward VI's prayer book which had been temporarily used as a stop-gap in some places. Unlike the Anglican book, Knox's was never a rigid order, but rather a guide; deliberately elastic from the beginning. Even in the sacraments there was scope for a man to build up his own service, choosing as he liked from 'such comfortable passages as appealed to him', or 'such prayers as these'. Knox would not fetter worship.

In the central act of the Lord's Table it was not on detail that emphasis was laid, but on sharing. As the minister broke bread to the elders, and they to the people, so did the people break bread with each other: there could be no possible division of class or colour here. So today the celebrant in the Scottish Kirk, unlike the Church of England or the Church of Rome, announces that it is 'his bounden duty as it is his privilege' openly to invite 'any member of any branch of the Christian Church whatsoever' to partake with them 'since this is not the Table of any one church, but the Table of the Lord'.

In Baptism too, the other sacrament, the order that became distinctively Scottish was Knox's own. He saw the child not only as the heart of the home, but as the heart of the community too. It was not enough for the parents only to be present, the whole 'family of God' must be there with them too, to welcome its newest and youngest member. And from thenceforward it was the responsibility not only of the parents but the whole community also. His Baptismal prayers are glorious. Knox was bitterly opposed to private baptisms in houses: and disciplined a minister later for carrying them out. He was still more bitterly opposed to the idea that an infant who died unbaptized was damned to hell. He called this 'the gross error by which many be deceived, thinking that children be damned if they die without baptism'. He also denounced 'whatsoever presumeth in baptism to use oil, salt, wax, spittle, conjuration or crossing'. They were to use only 'Christ's perfect ordinance'; always in face of the whole congregation, and preferably at the morning service.

The teaching of children was always tremendously important to Knox, and included in his book is the Catechism. This he claims was the 'most perfect' in use anywhere. A great part of the Book of Discipline too is given up to directions for their instruction: and those in remote 'landward' areas, without roads or access by sea, were specially remembered. Knox hoped that more gifted ministers would make a point of going to remote parishes that

F

they might teach there. Once a year the head of the house was to bring his whole household to church, and all those who had reached years of discretion were to be examined on the chief points of their faith. For no one should be admitted to the Lord's Table who did not have 'knowledge of God's Law and Commandments: the use and office of the same: the chief articles of our Belief: the right form to pray unto God: the number, use and effect of the Sacraments: the true knowledge of Christ Jesus, of His office and natures and such other points. . . .' Also – Knox's old point – 'the exercise of the children in every church shall be great instruction to the aged'.

Lethington once suggested that Knox's Kirk would prove 'but a pious imagination': and with an ignorant, illiterate people in a war-ravaged country it would seem quite likely. But Knox had complete faith in his vision. His Kirk demanded a totally literate, totally educated people; a quite unimagined, a genuinely incredible thing in his day. But in the big section of the Book of Discipline given over to 'The Necessity of Schools', he boldly planned how this could be achieved. 'Seeing that God hath determined that His Church here on earth shall be taught not by angels but by men', and 'seeing that men are born ignorant of all godliness and that the age of miraculous illumination has passed', then there is nothing for it but compulsory education. 'Of necessity therefore let every single church have a schoolmaster appointed' . . . A school in every parish was a brilliant plan: although not achieved till over a hundred years after Knox's death. The spying-out and encouraging of gifted pupils, sustaining the poor and compelling the rich, was also part of his scheme from the beginning.

He also gave minute and careful suggestions for the university courses; and proposed to add two new ones to the ancient foundations of St. Andrews, Glasgow and Aberdeen: this led to the founding of Edinburgh University in 1582, and of Marischall College, Aberdeen, in 1593, both after his death.

Knox's parish ministers and their sessions came to see also to such things as poor relief, the sick and aged, trade disputes and the upkeep of roads and bridges. They also disciplined such minor crimes as 'drunkenness, excess, fornication, oppression of the poor by exactions, deceiving of them in buying or selling by wrong measures, wanton words and licentious living tending to slander'.

Greater crimes such as 'blasphemy, adultery, murder, perjury and other crimes capital' came under the 'civil sword'.

In the days between 1556 and 1560, when the Protestants met secretly in their own houses, elders had already been ordained with prayer. Knox ordered that both they and the deacons should keep properly audited accounts, so that 'corruption cannot suddenly enter'. Elders had the fearful responsibility of taking heed 'to the life, manners, diligence and study of their ministers. If he be worthy of admonition, they must admonish him: of correction, they must correct him'. From this difficult and intensely personal relationship has come sometimes intolerable friction, but often a deep and abiding loyalty and affection. All that this vital, inarticulate bond can mean is beautifully expressed in Ian Maclaren's delightful old book *Beside the Bonnie Briar Bush*.

'Not only may the life and manners of the ministers come under censure . . . but also of their wifes, children and family.' That was prophecy indeed. They were not to live extravagantly, and not meanly: yet above all 'careful solicitude of money and gear' was 'utterly to be damned in Christ's servants. In fact, they were to live in grinding poverty, almost destitution, for many years.

'Neither yet must a minister be permitted to frequent and commonly haunt the Court.' Nor was he to lodge permanently in a common ale-house or tavern. 'Neither yet must he be one of the Council in Civil Affairs, be he never judgent so apt for that purpose; but neither he must cease from the ministry (which at his own pleasure he may not do), or else from bearing charge in civil affairs, unless it be to assist Parliament if he be called.' Surely a word for our times, when ministers are apt to hanker after civil office as an escape from the hard parish round!

The patrimony of the Roman Church was to be divided into three: one part for the Church, one for the poor and one for the schools. (As it happened, Mary's extravagence in Holyrood ruined any chance that might have had of success.) Buildings were to be put in repair and if not done in the agreed time, 'because we know the slothfulness of men', then the *builders* were to be fined. Burial was to be decent, but never extravagant: and no more fuss made over the great than the simple: since by that time the earthly account was closed.

'Because that marriage, the blessed ordinance of God, in this cursed papistry hath partly been contempned' so Knox took steps for its regeneration. There were to be no more child-marriages: and those at present under contract might either accept or repudiate the same when they grew up. Minors who wished to marry could appeal to the magistrate or minister: and if the only objection was the usual one of lack of goods 'or because they are not so high-born as requisit' then the parents would be told the work of God ought not to be hindered. 'The work of God we call when two hearts (without filthiness before committed) are so joined that both require and are content to live together in that holy band of matrimony.' Did Knox in that phrase look back to his own secret marriage: and to the 'despiteful words' of Marjorie's uncle?

Ten superintendents were to be appointed as an emergency measure, for the first setting-up of the Kirk. Ministers were always to be the free choice of the people. Ministers were to make no distinction of persons, but to remember that their ministry belonged equally to 'the labourers and manurers of the earth as to the nobles'. There is probably no equivalent in any church anywhere to the Scottish 'call'.

To Knox's doctrine also belongs that emphasis on what the Covenanters, a hundred years later, were to call 'The Crown Rights of the Redeemer'. Knox frequently refers to the Lord as 'His Majestie' – the only one he was bound wholly to adore and to obey. This was not rebellion: but it was political independence.

The Sabbath was to be decently kept, but it should not be imagined that gloom was ordered, or Levitical details laid down. Knox on a Sunday journeyed, wrote letters, and after service entertained friends. Once, when asked for guiding rules on women's clothes, by two earnest Edinburgh women, he flatly refused to lay down any laws. 'Touching the apparel of women, to be usit by sic as profess godliness, it is very difficult and dangerous to appoint any certainty, lest in so doing we either restrain Christian liberty or else loose the bridle too far. . . . For if we shall condemn sic vain apparel as commonly now is usit among women, we shall be called rigorous and severe, and accusit as too much inclining to superstition.'

The body of the ordinary people were to take full part, not only in the sacraments, but in the worship. 'Men, women and children should be exhorted to exercise themselves in the psalms, that when the church conveneth, and does sing, they may be the more able together with common heart and voice to praise God.' Full-hearted congregational singing has always been the mark of the Reformed Church: and the congregation of St. Giles' sang then, as they often sing today, the Psalms of Israel. These songs of a small embattled nation in search of its soul were in so many lands the voice of the new faith.

It was in Geneva that the first full translation of the psalms into English had been attempted. Whittinghame, Knox's colleague, translated seven of them himself, including a charming version of the 23rd Psalm, with the lilt of a Border ballad:

> The Lord is only my support
> And he that doth me feed:
> How can I then lack anything
> Whereof I stand in need?
>
> He doth me fold in cotes most safe,
> The tender grass fast by:
> And after drives me to the streams
> Which runneth pleasantly.

Kethe, also one of Knox's congregation in Geneva, and a Scot, translated many more. Two of those best-known and best-loved today are identical both in words and tune with that first Geneva version. One, by Whittinghame, is the 'psalm of delivrance', Psalm 124, sung as thankfully after the World Wars as once it was after battles with the English or the French:

> Now Israel
> May say and that truly
> If that the Lord
> Had not our cause maintained,
> If that the Lord
> Had not our right sustained

When cruel men
Against us furiously
Rose up in wrath
To make of us their prey:

Then certainly
They had devoured us all.
And swallowed quick,
For ought that we could deem:
Such was their rage
As we might well esteem.
And as fierce floods
Before them all things drown,
So had they brought
Our soul to death quite down. . . .

Ev'n as a bird
Out of a fowler's snare
Escapes away
So is our soul set free:
Broke are their nets
And thus escaped we.
Therefore our help
Is in the Lord's great name
Who heav'n and earth
By his great power did frame.

The psalm of Kethe's which is still widely used, with its strong
simple words and tune to match, is the *Old Hundredth;* as known
and loved in the New World today as it was in the Old World of
its birth. Longfellow called it, 'the grand old Puritan anthem'.

All people that on earth do dwell
Sing to the Lord with cheerful voice,
Him serve with mirth, his praise forth-tell,
Come ye before him and rejoice. . . .

For why? The Lord our God is good,
His mercy is for ever sure,
His truth at all times firmly stood
And shall from age to age endure.

There are some kirks in Scotland still where no other praise but the Psalms of David is ever heard.

Knox never offered an easy road: his charter of democracy was not bread and circuses. He did not put the Church into the hands of the common man by cheapening its truths or watering down doctrine. Up to the First World War, if you had asked any barefoot, barely-fed child out of a Scottish worker's hovel: 'What is the chief end of man?' you would have got the superb answer:

'Man's chief end is to glorify God, and to enjoy Him forever.'

This was the first Question and Answer in the Scottish Shorter Catechism. Also, this was the Kirk that Knox built: the Kirk of Scotland.

17

The Minister of St. Giles'

Knox did not rest. As once he had rallied the people by his preaching, so now from the pulpit of St. Giles' he wrestled almost daily with their doubts and fears. Having started so late, he was always conscious of the running-out of time.

Randolph, the English envoy, was amazed and rather scandalized at the speed of the proceedings. He was for putting them off and toning them down: but Knox's whitehot fervour drove them through. The Englishman did not think the Estates would pass the Confession of Faith and Book of Discipline, for many of the bishops and great churchmen of the Roman Church still sat with them. But 'in free and lawful assembly' as Knox triumphantly wrote, they were voted through: and with them two Acts, one abolishing the authority of the Pope throughout Scotland, and the other proclaiming the Mass wholly illegal:

'I never heard,' Randolph wrote south, 'matters of so great importance neither sooner dispatched nor with better will agreed to.'

Many of the lords who had been lukewarm now fully declared themselves, as they fully compassed Knox's vision. Lord Lyndesay, the oldest, said he could now say with Simeon: 'Nunc dimittis'. Winram, sub-prior of St. Andrews, defied his own bishop (one of the three dissenting), and spoke out clearly and boldly for the new Kirk. Winram was one of the guiding spirits of the Book of Discipline, which was translated into Latin and sent to Geneva to Calvin, Viret and Besa: and to Peter Martyr, Bullinger and others in Zurich.

Yet the Book must have been a disappointment to Randolph too: he had been steadily sounding them out on the possibility of 'uniformity in religion' with England. But he found them, while willing, 'so loath to remit anything of that they have received, that I see little hope thereof'.

'Lord St. John' (young Sandilands) went to the French Court
to ask for ratification of these documents: less from hope to
succeed than from determination to be legally correct. Elizabeth
and Cecil also constantly asked Mary to ratify the Treaty of Leith
and this she as consistently evaded.

But so long as Marie Stewart was Queen of France, there was
little fear of her coming to Scotland: so her lack of consent
mattered less. It was as well. That very spring of the Reformation
in Scotland there had been a horrible killing of Huguenots in
France. They had made an abortive rising at Amboise: and the
Cardinal had rounded them up. There was no longer Henri II to
counsel restraint, Mary's husband Francis II being young, weak
and ailing: so the Cardinal decided to slaughter the lot. Grand-
stands were built in the market-place and 'there was not a hang-
man in all France but was there'. Special seats were reserved in a
place of honour for the young King and Queen: and throughout
the sweet spring day the work went on. The psalm that had been
sung by fifty-seven prisoners dwindled to one dauntless voice:
the King might have saved this last, but the Cardinal overbore
him. So Scotland heard of its Queen.

While the Estates met that summer, Knox preached continually,
enlightening the people. Having made a people's Church, he had
still to make a church-minded people. One Sunday he preached
on the prophet Haggai 'whose doctrine was very proper for the
times'.

'In the second year of Darius the King, in the sixth month in the
first day of the month came the word of the Lord by Haggai the
prophet, saying:

"Thus speaketh the Lord of Hosts, saying, This people say, the
time is not come, the time that the Lord's house should be built.

"Is it time for you, O ye, to dwell in your ceiled houses, and this
house lie waste?

"Now therefore, thus saith the Lord of hosts: Consider your
ways.

"Ye have sown much, and bring in little; ye eat, but he have not
enough; ye drink, but ye are not filled with drink; ye clothe you,
but there is none warm: and he that earneth wages earneth wages
to put it into a bag with holes.

"Thus saith the Lord of Hosts: Consider your ways.

"Go up into the mountain, and bring wood, and build the house; and I will take pleasure in it, and I will be glorified, saith the Lord.

"Ye looked for much and lo, it is come to little; and when ye brought it home, I did blow upon it. Why? said the Lord of Hosts. Because of mine house that is waste, and ye run every man unto his own house." '

The book gave Knox a glorious text 'in application whereof he was so special and so vehement' that Maitland of Lethington, Speaker of the Parliament, felt himself 'pricket' and was heard to say: 'We maun now forget ourselves, and bear the barrow to build the houses of God!'

Yet there is a further and magnificent passage in Haggai, which Knox may also have used to encourage them:

'In the four and twentieth day of the sixth month in the second year of Darius the king . . . came the word of the Lord by the prophet Haggai, saying:

"Who is left among you that saw this house in her first glory? and how do ye see it now? is it not in your eyes in comparison of it as nothing?

"Yet now be strong, O Zerubbabel, saith the Lord: and be strong, O Joshua, the High Priest: and be strong, all ye people of the land, saith the Lord, and work: for I am with you, saith the Lord of Hosts. . . .

"The silver is mine, and the gold is mine, saith the Lord of hosts.

"The glory of this latter house shall be greater than of the former, saith the Lord of hosts: and in this place will I give peace, saith the Lord of hosts." '

Knox knew his hour of triumph was not an end but a beginning. The bulk of the Roman clergy had happily agreed to be pensioned off: but the new Kirk was still to be built. It was laid on democratic foundations. Knox himself had been called to be minister of Edinburgh: Willock went to Glasgow and the west: Goodman, who had been in Ayr since his arrival, and as far as the Isle of Man, went to St. Andrews: Adam Heriot to Aberdeen: Paul Methven ('to whom was no infamy then known') to Jedburgh: and travelling superintendents were appointed as an emergency measure to organize the first parishes. 'Master John Spottiswood for Lothian: Master John Winram for Fife: Master John Willock for Glasgow: the Laird of Dun' (a layman) 'for Angus and Mearns: Master John Carswell for Argyle and the Isles.'

Knox himself, not even entitled to be called 'Master' as a graduate, was not a superintendent. As Randolph noted, perhaps with surprise: 'Mr. Knox thinketh his estate honour enough, if God give him strength to persist in that vocation he hath placed him in, and will receive no other'.

The superintendents were not appointed without the full consent of the churches of each area, as far as it could be made out. In the service Knox drew up for their election the people were asked several questions as to their approval, and as to their loyalty and support: and the proposed man had in turn to answer searching questions on 'life and doctrine'. Knox gives as specimen the election of John Spottiswood to the Lothians, which was held in St. Giles': and which concluded by the singing of the 23rd Psalm, the pastor's psalm. There was a similar service for the ordination of elders, which is maintained to this day.

How heavy was the burden resting on Knox is shown by Randolph's dispatches to Cecil. On 25 August 'at eight o'clock in the morning' he writes:

'The number of Noblemen is greater (it is said) than of long time it hath been in any Parliament. . . . Sermons are daily, and great audience. Though divers of the Nobles present are not resolved in Religion, yet do they repair daily to the preaching, which giveth a good hope to many that God will bow their hearts. The Bishop of Dunblane is also now come, it is not to reason on religion, but to do, as I hear, whatsumever the Earl of Argyle will command him. If God has prepared him and his Metropolitan to die obstinate Papists, yet I would that they, before they go to the Divell, would show some token that once in their lives they loved their country, and set their hands to the Contract, as hardly I can believe they will.'

He adds that 'overmuch suspicion, where no cause was', had somewhat 'transported the spirits' of the Earl of Arran probably suffering again from depression. 'The pestilent counsel of three or four in this town, seduce many honest men both from good and their county. Mr. Knox spareth not to tell it them. . . .' Yet he added: 'The whole estate of the clergy is on our side, a few only excepted.'

The few included the Bishop of Dunkeld who 'remaineth as obstinate, as ignorant. Being moved to hear Mr. Knox, he gave answer that he would never hear an old condemned heretic. Mr. Knox hath been with him for it, since that time. . . .'

Yet there was no persecution: no hanging, burning, strangling or torture. Knox's hands are cleaner than Calvin's, Luther's, Cranmer's. The 'monks portions' – pensions paid to the Roman religious – were continued until 1590. For this was a Reformation too of the liberties of the people. They now had equal rights in their Kirk and in the ministry: they had freedom to debate and argue: and the Parliament that ratified the Confession of Faith also revived an Act of James I's of 1427, which gave the barons free voice in Parliament.

That autumn an embassy went to England, to propose Arran for Elizabeth's hand. This scheme had first been suggested by Henry VIII in the days of the siege of St. Andrews' Castle, when both were children. But it could hardly have been revived at a worse time. That summer Amy Robsart, Dudley's wife, had been found at the foot of the staircase with a broken neck. Dudley had not been there, but he had wished her dead often enough: and would Elizabeth not now marry her openly-loved favourite? Her ambassador in Paris confessed he was at his wits end to defend her reputation. She was, in fact, in much the same dilemma that later faced Mary: between the good of her throne and her heart's desire. She told Arran she 'would not marry hastily', so he need not hang on in hope. He cared little, preferring Mary, Queen of Scots and of France, to whom when widowed he wrote, sending a ring. But she also refused him: and this he 'bare heavily in heart'. 'Even more so,' said Knox, his adviser, 'than many would have wissed' (i.e. guessed).

Knox's own happiness did not last long. As winter shut down on Scotland, Marjorie's health faded. Towards the end of December she said farewell to her husband and her two little boys, to whom she left her special blessing, and died. She was only twenty-seven or twenty-eight and died when there was a bustle of

Christmas in the air: extra wares on the luckenbooths of the High Street, carols sung below the windows of their house:

> O my dear heart, young Jesus sweet
> Prepare Thy cradle in my spreit
> And I shall rock Thee in my heart
> And nevermore from Thee depart.
>
> And I shall praise Thee evermore
> With sangis sweet unto Thy gloir
> The knees of my heart sall I bow
> And sing that richt ba-loo-la-low.

It was a bitter blow that took her just when Knox could at last give her a home of her own, and the protection of his now honoured name. He too needed her now more than ever. Much of the harshness with which Knox has been charged is due to the bitterness that tinged him after her death. He became 'touchy', as lonely old men do.

About the same time he got word from a secret messenger in France – possibly Geordie Buchanan, the poet and schoolmaster – that Francis II, Mary Stuart's husband, was dying. At once he passed to 'the Duke's Grace' at his lodging at Kirk o' Field, to give him the news. He found the Great Duke with the Lord James, and these two consoled with him ('for he was in no small heaviness by reason of the late death of his dear bedfellow, Marjorie Bowes'), and while they 'were familiarly communing together' dispatches arrived from England confirming that the King of France had died. The Estates were hastily summoned for the 15th January: and some perused the Book of Discipline all over again, says Knox sarcastically, with 'pretended ignorance'.

It was settled at that convention that the Lord James should go to France at his own expense, to present their credentials to Mary the Queen, and possibly to sound out her views in case of her return. 'That she should have Mass publicly, he' (i.e. the Lord James) 'affirmed that he should never consent: but to have it secretly in her chamber, who could stop her? The danger was shown: and so he departed.'

The first general assembly of the Church of Scotland had been held that December, within days of the death of Francis. There were forty-two present, with Erskine of Dun as moderator: but only six were ministers. They must all have wondered what the changed situation would bring: would it mean Mary's return, and would she try to stamp out the Kirk as her mother had done? There was everything to fear from a de Guise.

In spite of personal grief and public rumours, Knox went steadily on with his ministry. This is an extract from the town treasurer and Dean of Guild's accounts:

'1561: Sunday, 2nd of March, the Communion ministered by John Knox in the High Kirk of Edinburgh.

Item, to John Cunningham and his 2 servants for making of 6 long forms and short, for serving the Tables, 2 days' labour . . . 16/-.

Item for 28 ells of broad blechit Bartan cloth of bartanye (i.e. Brittany) to cover the Tables, 6/- the ell . . . £8 8/-.

Sunday, 8th of June, the second Communion ministered in Edinburgh by John Knox: for 3 lbs. bread, 6d. the pecc . . . 30/-.

Item, for 8 gallons wine for 18d. the pint . . . £4 16/-.'

On 5 March Randolph wrote to Cecil: 'The Communion was ministered here upon Sunday last; I assure your Honour with great decency and very good order. There were none admitted but such as made open protestation of their belief, examined and admitted by the ministers and deacons to the number of 13 and odd.'

Randolph must have been moved to write so earnestly. It must indeed have been a memorable sight within the ancient stone walls of St. Giles'. No longer were there seventeen chapels like booths, with tawdry relics and images, before whom the people prayed and paid: no longer was there mumbling of Latin, incantation of gesture and incense, robes and mystic singing, celibate priest and 'hocus-pocus'. Now there was only white-washed walls, plain tables and benches: and the reality of the Fellowship as the great Lords, who had answered on their Faith, sat down to share common cup and common bread with the humblest of the poor who could do likewise.

Surely to Knox that moment was healing and fulfilment: and its memory a comfort.

Today there are still little country kirks where the single long table, spread with its bleached white cloth, is used for the sacrament: but the Kirk of Scotland lost immeasurably when it gave this up as general use.

Knox made the sacrament not only the heart of worship, but the well-spring of community life: here all were equal and all were one. They gathered as a family: and great communal good might have been built from that – if only there had been time!

But less than six weeks after Knox's second sacrament season in June, guns boomed through the white woolly sea-mist on the Forth. Mary Stewart had come back to Scotland.

They had all feared she would come with a French army, like her mother, if she came at all: that she would try to force Scotland. But she came only with two galleys dodging Elizabeth's ships in the Channel: and her 'army' was her company of poets, singers, musicians, her 'four Maries' and her three youngest de Guise uncles – the gayest of blades. Her most powerful weapons were her own beauty and her own charm: and her own high courage.

If it is true that Mary wept when she saw the Scottish 'cavalry' – shaggy ponies – then she quickly hid her tears, Brantome left a sarcastic account of her welcome, with the singing of discordant psalms under Holyrood Palace windows, '*Hé*! *Quelle musique*! *Et quel repos pour sa nuit*!' But Mary herself thanked the council graciously for it, and for their wine and torch-light procession. When, in the Masques done in her honour in the High Street, she was handed an English Bible she was quick-witted enough to hand it over at once to the keeping of 'the most pestilent Papist present'. At eighteen and alone Mary did splendidly.

Randolph poured forth an account to Throckmorton of her arrival and progress:

'All men welcome, all men well received, good entertainment, great cheer and fair words. I find no great alteration in things. Four days she was without Mass: next Sunday she had it in her chapel said by a French priest. There were only at that, besides her uncles and her own household, the Earl of Montrose, Lord Graham. The rest were at Mr. Knox's sermon, as great a number as ever was any days. The Earl of Cassilis was that Sunday at the preaching, and Monday at the Mass: it is said that since he hath repented it and this is but Tuesday . . . There are but two Bishops arrived, St. Andrews and Dunkeld, in long gowns and tippets, with hats upon their heads, but scarce dare put their noses out of doors for fear of after-claps.'

He adds a funny but lewd remark on the priest chittering with terror 'when he had his god at the highest'.

The Mass of course was illegal: and there was considerable outcry. Knox wrote: 'But the Lord James (the man whom all the godly did most reverence) took upon him to keep the chapel door. His best excuse was, that he would stop all Scottish men to enter in to the Mass. But it was and is sufficiently known that the door was kept that none should have entry to trouble the priest. . . .' And so there was 'great grief of heart'.

As the lords of the congregation one by one reached Edinburgh they were at the first coming 'wondrously offended, that the Mass was permitted: so that every man as he came accused them that were before him: but after that they had remained a certain space they were as quiet as were the former'. So that Campbell of Kinyeancleuch said to Ochiltree: 'My lord, now ye are come, and almost the last of all the rest: and I perceive, by your anger, that the fire-edge is not off you yet: but I fear, that after that the holy water of the Court be sprinkled upon you, that ye shall become as temperate as the rest. For I have been here now five days and at the first I heard every man say, "Let us hang the priest." But after that they had been twice or thrice at the Abbey, all that fervency was past. I think there be some enchantment, whereby men are bewitched.'

It was barely a year since the Church of Rome had been outlawed and the Kirk of Scotland established. Mary's smiles had already conquered more than all her mothers' cannon.

PART FIVE

THE BATTLE THAT CONTINUES

18

The Queen's Mass

EVERYONE was welcome now in Holyrood, except Bothwell
and Arran. They had been bitter enemies since Arran had
burned Bothwell's castle in revenge for the Hallowe'en raid and
Bothwell had sent him a challenge to single combat: so it was not
safe to let them meet. Otherwise, said Randolph, 'there is not one
that doth absent himself, or that is not well taken with for the
first face, saving John Knox that thundereth out of the pulpit, that
I fear nothing so much, that one day he will marr all. He ruleth
the roost, and of him all men stand in fear. Would God you knew
how much I am amended myself: but now again in earnest. . . .

'The French are dislodged out of Dunbar and the Inch . . .
proclaimation is already made upon the Borders for the continua-
tion of justice, and maintenance of amity with England. This is
much more than I thought my time would presently have served.'

As Mary's popularity grew, Knox's declined. But he did not
swerve from his path. If no one else would denounce the Mass, he,
in a sermon in St. Giles' soon did so. 'That one Mass, he said,
was more fearful to him than if ten thousand armed enemies were
landed. . . .'

Mary sent for him, to Holyrood. Surely she thought that her
charm, which had conquered so many, would disarm him also.
She saw him alone, save for her half-brother the Lord James, and
they argued for a long time.

She began by accusing him: of raising rebellion against her
mother and herself: of writing a book against her authority (the
Blast), of which she had a copy, and meant to have a reply made
by some learned scholar: of causing treason and slaughter in

179

England: and lastly of witchcraft: 'that all which he did was by necromancy'.

'May it please your Majesty,' he answered, 'patiently to hear my simple answers. First, if to teach the truth of God in sincerity, to rebuke idolatry, and to will a people to worship God according to His word, be to raise subjects against their princes, then I can not be excused.' He went on to say, after his defence, that 'touching that book' if any could adequately prove him wrong he would 'confess my error and ignorance'.

'Ye think then (quoth she) that I have no just authority?'

'Please your Majesty (saith he) that learned men in all ages have had their judgements free, and most commonly disagreeing from the common judgement of the world.' He cites Plato and his *Republic*, which Mary would have read: and suggests that so he could be 'as well content to live under your Grace as was Paul to live under Nero'. He adds, 'in verray deed Madame, that Book was written most especially against that wicked Jezebel of England'.

'But (said she) ye speak of women in general.'

'Most true it is Madame (said he) . . . for of late years many things which before were holden stable, have been called in doubt. . . .'

He then returned to her other two charges, and defended himself by a proud account of his ministry in England: and by citing the many times he had preached openly against witchcraft 'or any other art forbidden of God'. Although Knox calls his account of the interview a summary, it is a lengthy one. Mary returned to the attack.

'But yet,' (said she), 'ye have taught the people to receive another religion than their Princes can allow: and how can that doctrine be of God, seeing that God commands subjects to obey their Princes?'

'Madame (said he) as right religion took neither original strength nor authority from worldly Princes, but from the Eternal God alone, so are not subjects bound to frame their religion according to the appetites of the Princes. . . . If all the seed of Abraham should have been of the religion of Pharaoh . . . what religion would have been in the world? Or if all men in the days of the apostles should have been of the religion of the Roman emperors, what religion would there have been on the face of the earth? . . .'

'Yea (quoth she) but none of these men raised the sword against their Princes.'

'Yet Madame (quoth he) ye cannot deny but that they resisted: for these that obey not . . . in some sort resist.'

'But yet (said she) they resisted not by the sword.'

'God (said he) Madame, had not given them the power and the means.'

'Think ye (quoth she) that subjects having power may resist their Princes?'

This was the soul-searching question he debated so long: but now he had no hesitations.

'If their Princes exceed their bounds (quoth he) Madame . . . it is no doubt but they may be resisted, even by power. For what if a father should go mad, and try to kill his own children? Should they not seize him and take the sword or weapons from him by force? It is even so, Madame, with Princes that would murder the children of God that are subject unto them. Their blind zeal is nothing but a very mad frenzy . . . and therefore to take the sword from them, to bind their hands and to cast themselves in prison till they be brought to a more sober mind is no disobedience against princes, but just obedience, because that it aggreeith with the will of God.'

'At these words, the Queen stood as it were amazed, more than the quarter of an hour.'

How long it must have seemed in that silent room! Did she look out at the great park of Holyrood, at the driving rain or mist perhaps? Did she realize suddenly to how foreign a country and climate she had come, from the absolute monarchy of France? Did she even think of that May-day's butchery in Orleans.

If she did it was with a hardening of resentment. 'Her countenance altered, so the Lord James began to entreat her, and to demand: "What has offended you, madame?" '

At length she said, 'Well then, I perceive that my subjects shall obey you, and not me; and shall do what they list, and not what I command: and so must I be subject to them and not them to me.'

'God forbid,' answered he. . . . 'But my travail is, that both

princes and subjects obey God. . . . Yea, God craves of Kings that
they be as it were foster-fathers to his Church, and commands
Queens to be nourisses to his people. . . .'

'Yes (quoth she) but ye are not the Kirk that I will nourisse. I
will defend the Kirk of Rome, for I think it is the true Kirk of
God.'

'Your will (quoth he) Madame, is no reason: neither doth your
thought make that Roman harlot to be the true and immaculate
spouse of Jesus Christ . . . the Church of Rome is declined, and
more than five hundred years hath declined from the purity of that
religion which the apostles taught and planted.'

'My conscience (said she) is not so.'

'Conscience, Madame, (said he) requires Knowledge. And I fear
that right knowledge have ye none."

'But (said she) I have both heard and read.'

'So, (said he) Madame, did the Jews that crucified Jesus Christ
read both the Law and the Prophets, and heard the same interpret
after their manner. Have ye heard (said he) any teach but such as
the Pope and his Cardinals have allowed?'

'Ye interpret the scriptures in one manner, (said she) and they
interpret in another: whom shall I believe? Or who shall be
judge?'

He referred her to his final authority: the word of God revealed
in the Bible: and finished by citing his old contrast – the elabora-
tion of the Mass as against the simplicity of the Last Supper.

'Ye are ower sair for me (said the Queen) but and if they were
here that I have heard, they would answer you.'

'Madame, (said he) would God that the learnedest Papist in
Europe . . . were present to sustain the argument. . . .'

'Well, (said she) ye may perchance get that sooner than ye may
believe.'

'Assuredly, (said he) if ever I get that in my life, I get it sooner
than I believe . . . they are never able to sustain an argument,
except fire and sword and their own laws be judges.'

'So say ye, (said the Queen).'

'It has been so to this day, (said he). . . .'

And with this the Queen was called upon to dinner, for it was
afternoon. At departing John Knox said unto her: 'I pray God,
Madame, that ye may be as blessed within the Commonwealth of

Scotland if it be the pleasure of God, as ever Deborah was within the Commonwealth of Israel.'

They had measured steel: in the faith of the shabby little preacher, scarcely up to her shoulder in height, Mary met a rock she could neither move nor soften. In the tall, charming young widow, with the gracious, artless manner, Knox discerned 'a proud mind, a crafty wit and an indurate heart against God and his truth. . . .'

In autumn the Queen, with ten new hackneys, went on a royal progress to Perth and Dundee, taking the Mass with her. She was welcomed with gifts, yet shown by broad hints in the pageants that the people's loyalty lay with their own faith. Yet she won more hearts, while Knox was losing those he had had. They sang about him now in the High Street taverns:

> The subject now is grown so great
> That Knox becomes a King
> All that he wills obeyit is
> Wha made the bishop hing!

The last line was poetic licence: and the rest out of date. There were already differing factions in the town: Mary could win support by pardons: and when the Provost was bold enough to offend her ,she deposed him and made a new one. Even Mrs. Locke no longer wrote: she was to re-marry, and perhaps her new husband distrusted it. Knox wrote to her that October:

'I have received your token, dear sister, without writing. I understand your impediment, and therefore, I cannot complain Yet if you understood the variety of my temptations, I doubt not but ye would have written somewhat. . . . I thirst to change this earthly tabernacle, before that my wretched heart should be assaulted with any such new dolours.' He pours out his grief and disappointment, and ends: 'Our Queen weareth the dule, but she can dance, daily dule and all.'

Secretary Lethington was enchanted with the dancing, the Court, the Queen; and already in love with Fleming, one of her Maries. When assembly time came in December, he and the Court faction queried the right of the Church to hold meetings without the Queen's permission and approval. But Knox stood firm on the right of every man to hear and to be heard: 'Take from us the freedom of assembly, and you take from us the Evangel'.

He was less successful in his fight to get the Kirk's rightful revenue. It was his endless, weary, fruitless labour for the last years of his life. Lethington 'ashamed not to affirm' that if the ministers were sustained, the Queen would not have 'at the year's end to buy her a pair of new shoes'. There were all the hungry lairds also who would not, said Knox, 'lack their share of Christ's coat'.

If life was hard in the manse, it was merry in the palace. 'Her common talk was, in secret, she saw nothing in Scotland but gravity, which repugned altogether to her nature,' wrote Knox, adding the phrase we remember, 'for she was, as she said, brought up in joyousity.' But it went too far in December when Bothwell with one of the de Guise uncles and another royal bastard called Lord John staged a riot in the town and broke open a magistrate's house to reach his daughter: this was chiefly to spite Arran, whose light o' love she was said to be.

In February came another celebration, but this time better ordered. The Lord James was married in St. Giles' to the Earl Marischall's daughter – 'after long love'. Knox blessed them, and added the humorous warning to the bridegroom: 'Unto this day the Kirk of God hath received comfort by you, and by your labours: in the which, if hereafter ye shall be found fainter than ye were, it will be said that your wife hath changed your nature.'

The whole procession then went down the Royal Mile to Holyrood, where Mary gave a magnificent banquet, followed by a masked ball: in the course of it she drank a toast to Elizabeth from a splendid gold cup, which she gave Randolph to keep. She also knighted ten of Lord James's friends, including Kirkcaldy of Grange and a Wishart of Pittarrow.

Randolph reported to England that February that Mr. Knox 'upon Sunday last, gave the Cross and the Candle such a wipe, that as wise and learned as himself wished him to have held his peace. He recompensed the same with a marvellous, vehement and piercing prayer in the end of his sermon for the continuance of amity and hearty love with England. . . .'

All through that spring Mary was arranging a Border meeting with Elizabeth. Lethington was at the English Court, holding his

own in wit with the Queen herself. Mary was in Fife, after
banishing Earl Bothwell from Edinburgh for yet another riot in
the streets, which had threatened to become a battle. Then Barron,
Knox's old friend and Bothwell's chief creditor, asked him to
meet with the earl.

Knox did so by night, first in the earl's lodging, then in his own
study. Bothwell said he 'lamented his former inordinate life', and
his many quarrels, including crowning Sandy Cockburn of
Ormiston in the Hallowe'en raid: and in particular his feud with
Arran. On account of these he had to maintain a tail of so many
'wicked and unprofitable men that his living was consumed'.

Knox gave him a good welcome, for the sake of old local
loyalty. He had, he said, 'borne a good mind to your house; and
have been sorry at my heart of the troubles I have heard you to
be involved in. For my Lord, my grandfather, godsire and father
have served your Lordship's predecessors: and some of them have
died under their standards; and this is a part of the obligation of
our Scottish kindness; but this is not the chief'.

There was a slight hitch when it was found that that very night
some of Bothwell's men had again taken the unfortunate laird of
Ormiston: but he was released with excuse: so Knox tried again,
and got Arran and Bothwell to meet at Kirk-of-field, with witnesses. When Bothwell entered, Arran went straight to him and
embraced him, and Knox made a speech, and all went well.
Next day they both came to St. Giles' to the service 'whereat
many rejoiced', and later they dined together.

But on Good Friday, straight after the service, Arran came
down to Knox's Manse. Knox had not finished his writing (note-
making?) which was his habit after preaching: but when he did go
in the earl cried that he was 'treasonably betrayed' and burst into
tears.

'My Lord, who has betrayed you?' asked Knox.

'Ane Judas or other,' said he, 'but I know it is but my life that is
sought: I regard it not.'

Knox tried to calm him: and he poured out a long, incoherent
tale that Bothwell meant to abduct the Queen, and throw the
blame on him. Nothing would stop him from riding straight off to
the Queen to warn her. He went: and his 'phrensy', growing more
violent, 'could not be hid'. He raved of plots and enemies, of the

stars, of the Queen in whose bed he would be: he escaped crazily and violently from his first prison. He ended, the lad who might have married either Queen, with the manacles, straw and dungeon-oblivion that was the lunatic's portion.

His father, the Great Duke, knelt before the Queen with tears running down his face like a whipped child. Knox wrote to Mrs. Locke:

'Our estate here is troublesome. God hath further humbled me since that day which men call Good Friday, than ever I have been in my life, in my business that God put in my hands.'

Bothwell, who had not heard of Arran's breakdown, went to Court, and was promptly arrested and put in Edinburgh Castle. From there he later escaped, and sailed for Frence, but was wrecked on the coast of England, where he remained some time.

The plans for the two Queens to meet came to nothing. That late spring the Duc de Guise made a new push to regain power in France: and he armed the mob against the Huguenots. Cruelty raged again in Paris. Elizabeth cancelled the meeting: and in Scotland Knox's preaching was suddenly popular once more.

Her hopes dashed, Mary set off abruptly on a progress to the far north. Goodman went that way also, to strengthen the young kirks, and Knox went to the west 'as far as his language would bear him' (much of the west was Gaelic-speaking only). Before Knox left he applied to Cecil through Randolph for a pass for Mrs. Bowes, who must have gone south in spring, to come back and look after his two little boys. 'Mr. Knox being now, as he saith, a sole man . . . that she may be a relief unto him in the burden of household, and bringing up of his childer, her daughter's sons.'

Randolph went with Mary, perhaps the first Englishman to spend an autumn holiday in the Highlands. He did not enjoy it. It was 'a terrible journey both for horse and men. The country is so poor, and victuals so scarce. . . .' Travelling he found 'cumbersome, painful and marvellous long: the weather extreme foul and cold: all victuals marvellous dear: and the corn that is, never like to come to ripeness'. He buried his best servant, ruined his horses, and had to share a bed with Lethington.

But Mary led them on, by Glamis and old Aberdeen to Inverness. There she was refused admission to the castle in the name of Lord Gordon of Huntly – 'The Cock o' the North'. But she rallied the country, the castle surrendered and the captain was hanged. Randolph wrote:

'In all these garboils I assure you I never saw her merrier, never dismayed, nor never thought that so much to be in her that I find. She repented nothing but . . . that she was not a man to know what life it was, to lie all night in the fields, or to walk in the causeway with a jack and a knapskull, a Glasgow buckler and a broad-sword.'

Mary in action was Mary at her radiant best.

Although Gordon of Huntly was the chief Roman Catholic of her realm, Mary decided to crush him. She called in Kirkcaldy of Grange, who defeated him completely at Corrichie at the end of October, where he died. He was embalmed, brought to Edinburgh and tried for treason in his coffin, in Mary's presence, the following spring. The Lord James received the rich Moray-shire lands that had been Huntly's, and became Earl of Moray – later 'Regent Moray'.

While in Galloway in the west, Knox had been challenged by Quentin Kennedy, abbot of Crossraguel, to a public debate: but the abbot took his stand on that misty character, Melchisidec, so it came to little. When he came back to Edinburgh the Great Duke asked Randolph to join him at dinner in Knox's Manse on Sunday evening, at the end of November, and there he made Knox three promises, with Randolph as witness. First, he promised loyalty to Christ's word and its setting-forth: second, to be an obedient subject of the Queen, as far as in duty and conscience bound: and third, never to swerve from his promise to maintain peace and friendship between the two realms.

Those early years were the best in Mary's reign: when she leant on the Protestant lords, who were the best in the realm; and when Knox exerted himself to keep the country united. But, as Randolph noted, 'little liking there was between them of th' one or th' other. . . .' Optimists might believe that Mary would yet turn Protestant, but Knox, who had seen de Guise power in France, knew better.

'He is so full of mistrust of all her doings, words and sayings,' wrote Randolph, 'as though he were either of God's privy counsel . . . or that he knew the secrets of her heart. . . . Upon Sunday last he inveighed sore against the Queen's dancing, and little exercise of herself in virtue or godliness; the report hereof being brought unto her ears yesterday, she sent for him. She talked long time with him. . . .'

This time Mary received him in her bedchamber, with her ladies, her servants, various lords including the Lord James, Morton and Secretary Lethington: and those who had accused Knox. He had with him only Black Sandy Cockburn, his old pupil and the victim of the Hallowe'en raid. He was accused of having irreverently spoken of the Queen, having sought to bring her in contempt, and of having exceeded the bounds of his text: 'and upon these three heads made the Queen herself a long harangue or oration'.

When Knox got a chance to reply, he pointed out that if her reporters had been honest men 'they would have reported my words and the circumstances of the same. . . . For, Madam, if your own ears had heard the whole matter that I entreated, if there be in you any spark of the Spirit of God, yea, of honesty or wisdom, you could not justly have been offended with anything that I spak.' He rehearsed his sermon: 'And of dancing, Madam, I said, that albeit in Scriptures I found no praise of it . . . yet do I not utterly damn it, providing that two vices be avoided.' These were, that vocation be not neglected for the pleasure of dancing: 'Secondly, that they dance not, as the Phillistines their fathers, for the pleasure that they take in the displeasure of God's people. For if any of both they do, they shall receive the reward of dancers, and that will be to drink in Hell. . . .'

The Queen looked about to some of the reporters, and said: 'Your words are sharp enough as ye have spoken them: but yet they were told to me in another manner. I know,' said she, 'that my uncles and ye are not of one religion, and therefore I cannot blame you albeit you have no good opinion of them. But if you hear anything of myself that mislikes you, come to my self and tell me, and I shall hear you.'

'Madam,' quoth he, 'I am assured that your uncles are enemies to God, and unto his son Jesus Christ; and that for the main-tenance of their own pomp and worldly glory, that they spare not to spill the blood of many innocents. . . . But as to your own personage, Madam, I would be glad to do all that I could to your Grace's contentment, provided that I exceed not the bounds of my vocation. I am called Madam, to ane public function within the Kirk of God, and am appointed by God to rebuke the sins and vices of all. I am not appointed to come to every man in particular to show him his offence: for that labour were infinite. If your Grace please to frequent the public sermons, then I doubt not but that ye shall fully understand both what I like and mislike, als well in your Majesty as in all others. Or if your Grace will assign unto me a certain day and hour when it will please you to hear the form and substance of doctrine which is proponed in public to the churches of this realm, I will most gladly await upon your Grace's pleasure, time and place. But to wait upon your chamber-door, or else-where, and then to have no farther liberty but to whisper my mind in your Grace's ear, or to tell to you what others think and speak of you, neither will my conscience nor the vocation whereto God hath called me suffer it.'

Knox, having seen through Mary's flatteringly-baited trap to silence him, could not resist a jeer.

'For albeit at your Grace's commandiment I am hear now, yet can not I tell what other men shall judge of me, that at this time of day am absent from my book and waiting upon the Court!'

'Ye will not always,' said she, 'be at your book.' And so turned her back. And the said John Knox departed with a reasonable merry countenance; whereat some papists, offended, said: 'He is not afraid.'

Which heard of him, he answered, 'Why should the pleasing face of a gentlewoman affray me? I have looked in the faces of many angry men, and yet have not been afraid above measure.' And so left he the Queen and the Court for that time.

Knox ends his account of that second interview with the sense that he had held his own.

19

Queen and Preacher

THAT same December Mary celebrated as usual the death of her husband with a solemn Requiem Mass: and spent the next day 'with mirth and pastime on the sands of Leith'. Both Randolph and Knox are sarcastic at this demonstration of sorrow.

Then winter shut down sharply, blocking all movement, pinching the blue flesh. Beyond the usual winter hunger there was dearth in Scotland that year: and, in the north, men, women and children died of starvation.

But in Holyrood there was music and dancing, dicing and feasting: with 'Lusty' Livingstone, one of the Maries, crowned Queen of the Bean on Twelfth Night. To those who suffered with the common people it could only look heartless. Yet perhaps it was the answer of Mary's gay, courageous spirit to the depression of the northern winter, the weary months of cold and darkness.

Melville, who had now given his service wholly to Mary, describes her at this time as 'somewhat sad and solitary, and glad of the company of such as had travelled'. The Court had a new favourite in the poet Chastelard, nephew of Chevalier Bayard, new come from France with all the latest dances, sonnets, love-songs and fashions. He must have been a god-send for the long evenings. They now danced 'The Purpose', in one figure of which the partners exhange secret whispers: and for this 'the Queen chose Chastelard, and Chastelard chose the Queen'.

The flirtation ended badly. Chastelard, says Melville cautiously, was 'transported to miscarry himself by her affability': and twice found hiding in Mary's bedroom. The second time Mary cried to Moray to run him through: but he preserved him for legal trial.

Courteously, the poet neither excused nor accused: he went to the scaffold carrying a book of Ronsard's poems which he kissed, with a graceful: '*Adieu, la plus belle et cruelle Princesse!*'

'And so,' adds Knox, 'received Chastelard the reward of his dancing. . . .'

Meanwhile the preachers pled for the poor: 'who be of three sorts: the poor labourers of the ground: the poor desolate beggars, orphelins, widows and strangers: and the poor ministers of Christ Jesus his Holy Evangel' . . . This was denounced as 'railing': and as Huntly's embalmed corpse was brought to Edinburgh for trial, Knox used the dead man as an illustration to his sermon in St. Giles':

'It has come to our ears that we are called railers . . . yet we are not ashamed, seeing that the most worthy servants of God . . have been so styled. But unto you do I say that that same God, who from the beginning has punished the contempt of his Word, and has poured forth his vengeance . . . shall not spare you. Have ye not seen a greater than any of you sitting where presently ye sit, pick his nails, and pull down his bonnet over his eyes, when idolatry, witchcraft, murder, oppression and such vices were rebuked? Was not his common talk, "When these knaves have railed their fill, then will they hold their peace?" Have you not heard it affirmed to his own face, that God would revenge that his blasphemy, even in the eyes of such as were witnesses to his iniquity? Then was the Earl of Huntly accused by you. . . . Him has God punished, even according to the threatenings that his and your ears heard. . . . If God punish not you, that this same age shall see and behold your punishment, the Spreit of righteous judgement guides me not.

That Easter, when the men of Kyle in the west saw the Mass being openly celebrated in different places in defiance of the law, they took the matter into their own hands and laid hold on the priests. Mary was furious and sent for Knox to come to her at Lochleven, in Fife, where she was hunting.

Lochleven Castle, on its tiny island, was the home of Lady Margaret Douglas. This remarkable woman had seven illegitimate children by Mary's father, James V: the best of them being the Lord James Stewart, now Earl of Moray. After the King's death, she married Douglas of Lochleven by whom she had another ten children. She was liked and respected: and seems to have been good to Mary both now as her hostess and later as her gaoler.

For two whole hours before supper the Queen struggled to

persuade Knox to quieten the people, particularly the men of Kyle, so that no man would be punished for his religion. Knox could do it, she insisted: and why should every man not worship God as he pleased?

He could indeed promise quietness, returned Knox, if the Queen would but enforce the laws of the land: one of which outlawed the Mass. In short, he was not going to be bought by flattery any more than by bribes: and this is inferred in his play on phrases: If 'your Majesty', he said to her, would delude the laws, there were those who would not allow 'God's Majesty' to be so offended.

'Will you allow,' she cried, 'that they shall take my sword in their hand?'

'The Sword of Justice, Madam, is God's. . . .' Knox spoke to her of the duties of rulers, and of their 'mutual contract' with their people. What shocking heresy it must have sounded to her!

'They are bound to obey you, and that not but in God. You are bound to keep laws unto them. Ye crave of them service: they crave of you protection and defence against wicked doers. Now, Madam, if ye shall deny your duty unto them, (which especially craves that ye shall punish malefactors) think ye to receive full obedience of them? I fear, Madam, ye shall not.'

'Herewith, she, being somewhat offended, passed to her supper.' Knox sought out Moray, and told him all that had passed at the interview. He knew well there was no hope of a compromise: and intended to go straight back to Edinburgh without further word with the Queen.

But Mary was too clever for him. Next morning, 14 April, in the chilly greyness before dawn, two of the Queen's gentlemen came to his room, to command him not to leave without further speech with her. He obeyed, and 'met her at the hawking be-west Kinross'.

If northern winters are cruel, the spring is all sweetness. Tenderly blue is the sky above Perthshire peaks, still streaked with snow: azure mists of hyacinths wash the valleys where the golden birches are 'letting down their hair', in country phrase. There is no other howe in all Scotland so bird-dizzy with song as that dawn-chorus in the month of April.

So Knox stood at Mary's belled and sparkling bridle-rein, while the courtiers and falconers drew back. And the Queen too was all

G

radiant sweetness and gaiety. What did Master Knox think? Lord Ruthven had offered her a ring: 'whom I cannot love,' she said, '(for I know him to use enchantment), and yet is he made one of my privy counsel.'

'Whom blames your Grace thereof?'

'Lethington,' she pouted, 'was the whole cause.'

'That man is absent,' said Knox, 'for this present, Madam: therefore I will speak nothing in that behalf.'

'I understand,' said the Queen, 'that ye are appointed to go to Dumfries, for the election of a superintendent to be established in thae countries.'

'Yes,' said he, 'these quarters have great need, and some of the gentlemen so require.'

'But I hear,' said she, 'that the Bishop of Athens' (i.e. Alexander Gordon) 'would be superintendent.'

'He is one, Madam, that is put in election.'

'If ye knew him as well as I do,' said the Queen, 'ye would never promote him to that office, nor yet to any other within your Kirk.'

Knox was plainly startled.

'What he has been, Madam,' said he, 'I neither know, nor yet will I enquire: for, in time of darkness, what could we do but grope and go wrang even as darkness carried us? But if he fear not God now, he deceives many mae than me. . . .'

'Well,' said the Queen, 'do as ye will, but that man is a dangerous man.'

'And thereuntill was not the Queen deceived'; so continues Knox's account in parentheses. For he took heed of the warning, and postponed the election: which it was then discovered Gordon had tried to rig. 'And so was the bishop frustrate of his purpose for that present. And yet was he, at that time, the man that was most familiar with the said John in his house and at table.'

They had talked long, while the rising sun smoked the mists off the hill-tops. Knox was aware of the impatience of the Court, their side-long looks and muttering: of the jingling of bits as horses sidled and snatched, the tinkling of bells on the hawks jesses as they half-roused. But each time he would have taken his leave the Queen called him back.

Now she bent more flatteringly than ever from the saddle.

'I have one of the greatest matters that have touched me since I came in this realm to open upon you,' she began, 'and I maun have your help into it.' She began a long tale about her (illegitimate) sister, the Lady Argyle, and her indiscretions: and the corresponding sins of her husband the earl: and of how their marriage was breaking up.

Knox, who had patched up this marriage once before, was half convinced. Yet he would like to have heard from their own mouths.

'Well,' said the Queen, 'it is waur than ye believe. But do this meikle for my sake, as once again to put them at unity. . . .'

Having thus put a nice little bit of mischief to Knox's hand, one can imagine the ravishing smile with which she ended:

'And now, as touching our reasoning yesternight, I promise to do as ye required: I shall cause summoned all offenders and ye shall know that I shall minister justice.'

With Knox's farewell salutation, she gave her hackney its head at last: and as they all galloped off into the April sunlight, the young Queen leading, it must have been a sight to catch the heart.

Knox duly wrote to the Earl of Argyle, and so caused lasting offence. Mary was cleverer still. She kept her promise to summon the Roman bishops who had been celebrating the Mass: and so took a grievance away from the men of Kyle, and also greatly increased her own growing popularity. The bishops came in procession to court, 'a merrie fellow' solemnly carrying a great steel hammer in front of them for crozier. Their punishment seems to have been nominal: but the benefit to Mary, in popular goodwill, was tremendous.

On 20 May Mary rode up the cobbled Royal Mile from Holyrood to the Tolbooth – that is, at St. Giles' – to open Parliament. Mounted on a white horse and beautifully dressed, with all the court gorgeously dressed behind her, she won every heart. All Edinburgh thronged the streets, or leant from the windows of the tall tenements, cheering and shouting: 'God save that sweet face!'

Three days running Mary made that procession, and the people loved it. But only on the first did she actually address the Estates in a short speech, which captivated her hearers. '*Vox Dianae!*' cried the court: and even careful Randolph wrote glowingly to

England that it was very pretty: 'I am sure she made it herself, and deserves great praise for uttering the same.'

Protestant lairds were restored at that Parliament: Henry Balnaves, Kirkcaldy of Grange, John Lesley and old Alexander Whitelaw. Huntly's corpse in its coffin had been tried, and forfeited: and the Lord James confirmed in his new title of Earl of Moray. To every man his price!

For Knox knew in his bones that all was not well: that this show of toleration masked some plan of Mary's. But when he tried to urge practical measures for the Church 'the matter fell so hot' between him and the Earl of Moray that they quarrelled bitterly and painfully. Knox 'gave a discharge to the earl of all further intromission or care with his affairs. He made unto him a discourse of their first acquaintance: in what estate he was when that first they spake together in London' – when Knox was Court preacher and James a disregarded bastard – 'how God had promoted him and that above man's judgement;' and in the end made this conclusion: 'But seeing that I perceive myself frustrate of my expectation, which was, that ye should ever have preferred God to your own affection, and the advancement of His truth to your singular commodity, I committ you to your own wit, and to the conducting of those who better can please you. . . .'

'All things misliked the preachers.' When they spoke against the trailing extravagant dresses and 'stinking pride' of the court ladies, they were 'scripped at'. People were in a summer mood, all things looked fair and hopeful to them.

The Church too had lost face, since it had been proved that Paul Methven, one of their first preachers, had in the absence of his elderly wife got a servant lassie into trouble. It fell to Knox to try the case, sifting it to its sad conclusion. Methven was given a penance so humiliating that he broke down and fled.

So Knox growled like an unheeded old watch-dog over the country's affairs. And yet he was right. Mary had that spring one paramount concern: the Spanish match. She longed for marriage, both as a woman and as the head of an isolated little country. But it must be a rich and splendid match, to suit her pride and give her security. Don Carlos, only son and heir of Philip of Spain, could give her magnificence, and the strength of Spain and the Pope's approval. So, although he was mentally and physically crippled – which she may not have known – Mary had set her whole heart on this.

All winter and spring she had worked on it: and Lethington now absent in England and France carried secret messages to della Quadra, Bishop of Aquila, the Spanish Ambassador in London. Even Philip was caught by it: seeing Mary as 'the one door' through which the Pope's power might come once again to dominate not only Scotland but England. So well had things gone, it seemed possible that year.

For that was the reality that lay behind the mirth and pastime of the winter and spring: it lay behind all the flattering and encouraging of the Protestant lords: behind the gay, kind words to Knox, and the summoning of the bishops: even behind the glamour of the gorgeous clothes and speeches of the opening of Parliament. It was the reality of the Spanish Inquisition.

Elizabeth's spies got wind of it, and she issued a warning: but, powerless in Scotland, it must have been a nightmare to her. Knox, with correspondents everywhere, eventually learnt of it too: and learnt that not only did Lethington approve and connive at it, but that Moray also knew, and kept silence.

So the lords of the congregation had departed, and he had no friends left to count on: the populace had been won away from him, and he had neither the means nor inclination to win them back. He had no longer power, nor influence, and he had never had wealth or place. He had only the low, crudely made wooden pulpit like the one which is now in Queen Street Museum in Edinburgh.

So he mounted its few wooden steps one hot Sunday before Parliament ended; and facing a large congregation including many nobles and courtiers, he began one of the most courageous sermons of his life.

'I praise my God, through Christ Jesus, that in your own presence I may pour forth the sorrows of my heart . . . for from the beginning of God's mighty working within this realm, I have been with you in your most desperate temptations. Ask your own consciences and let them answer you before God, if that I (not I, but God's Spirit by me) in your greatest extremity willed you not ever to depend upon your God. . . .'

'In your most extreme dangers I have been with you: St.

Johnston, Coupar Muir, and the Crags of Edinburgh are yet recent in my heart: yea, that dark and dolorous night wherein all ye, my lords, with shame and fear left this town, is yet in my mind: and God forbid that ever I forget it. . . . Shall this be the thankfulness that ye shall render unto your God, to betray his cause, when ye have it in your own hands to establish it as ye please?'

'The Queen, say ye, will not agree with us: Ask ye of her that which by God's word ye may justly require, and if she will not agree with you in God, ye are not bound to agree with her in the Devil. Let her plainly understand so far of your minds, and steal not from your former stoutness in God, and he shall prosper you in your enterprises. But I can see nothing but such a recoiling from Christ Jesus, as the man that first and most speedily flyeth from Christ's ensign holdeth himself most happy. . . .'

'And now, my lords, to put an end to all, I hear of the Queen's marriage. Dukes, brethren to emperors, and kings strive all for the best game. But this my lords will I say (note the day, and bear witness after) whensoever the nobility of Scotland, professing the Lord Jesus, consents that an infidel (and all papists are infidels) shall be head to your sovereign, ye do so far as in ye lieth to banish Christ Jesus from this realm: ye bring God's vengeance upon the country: a plague upon yourself and perchance ye shall do small comfort to your sovereign.'

Knox's congregation reacted instantly.

'These words and this manner of speaking was judged intolerable. Papists and Protestants were both offended: Yea, his most familiars disdained him for that speaking. Placebos and flatterers posted to the Court to give notice that Knox had spoken against the Queen's marriage. The Provost of Lincluden . . . gave the charge that the said John should present himself before the Queen: which he did soon after dinner. The Lord Ochiltrie and diverse of the faithful bare him company to the Abbey: but none passed in to the Queen with him in the cabinet but Erskine of Dun, then superintendent of Angus and the Mearns.'

'The Queen, in a vehement fume, began to cry out, that never Prince was handled as she was.'

'I have borne with you in all your rigorous manner of speaking, both against my self and against my uncles. Yea, I have sought your favours by all possible means. I offered unto you presence and audience whensoever it pleased you to admonish me: and yet I cannot be quit of you!'

At this point Mary's passion got the better of her altogether. She finished in an indiscreet burst, and a flood of tears:

'I vow to God, I shall be once revenged!'

'And with these words, scarcely could Marna, her secret chamber-boy, get napkins to hold her eyes dry for the tears: and the owling, besides womanly weeping, stayed her speech.'

The word 'owling' conveys a vivid sense of woo-hooing.

Knox 'did patiently abide the first fume', till he got a chance to answer.

'True it is, Madame, your Grace and I have been at diverse controversies. . . . Without the preaching place, Madam, I think few have occasion to be offended at me; and there, Madam, I am not master of my self, but maun obey Him who commands me to speak plain, and to flatter no flesh upon the face of the earth.'

'But what have *you* to do,' said she, 'with my marriage?'

'If it please your Majesty patiently to hear me, I will show the truth in plain words. I grant your Grace offered unto me more than ever I required: but my answer was then, as it is now, that God hath not sent me to await upon the courts of princesses nor upon the chambers of ladies: but I am sent to preach the evangel of Jesus Christ, to such as please to hear it. And it hath two parts, Repentance and Faith. And now, Madam, in preaching Repentance. . . .'

It was too much. Mary had won over all Scotland, rich and poor: her marriage negotiations had been well received in Spain, even by the great Philip himself. What right had this shabby, ill-born nobody to interfere? When Queen of France, a wave of her hand would have sent him to inhuman torture and death: and even as Queen of Scots Repentance and Faith were really too much. She broke in:

'What have *ye* to do with my marriage? Or what are *ye* within this Commonwealth?'

We infer the passion of scorn that stung Knox to one of the noblest answers in history:

'A subject born within the same, Madam!'

He went on: . . . 'yet has God made me (how abject that ever I be in your eyes) a profitable member within the same. Yea,

Madam, to me it appertains no less to forewarn of such things as may hurt it, if I foresee them, than it does to any of the nobility: for both my vocation and conscience craves plainness of me.' So he then repeats his call for opposition to any infidel husband.

'At these words, owling was heard, and tears might have been seen in greater abundance than the matter required.' Erskine did his best to calm her with soothing remarks and 'pleasing words of her beauty' and so forth: which did but 'cast oil on the flaming fire'.

Knox endured this moral onslaught 'for a long season' without giving way: but even he weakened under its impact. It seems clear that Mary accused him of not caring, and even 'delighting' in the sight.

'Madam, in God's presence I speak: I never delighted in the weeping of any of God's creatures: Yea, I can scarcely well abide the tears of my own boys whom my own hand corrects; much less can I rejoice in your Majesty's weeping. But seeing that I have offered unto you no just occasion to be offended, but have spoken the truth, as my vocation craves of me, I maun sustain (albeit unwillingly) your Majesty's tears, rather than I dare hurt my conscience or betray my Commonwealth, through my silence.'

'Herewith was the Queen more offended.' And he was ordered out of the cabinet into the main chamber, to await further orders.

In this outer chamber were all the Queen's ladies in their gorgeous clothes, the lords of the court, their pages and hangers-on, and all the bustle of messengers and servants coming and going: and Knox stood among them all for nearly an hour 'as one whom men had never seen'.

Even for the righteous, to be cut dead still cuts deep. Men were afraid to be seen even knowing him: and so hurried past. The ladies did their best to underline that he was a hopeless outsider: sweeping past with trailing 'targetted' skirts drawn back, not to touch the shabby figure: the contrast of their elaborate beauty – dyed and dressed hair, jewels, costly perfumes – forced upon him. Till suddenly his powerful compelling voice, tinged with irony, rang out:

'O fair ladies, how pleasing were this life of yours, if it should ever abide, and then in the end that we might pass to heaven with all this gay gear! But fie upon that knave Death, that will come whether we will or not! And when he has laid on his arrest, the foul worms will be busy with this flesh, be it never so fair and so tender; and the sillie soul I fear shall be so feeble, that it can neither carry with it gold, garnishing, targetting, pearl nor precious stanes. . . .'

Did they all cower away from this suddenly terrible little man, and feel cold?

Then at length he could go. The Queen had been counselled not to proceed against him, as she longed to do. 'And so that storm quieted in appearance, but never in the heart.'

20

Trial for Treason

THAT summer the Maries were busy sewing a new costume for the Queen: 'Highland apparel' for her autumn hunting trip in Argyle. Was it a tartan plaid? – Royal Stewart, or a darker hunting sett? Either way, her tall figure and (dyed) auburn hair would suit it magnificently.

Lethington now returned from his negotiations abroad for the Spanish match. He blandly denied that it had ever been suggested, and the people saw it all as a delusion of Knox – of an old man blinded with prejudice. So he was, he writes himself, wholly discredited.

Parliament rose in June, and the Queen went by Glasgow to the west: taking her Mass through those very parts most resentful of her religion that spring. At the same time, the arrested priests were quietly released.

But while she took her Mass with her, she also left it behind. It was no longer a question of Mary's private celebration: it was already, as Knox had always known it would be, an outpost of restoration.

So while she made a parade of it in the west, it was celebrated with increasing boldness in the chapel of Holyrood House, and especially when the Sacrament of the Lord's Supper was celebrated in St. Giles'. So the capital was already torn in two, as the country soon would be. Knox's commonwealth was broken, and his one great flock 'shed'.

On 15 August the Provost and town council came to St. Giles', as they still do on special occasions, and most of the townsfolk came with them. But some of the brethren had gone down to Holyrood, to take note of those who had backslid to Rome. They had better have gone to their prayers. Words soon passed, and passed to blows: men cursed, and the Frenchwomen began to scream. Madame Rollet sent someone running up the Royal Mile to St. Giles' to whisper to the Laird of Pitarrow, the controller, that riot had broken out. Up he rose and left, and up rose the Provost and the magistrates and – irresistibly – up rose most of the congregation, and away they all rushed down to Holyrood, leaving Knox with his message undelivered, and much displeased.

Mary was back in Stirling Castle in September. She was furious at the news of the riot and threatened full vengeance. Several Protestants had been arrested and charged with malice afore-thought 'felony, hame-sucken, violent invasion of the Queen's Palace, and spoliation of the same.'

The congregation in alarm came to Knox: and at their request he wrote a letter to 'cause summon the brethren', as he had done before in the days of Rome's tyranny: to ensure, by sheer weight of unarmed witness, that justice was done. And also, as he wrote, because there were many matters that required full discussion.

Copies of the letter went all over the country: so one came to the minister of Failford, a traitor, who handed it to the principal of the College of Justice, styled the Bishop of Ross: this man hated Knox for having said that bishops who did not feed their flock as pastors were but thieves and murderers. So the bishop gave the letter to the Queen: and Mary saw with joy that now, at last, she might be 'once revenged'.

Her secret council agreed that the letter was high treason. It was decided to summon the nobility to an especially full council in mid-December, at which Knox would be tried on such a charge.

So, as winter began, the whole council and nobility rode in; including the old Laird of Lethington, and the Earl of Moray, who had the matter related by secretary Lethington 'as best pleased him'. The Master of Maxwell, later Lord Herries, was one of those who came. Once, his magnificent fighting had held off the French, that last desperate winter of 1559–60, when the Reformation hung in the balance. Now he came to Knox in a different guise. He came to the Manse to give him 'as it had been, a discharge of the familiarity which before was great betwixt them' unless Knox would apologize to the Queen's satisfaction.

Knox denied any offence.

'No offence,' said he, 'to convocate the Queen's lieges?'

'Greater things,' said Knox, 'were repute no offence within this two years. . . .'

'The time is now other,' said he, '. . . now she is present.'

'It is neither the absence nor the presence of the Queen that rules my conscience,' said Knox, 'but God speaking plainly in his word; what was lawful to me last year is yet lawful, because my God is unchangeable.'

'Well,' said the Master, 'do as ye list: but I think ye shall repent it, if ye bow not to the Queen.'

He had never, retorted Knox, made himself 'an adversary party' to the Queen's Majestie: 'except in the head of religion, and thereuntill I think ye will nocht desired me to bow.'

'Ye are wise enough,' said the Master, 'but you will find that men will nocht bear with you in times to come as they have done in times bypast.'

'If God stand my friend,' said Knox, 'as I am assured He of His mercy will, so long as I depend upon His promise, and prefer His glory to my life and worldly profit, I little regard how men behave themselves towards me.' He did not know how men had had to bear with him 'in times past', unless it was that by his mouth they had had to hear the word of God: which if 'in times to come, they refuse, my heart will be pierced, and for a season will lament: but the incomodity will be their ain.'

The Laird of Lochinvar was with the Master: and at these final words they both rose and left him: never to meet in friendship again, adds Knox sadly in his record: 'unto this day the 17th December, 1571.' That was, within months of his death.

Next to abandon him formally were Lethington and Moray. They were now too grand to come to the Manse, Knox notes sarcastically in the margin. They sent for him instead, to attend them at the Clerk of Registers' house. There they 'began to lament that he had so highly offended the Queen's Majesty', and to show 'what pains and travail they had taken to mitigate her anger, but they could find nothing but extremity, unless he himself would confess his offence and put him in Her Grace's will.'

'I praise my God through Jesus Christ,' said Knox, 'I have learned not to cry conjuration and treason at everything that the godless multitude does condemn, neither yet to fear the things that they fear. . . . I have done nothing but my duty, and so whatsoever shall thereof ensue, my good hope is that my God will give me patience to bear it. But to confess an offence where my conscience witnesseth there is none, far be it from me.'

'How can it be defended?' cried Lethington, 'Have ye not made convocation of the Queen's lieges?'

'If I have not a just defence,' said Knox, 'let me smart for it.'

'Let us hear,' said they, 'your defences; for we would be glad that ye might be found innocent.'

'No,' said Knox, out of the bitterness of his heart: 'for I am informed . . . even by you my Lord Secretary, that I am already condemned and my cause prejudged: therefore I might be reputed ane fool, if I would make you privy to my defences.'

'At these words they seemed both offended,' wrote Knox later, 'and so the secretary departed.' But Moray lingered. Perhaps he wished to offer an olive branch: perhaps he thought Knox did not fully understand the danger in which he stood. He 'would have entered in farther discourse of the estate of the Court with the said John', who turned away, cutting him short with: 'My Lord, I understand mair than I would of the affairs of the Court: and therefore it is nocht needful that your lordship trouble you with the recounting thereof. Gif ye stand in good case I am content. . . . I can do nothing but behold the end, which I pray God be other than my troubled heart feareth.'

But the music and candle-blaze in Holyrood made his words sound meaningless. The Court was full of gaiety and excitement. Horsemen clattered in and out, there was feasting and dancing every night, and excellent singing. Davie Rizzio, the Italian, was promoted to be bass in the Queen's singers. It was all youth, life, laughter and love-making.

In the Royal Mile, St. Giles' Manse, that had once been the centre of the day's business, now stood deserted as a plague-house. Knox sat alone in the little 'dallas-lined' study that the town had had made for him. It was, once again, his hour of darkness.

One knock came, secretly, to the darkened door. It was, of all impossible visitors, the Queen's own advocate, Spens of Condie. He came, as the driest Edinburgh lawyer can sometimes come, on a Nicodemus-like quest: to learn how it fared with Knox, because he was one who 'has received the Word of Life which you have preached'. Knox trusted him instantly, told him all, and showed him a copy of the letter.

'I thank my God,' said the lawyer, 'I came to you with ane fearful and sorrowful heart . . . but I depart greatly rejoiced, alswell because I perceive your own comfort even in the midst of your troubles, as that I clearly understand that you have committed no sic crime as ye are burdened with: ye will be accusit' (said he) 'but God will assist you.' And so he departed, wrote Knox.

The summons to be tried for treason before the council in Holyrood came to Knox between six and seven at night, a few days before Christmas 1563. 'The bruit rising in the town that John Knox was sent for by the Queen, the brethren of the Kirk followed in such numbers that the inner close was full, and all the stairs, even to the chamber door where the Queen and council sat. . . .'

'The lords were talking ilk ane with other . . . but upon the entry of Knox, they were commanded to take their places, and so they did, sitting as councillors one against another. The duke, according to his dignity, began one side. Upon the other side sat the Earl of Argyle, Moray, Glencairn, the Earl Marshal, the Lord Ruthven, Pitarro the controller, the justice clerk, Spens of Condie, advocate, and divers others.'

So the court was ready. Then there was 'no little wordly pomp' for the Queen's entry – a fanfare perhaps? A cry certainly of 'The Queen!' and all the lords would bow low. In she swept, in her rich dress with jewels in her hair: and so was placed in her throne at the head of the council table. Like a double blow in Knox's face was the sight of the two courtiers who stood to either hand at her chair, leaning to her whispers and laughing eagerly at her every smile: for they were the Master of Maxwell and Secretary Lethington.

Mary looked long at the bent little figure of the preacher, standing bareheaded and alone at the other end of the long table.

'She first smilit, and after gave ane gawf laughter.' The two courtiers hastened to do the like.

'This is ane good beginning,' said the Queen merrily: 'But wat ye whereat I laughed? Yon man garred me greet, and grat never tear himself: I will see if I can gar him greet!'

'At that word the secretary whispered her in the ear, and she him again, and with that gave him a letter'. So he turned to Knox.

'The Queen's Majesty is informed, that ye have travailed to raise a tumult of her subjects against her, and for certification thereof there is presented to her your own letter subscrivit in your name . . . she has convened you before this part of the nobility, that they may witness betwixt you and her.'

'Let him acknowledge,' said she, 'his own hand-writ, and then shall we judge of the contents of the letter.'

'And so the letter was presented from hand to hand to John Knox, who . . . said: "I gladly acknowledge this to be my hand-writ. . . ." ' He had given signed blanks to scribes, whom he trusted: so he acknowledged both 'the hand-writ and the dyte-ment'.

'Ye have done more,' said Lethington, 'than I would have done.'

'Charity,' said Knox, 'is not suspicious.'

'Well, well,' said the Queen, 'read your own letter, and then answer to such things as shall be demanded of you.'

'I shall do the best I can,' said Knox meekly, 'and so with loud voice he began to read. . . .'

Here Mary blundered. Knox's voice, reading his own words, had compelling power:

'It is not unknown unto you, dear Brethren, what comfort and tranquillity God gave unto us, in times most dangerous, by our Christian assemblies and godly conferences, as oft as any danger appeared to any member or members of our body: and how that since we have neglected . . . our conventions and assemblies . . . the holy Sacraments are abused by profane Papists. Masses have been (and yet are) openly said and maintained. The blood of some of our dearest ministers has been shed, without fear of punishment or correction craved by us. And now last, are two of our dear brethren . . . summoned to underly the law. . . .

'. . . this fearful summons are directed against them to make (no doubt) preparation upon a few, that a door may be opened to execute cruelty upon a greater multitude. . . .

'And now I, whom God has of his mercy made one amongst many to travail in setting forward of his true religion within this Realm, seeing the same in danger of ruin, can not but of conscience crave of you, my brethren of all estates, that have professed the truth, your presence, comfort and assistance at the said day in the town of Edinburgh, even as ye tender the advancement of God's

glory, the safety of your brethren and your own assurance'
together with the preservation of the Kirk in thir appearing
dangers. It may be perchance that persuasions be made in the
contrary, and that ye may be informed, that either your assembly
is not neccessair, or else that it will offend the upper powers: but
my guid hope is, that neither flattery nor fear shall make you so
far to decline from Christ Jesus. . . .'

After Spens had accused him (but 'very gently'):

'Heard ye ever, my lords,' cried the Queen, looking round the
table, 'ane mair despiteful and treasonable letter?'

'Master Knox,' said Lethington, 'are ye not sorry from your
heart, and do ye not repent that sic any letter has passed your
pen, and from you is comen to the knowledge of others?'

'My Lord Secretary, before I repent I maun be taught my
offence.'

'Offence! If there were no more but the convocation of the
Queen's lieges, the offence cannot be denied.'

'. . . what convocation of the brethren has even been to this day
unto which my pen served not? Before this no man laid to my
charge as ane crime.'

'Then was then, and now is now. We have no need of such
conventions as sometimes we have had.'

'The time that has been is even now before my eyes; for I see
the poor flock in no less danger than it has been at any time
before, except that the devil has now a vizer upon his face. . . .'

'What is this?' said the Queen, 'methink ye trifle with him.
Who gave him authority to make convocation of my lieges? Is
not that treason?'

'Na, Madam,' said Lord Ruthven, 'for he makes convocation
of the people to hear prayer and sermon almost daily, and
whatever your Grace or others will think thereof, we think it no
treason.'

'Hold your peace!' cried the Queen, 'and let him make answer
for himself.'

'I began Madam,' said Knox, 'to reason with the secretair,
whom I take to be ane far better dialectician than you Grace is,
that all convocations are not unlawful; and now my Lord Ruthven
has given the instance. . . .'

'I will say nothing,' said the Queen, 'against your religion, nor against your convening to your sermons: but what authority have ye to convocate my subjects when ye will, without my commandment?'

'. . . I answer, that at my will I never convened four persons in Scotland: but at the order that the brethren has appointed, I have given diverse advertisements, and great multitudes has assembled thereupon. And if your Grace complain that this was done without your Grace's commandment, I answer, so was all that God has blessed within this realm from the beginning of this action. And therefore Madam, I maun be convicked by ane just law that I have done against the duty of God's messenger in writing of this letter, before that either I be sorry or yet repent. . . . For what I have done, I have done at the commandment of the general Kirk of this Realm: and therefore I think I have done no wrong.'

'Ye shall not escape so! Is it not treason, my Lords, to accuse a Prince of cruelty? I think there be Acts of Parliament against sic whisperers.'

Mary had a good point there. And she made Knox read out the part of his letter to a door that may be opened 'to execute cruelty upon a greater multitude'. Might he speak frankly in his defence, asked Knox?

'Say what ye can, for I think ye have much ado.'

Knox then spoke of the earnest desire of all true papists to exterminate the Protestants and their Church. (God forbid, murmured all the lords, that 'the lives of the faithful or the staying of the doctrine', stood in the power of the papists. They had experienced their cruelty.) He went on to speak of their craft, and of the zeal of their Holy War: his voice rang out, till the Queen perhaps shifted in her throne.

'Ye forget yourself,' she broke in. 'Ye are not now in the pulpit.'

'I am in the place where I am demanded of conscience to speak the truth: and therefor I speak.' He warned the Queen against papish councillors. ('As this was said, Lethington smiled and whispered to the Queen' who responded.) She then changed her tack, and accused Knox again – how the charge has survived the centuries! – of having made her weep, and of having been indifferent to her tears. So he repeated his account of that private interview.

'. . . ye said, what ado had I to speak of your marriage? What was I, that I should meddle with sic matters? I answered, As touching nature, I was ane worm of this earth, and yet ane subject of this Commonwealth; but as touching the office whereuntil it has pleased God to place me, I was a watchman both over the Realm and over the Kirk of God gathered within the same. . . .'

Lethington had another conference with the Queen, and then told him: 'Master Knox, ye may return to your house for this night.'

'I thank God and the Queen's Majesty,' returned the accused: 'And Madam, I pray God to purge your heart from papistry, and' – did the piercing grey eyes rest on Lethington and the Master of Maxwell? – 'to preserve you from the counsel of flatterers; for how pleasant that they appear to your ear and corrupt affection for the time, experience has told us in what perplexity they have brought famous princes.'

It was a magnificent exit. The Queen retired, and the whole council voted. They were unanimous: 'Not Guilty!' Lethington and others raged, and the Queen was brought again to her chair of state, to see the votes given. This was another blunder. Would they, argued the rugged lords, be intimidated by a woman, or take orders from Lethington? When the Queen saw the Bishop of Ross, the informer, give his vote for Knox with the rest, she turned on him in transports of fury:

'Trouble not the bairn! – I pray you, trouble him not! For he is newly wakened out of his sleep. Why should not the old fool follow in the footsteps of them that have passed before him?'

The bishop answered coldly: 'Your Grace may consider, that it is neither affection to the man, nor yet love to his profession, that moved me to absolve him; but the simple truth, which plainly appears in his defence. . . .'

'That night was neither dancing nor fiddling in the Court,' runs Knox's account: 'for Madam was disappointed of her purpose. . . .'

Yet something broke in Knox himself, from that hour when he had had to stand quite alone at the bar. At the assembly immediately after he kept silent through all the debates, though 'many wondered'. Only at the end he rose to address them:

'I have travailed, right honourable and beloved Brethren, in an upright conscience before my God . . . and yet of late days I have been accused as ane seditious man, and ane that usurps unto my self power that becomes me nocht.' Wearily he repeated the defence of his letter: '. . . for I say that by you, that is by the charge of the general assembly, I have as just power to advertise the brethren from time to time of dangers appearing as that I have to preach the word of God in the pulpit of Edinburgh; for by you I was appointed to the one and to the other; and therefore in the name of God I crave your judgements. The danger that appeared to me in my accusation was nocht so fearful as the words that came to my heart. . . .'

(Lethington had jeeringly said: 'What can the Pope do more than send forth his letters and require them to be obeyed?')

The Court party protested. The Justice Clerk cried out: 'Shall we be compelled to justify the rash doings of men?'

'My Lord,' said Knox, '. . . of you I crave nothing. But if the Kirk that is here present do not either absolve me, or else condemn me, never shall I in public or in private, as a public minister, open my mouth in doctrine or in reasoning.'

He then withdrew. 'After lang contention' the whole Kirk cleared him, saying he had but carried out his commission.

So he settled down to his parish. That March he married Ochiltree's daughter, Margaret Stewart. 'The Queen stormeth wonderfully,' gossipped Randolph in his English despatch, 'because she is of the blood and name.' Later generations have been shocked at the disparity in their ages – she was not yet twenty: but the people of the time were shocked only at the disparity in rank. Yet she may well have wanted to marry one of the first men of her day. A papist writer says she was so in love that Knox had surely used enchantment. She bore him three daughters, nursed him through his last days, and later married a laird, Ker of Fawdonside.

So he had some peace. Yet written across the end of his 'History', quite out of context and as an addition, he wrote:

'In all that time was the Earl of Moray so fremmit to John Knox that neither by word nor write was there any communication betwixt them.'

And it reads like a cry of pain.

21

'The Reward of Dancers'

THE new year of 1564 began with savage cold. On 20 January heavy rain froze as it fell, till the earth was 'but ane sheet of ice. The fowls, baith great and small, freezit and might not flee: many dyed, some were taken and laid beside the fire, that their feathers might resolve.' Perhaps Knox's boys did that. Mary shut out the winter with 'banqueting on banqueting' in Holyrood. She hid her disappointment over her defeat with her usual grace and courage, and feasted the lords more especially.

Yet that year she was unwell and depressed. She took her hunting trip through Athole, and home by Aberdeen: but she was dispirited. Elizabeth of England had shown her teeth at the possibility of any foreign match whatever. Mary must have felt frustrated and helpless. After her twenty-first birthday that autumn she was ill again.

'Then began Davie to grow great in Court'. Rizzio, 'Signor Davie', became her chief secretary in place of Rollet. It is true she had to correct and re-write his French dispatches: but his love of music and masques, of the Mass and, above all, of intrigue must have endeared him. He was 'ane good fellaw' to all; accommodating: bribeable.

That summer there took place the last assembly reported by Knox. At the bi-annual meeting the lords and the Court party had made themselves a sort of Upper House, apart from the common ministers and elders of the main assembly. The Laird of Lundie spoke boldly against this as a thing 'verie prejudicial to the liberty of the Kirk'. He further proposed 'humbly requiring them, if they be Brethren, that they will assist their Brethren with their presence and counsel, for we had never greater need. And if they be minded to fall back from us, it were better to know it now than afterward.'

The lords were offended, but remained aloof. The whole point
of the assembly, indeed the foundation of the democratic Kirk of
Scotland, was the full and free discussion of every point on the
open floor: as against decision by any secret council, cabal or
inner ring. Finally, the lords said they had private complaints
of which 'the principal complaint touchit John Knox'. So a
debate was staged; and his report gives a summing-up of his views.

Lethington, 'leaning on the bosom of the Master of Maxwell'
spoke for the Court: for the divine right of kings, and the duties
of subjects. Knox speaks clean out of century: he would have
shocked the Victorians almost as much as the Elizabethans.

The courtier wanted thanks given for the Queen's toleration
of the Kirk. He denied Knox's doctrine that a people were
responsible for their ruler, or could be punished for her sins.
For instance, she thought the Roman Mass not idolatry but
'good religion'.

'So thought they,' said Knox drily, 'that sometimes offered their
children unto Moloch. . . .'

Did Knox actually mean that subjects might disobey their
ruler's commands, if they thought them unjust?

'In very deed,' said Knox, who had once agonized in soul and
travelled Europe to answer that, 'of that same judgement I have
long been, and so I yet remain.' And later: '. . . it is plain, that
God craves not only that a man do no iniquity in his own person,
but also that he oppose himself to all iniquity as far as in him lies.'

'Then will ye make subjects to control their princes and leaders!'

'And what harm,' retorted Knox, 'should the Commonwealth
receive if . . . ignorant rulers were moderated and so bridled by the
wisdom and discretion of godly subjects?'

'Prove that, and win the play!' cried Lethington, plainly
scandalized. By what authority could such a thing be done?

'By the people of God,' answered Knox firmly: 'for the commandment was given to Israel, as ye may read: "Hear, O Israel!"
says the Lord' . . . He enlarges on his startling new phrase: 'The
People of God': '. . . for I speak of the people assembled together
in ane body of ane Commonwealth. . . .' Had not all Scotland
been called, like Israel of old? He appeals to the lords to witness
that God has 'wrocht no less miracle upon the Commonwealth of
Scotland than upon the seed of Abraham:' so few short years

ago 'you and it were both in bondage of ane strange nation and ...
tyrants ruled over your conscience.' He adds his conclusion: 'that
to resist a tyrant is not to resist God.' He produced a copy of the
Apology of Magdeburg, signed by Lutherans against the Emperor.

'*Homines obscuri!*' scripped Lethington.

'*Dei tamen servi,*' answered Knox.

Lethington then called for a vote, by those present, on the
Queen's Mass; at which Knox hotly protested, reminding them
of their promise that everything should be 'debateit in public' and
voted on by 'the whole of the assembly' or not at all.

It was not reasonable that 'sic an multitude' should vote on
the Queen's affairs, insisted Lethington. After a long and heated
argument, he persuaded them to vote first and to inform the
assembly after. Knox would have none of it.

'That appears to me,' he said, 'not only a backward order, but
also a tyranny usurpit upon the Kirk.'

With this debate, apart from the heart-cry over Moray, he
closes his great and vivid 'History'. The fifth book, compiled from
his notes after his death by Buchanan, lacks all his fire.

By the new year, Mary and her ladies were 'playing house' in
plain lodgings in St. Andrews. She gaily told Randolph that the
Queen was not there: 'I know not myself where she is gone!' She
returned along the Fife coast: and at Wemyss Castle in February,
Harry Stewart Lord Darnley, new released from England, knelt
to kiss her hand.

He was, she said, 'the properest long man she had seen'.
Perhaps she had the tall woman's satisfaction at being out-topped.
He was a possible match by birth: and providential to her wishes.
She fell deeply in love, encouraged by the Maries and by Rizzio,
and decided forthwith to make him her husband and King.

She created him Earl of Ross, and proposed making him Duke
of Rothesay, the traditional royal title. She gave him the Crown
Matrimonial, reviving unpleasant memories of her first husband,
Francis of France: and did this in spite of opposition from Moray
and other lords. She would not wait for the Estates approval, but
married him in July in her chapel: and shortly after had Moray
and his friends 'put to the horn'.

'All things now grow too libertine, and the Queen taketh upon
herself to do as she pleases,' ran an English dispatch. Buchanan is

briefer: 'Will shall rule all.' Darnley was younger than Mary, and a hopelessly weak character. Only his father could be found to cry: 'God save the King!' to him.

Nobles and commons now signed a new bond, and the anxious people flocked back to St. Giles'; deciding, too late, that Knox had been right. When he prayed for the banished lords, even Lethington refused to complain. On 19 August, King Henry made the gesture of attending morning service in St. Giles', sitting in a traditional royal seat, specially installed for him.

Knox was preaching on Isaiah xxvi, v. 13 (Geneva version): 'O Lord our God, other lords beside Thee have ruled us: but we will remember Thee only and Thy name.'

He was again on the theme of power and responsibility: wicked princes were a plague sent to sinful people. He linked the prophecies and teaching of Isaiah with his times – the stirring history of 2 Kings: and surely the congregation would not be slow to see the application. 'And I will appoint, sayeth the Lord. children to be their princes and babes shall rule over them. Children are extortioners . . . and women have rule over them.' (Did they glance at the sulky boy in the royal pew?) And again, they heard that God justly punished Ahab because he did not take order with Jezebel his wife, who painted her face and tired her hair and worshipped images.

Darnley went home so furious he did not even sit down to dinner, although Knox had preached 'an hour or more' longer than usual: he flung himself on horseback and rode straight off to the hawking; and Knox was summoned at once before such of the council as were available. There, Lethington desired him to abstain for preaching and let Craig act as supply.

Knox maintained he had 'spoken nothing but according to his text; and if the Kirk should command him to speak or abstain, he would obey, so far as the word of God would permit him.' As for Darnley, he had dishonoured God by attending Mass for the Queen's pleasure: 'so should He in His justice make her the instrument of his overthrow'. This was reported to Mary, and caused another outburst of angry tears.

That summer Bothwell, Moray's enemy, was recalled. He was welcomed by Mary and made Lieutenant of the Marches.

Mary then took the field against the rebel lords. She rode at the head of her troops with Darnley by her side, wearing scarlet and gold over light armour, a shining steel casque on her head, and carrying pistols and dagger at her saddle-bow. She was again in highest spirits, ready to 'sleep in the heather with a dirk by her side'. On the long bleak march between Glasgow and Edinburgh they ran into a raging storm of wind and rain: but 'albeit the most part waxed weary, yet the Queen's courage increased man-like so much, that she was ever with the foremost'. This, the 'Chase-about Raid', ended with Moray and the others driven helter-skelter over the Borders.

Mary was victorious: but unhappy. She was already tired of Darnley and was quarrelling with him. She loved physical courage, and the King was extremely timid. He had the excuse of having been brought up in the Tower by a mother who was said to be 'more feared than the French'. The 'lady-faced' boy may even have been as backward in bed as on the battlefield. Buchanan says of him: 'he passed his time in hunting and in hawking and in such other pleasures as were agreeable to his appetite, having in his company gentlemen willing to satisfy his will and affections.'

Yet nothing can justify the speed with which Mary turned to Rizzio, the bass singer. By autumn she sat with him early and late: she had a copy of the King's signet made for him: and finally, to the scandal of the country, gave him the Great Seal of Scotland. Even if their relations were innocent, her conducting of them was scandalous. And when, that autumn, she conceived, her husband never doubted that the child was Rizzio's.

That, of course, was the point of his public murder. There were various schemes in hand to dispose of Rizzio – rumours of which were known even to Knox and Cecil: but it was the King's one firm decision, in signing a bond with others, that the deed must be done in the Queen's presence, and so publish her shame to the world.

Knox was busy too that summer. He had visited the churches in the north and east the year before, now he visited those in the south of Scotland. He wrote, at the request of the assembly 'a comfortable epistle' to encourage the ministers, exhorters and readers throughout the country, 'to preserve'. He also began to draw up an order for a national fast, because of the unhappy state of the country. There were to be mourning clothes and no games for a week, and special daily readings and prayers: but only abstention from meat for twenty-four hours on the sabbath itself, and then not for the weak or sick, or those who felt driven to eat 'privily'. Knox was only too aware how precarious was the life of the Protestant churches in his day. There was a very ugly side to the ideal of 'one flock, and one apostolic governour and pastor' – in Rome.

Consider, he wrote, 'the last Council of Trent, who in one of their Sessions, have thus concluded: "All Lutherans, Calvinists, and such as are of the new religion shall utterly be rooted out" ... the danger may be nearer than we believe, yea, perchance a part of it hath been nearer to our necks than we have considered. . . .'

'With the help of God and your Holiness,' Mary wrote to the Pope, 'I will leap over the wall.'

She had already restored the Roman ecclesiastics to their place in Parliament. She now summoned the Protestant rebel lords to be tried before them on 12 March. That February 1566, a messenger came to the Scottish Court from Mary's uncle the Cardinal de Lorraine, with a copy of the Catholic League: and this Mary secretly signed. Wooden altars were said to have been made ready for St. Giles'.

Sunday, 3 March, was the first day of the great national fast for the sad state of Scotland and the danger to its Kirk. The day was specially chosen. For on Thursday, 9 March, Mary rode up the Royal Mile from Holyrood to open Parliament, in 'wondrous gorgeous apparel'. There would be few people to cheer. The Protestant lords were due to be tried on the Tuesday: and all Protestants had reason to fear what might follow.

On the Saturday night, when all douce folk were preparing for the second sabbath of the fast, Mary sat late at supper in a tiny closet-room, with one or two of her ladies and Rizzio close by her side. The door was flung open and in came Darnley, half-drunk, with Ruthven, Ker of Fawdonside and some other lords. The table with its candles was overthrown and Rizzio was torn screaming from Mary's skirts and stabbed repeatedly as they dragged him out. Fifty-three wounds were said to have been counted in him: and the King's whinger was still sticking in his carcase as they flung it down the back stairs.

When Mary heard he was dead, she grew quite calm. She soon

detached Darnley from his friends – Ruthven says she invited him straight away to her bed, but that he fell asleep first. She certainly persuaded him to join her in an escape, organized by Bothwell, and they rode towards Dunbar. There others joined her, and soon she rode back in strength to the capital. Lethington hurriedly left it, but made peace later. Knox, forbidden to preach, 'passed to Kyle'. But Parliament was prorogued: the danger to the Kirk was averted.

Beyond doubt, Mary thirsted for revenge: but she had to get her child acknowledged. So once more she kept her head and hid her feelings. James VI and I was born in Edinburgh Castle on 19 June. Mary swore to Darnley that he was his son: 'so much so, I fear it will be the worse for him hereafter'. In a surprisingly short time she was off to the hawking she loved, riding with Bothwell who 'had now of all men greatest access and familiarity with the Queen'.

The King was 'contemned of all men, seeing that the Queen cared for him not'. He wandered the country with barely six horses to his name, 'desolate and half desperate'. He complained of Mary's policy to foreign rulers, and she sent for him, and both scolded and threatened. Yet she still needed his presence at the christening.

That summer Bothwell was slashed over the head by a Liddles- dale raider: according to guide books, you can still see the scar on his mummified head in Denmark. Mary rode at reckless length to visit him: and was after seriously ill. But by autumn she completed her progress to within sight of Berwick.

The Prince was christened in the Great Hall of Stirling Castle on 17 December and Mary spared no expense. Elizabeth sent a font of solid gold (afterwards melted down to pay Bothwell's soldiers). The nobility came, though they would not assist at the Roman rites. Darnley did come, but scarcely appeared. 'It is greatly to be feared,' wrote Randolph, 'he can have no long life among this people.' He seemed already a ghost: and, straight after, he left 'without goodnight' for the sanctuary of his father's house, Provand's Lordship, in Glasgow. So long as he stayed there, he was safe.

At that time the Kirk of Scotland was one link in a ring of lively churches: now a letter came from the churches of Geneva,

Berne, Basel, and other Reformed churches of Germany and France, containing the sum of their Confession of Faith, and desiring to know if Scotland agreed in doctrine. At a conference at St. Andrews the Scots churchmen found that they differed in nothing from them, except in the keeping of some festival days: for only the sabbath was kept, as a wholly dedicated day, in Scotland.

Knox presumably attended the December assembly. Mary had just restored the Archbishop of St. Andrews for a secret scheme of her own. Not even Knox could have guessed what that was, but he saw the danger of the precedent: and in the name of the assembly drew up two letters, warning the nobility and the brethren against it. He also wrote a letter on their behalf to the Church of England, deploring surplices. He got their permission to visit England, to see his sons, on condition he returned again soon.

Knox's boys had gone south a little time before to stay permanently with Grandmother Bowes. Presumably they were too big a handful for the young wife with a new baby. So now at long last, with Elizabeth's safe-conduct, Knox might re-visit his flock at Berwick and Newcastle, and see again old friends such as Whittinghame at Durham. He went also to 'officiate a while there as a minister of that church'. It is good to read of those days, when the Anglican communion was freely open to the Scots: and when ordination by the 'laudable form and rite of the Reformed Church of Scotland' was freely accepted by them.

So Knox was not in Scotland when Mary coaxed her husband out of his refuge in Glasgow. A few months before, Lethington had summed up her tragic situation: 'It is a heartbreak for her to think that he should be her husband, and how to be free of him she sees no out-gait'.

But a few weeks after she had seen him lodged in Kirk o' Field a shattering explosion provided the out-gait. Darnley was strangled in the garden. According to some witnesses, he 'made great debate for his life', pleading: 'I am but young'. He was only twenty.

The King was buried with a haste and lack of respect almost as shocking to the times as his murder. Bothwell was universally blamed: but the town was full of his armed ruffians, and the

Queen's devotion was quite open. She confirmed him in lands, and later made him Duke of Orkney. He stood a trial that was little more than a sham. His divorce was being negotiated by the restored Archbishop of St. Andrews – that prelate's one significant act – and now Mary announced that she would marry him.

Craig was obliged, as parish minister, to publish the banns in St. Giles'. But as he did so he called heaven and earth to witness that he abhorred and detested the intended marriage. Lethington excepted, the nobles were more or less united by the general horror. The Master of Maxwell, now Lord Herries, rode to Holyrood as he had once ridden to the Manse, to warn Mary against Bothwell, and to take leave of her. 'He had fifty horse with him for the time, and garred each of them to buy a new spear in Edinburgh ere he rode home.'

Honest James Melville also came to plead with her. He sent word by Lethington that it was 'a sore matter to see a good princess run to utter wreck'. Mary was furious: and Lethington begged Melville to 'retire diligently before the Earl of Bothwell come up from his dinner'.

Why did Mary have this indecent and unwise haste in marrying? Was it only because, as Kirkcaldy reported, 'she would go to the world's end in a white petticoat for him. Yea, she is so far past all shame'? . . .

Or was there a more definite reason? After she was defeated and imprisoned in Lochleven, in the care of the notable Lady Douglas, Moray's mother, she declared she was ill and sent for her French Court doctor. There she is believed to have miscarried. But it was also said at the time that she had, with characteristic courage, decided that the game was up; and had sent for this doctor, reckoned a skilled abortionist, to save her from final exposure.

Pregnancy seems the only possible explanation of Mary's desperate haste. Bothwell's abduction, in which not even Elizabeth could bring herself to believe, did make the marriage fact. It also made Mary indefensible. Fact-defying feats of faith have been achieved to whitewash her, even to make her a saint. But Buchanan has the last word. 'To lay all proofs aside,' he wrote, 'her marriage with Bothwell . . . notwithstanding all the advices and counsels . . . witness anent their guilt.' The divorce was clear

H*

on 7 May and they married on 15 May barely three months after her husband's murder.

A month later Bothwell narrowly escaped from the avenging lords at Borthwick Castle and rode for Dunbar. Mary, disguised in the page's doublet and hose so becoming to her long, slim legs, rode after him. This explains why, when the two armies met shortly after at Carberry Hill, she was wearing only an ordinary wifie's bodice and short petticoats: all she had been able to borrow.

Mary surrendered to Kirkcaldy of Grange, to whose chivalry she could trust. This gave Bothwell time to escape, which he swiftly seized. There is no suggestion anywhere that, apart from her value as a Queen, Bothwell cared a rap for Mary. Perhaps he had had too many women. Or perhaps Mary, so unlucky in all her husbands, was less desirable as a wife than as a prize.

When they brought her up the High Street of Edinburgh as a prisoner the crowd saw her at last for what she was, stripped of all glamour and majesty, the hair she could not dress herself hanging down her back. The cry went up: 'Burn the hoor'! They had to bring out the old Blue Blanket, the Flodden flag, and carry it in front to keep her from being torn to pieces.

Knox was home for the momentous assembly of that same month of June, at which so many things were settled. Articles were signed securing the Kirk in both its worship and just provision. The status of teachers came high on the list of priorities: and loyalty to the young Prince followed.

Mary was persuaded to abdicate in favour of her son, with Moray as Regent. Knox preached the sermon at the coronation of the young King James VI in Stirling on 29 July. His text was from 2 Kings: on Jehoash, who was crowned young.

Moray was installed in August, and he and Knox joined hands in settling the affairs of Church and State. On 15 December Knox preached at the kirking of Parliament in St. Giles': and the first business of the day on which it first met was the ratifying and establishing of the Church and its affairs.

Moray, the King's son barred from the king's throne, now came into his own as ruler of Scotland. His house was said to be 'more like a church than a court', and he earned the name 'The Good Regent'. The country had a moment of security and peace.

Knox maintained that there could be no lasting peace till Mary was brought to trial, and if necessary put to death: but he had no great support. Then, a year after she had been taken prisoner, Mary escaped. Young Willie Douglas dropped the napkin over the keys at suppertime: and presently Mary was galloping hard for the west.

At Langside she faced Kirkcaldy with superior forces: but without his touch of genius. He won: and then 'the Queen lost all courage, which she never had done before'. She rode night and day for Dundrennan Abbey, and from there took ship across the Solway to England: and to prison. There was no more dancing, hunting, hawking – or freedom. When the end finally came it must have been a release: and her last role was her finest.

But in escaping she completed her wreck of Scotland. She left behind civil war and plotting and feuding, for as long as she continued to live.

The Leslies and Balfours all met violent deaths. In the end Lethington took poison to escape the dreadful death of traitors. Kirkcaldy died with unflinching courage. But of all those who 'gat the reward of dancers and drank in Hell' none drank so deep as Earl Bothwell. Escaping brilliantly over the Orkney sandbanks after his flight from Carberry Hill, he was then seized by the King of Denmark on behalf of a Danish lady he had once ruined and left. He was thrown into a dungeon in an island keep, and kept close chained to a pillar: and there he slowly went mad. There he lived on, long, long after all had forgotten him: long after Mary had planned to marry the Earl of Norfolk, the last suitor to die savagely for her: long after all believed him dead. Once, tourists were shown the half-circle worn into the solid stone by the endless, endless, endless pacing of the Border riever's feet.

22

The Sure Anchor

O^N a January day in 1570 Regent Moray rode at the head of his men through the main street of Linlithgow. Then, from a balcony above him, muffled by mattresses and curtains, a shot rang out: and the Regent crumpled in the saddle.

Struck through the body, he lingered till evening, settling his affairs and commending the young King. He died with dignity and no bitterness: killed by a Hamilton whose life he had previously spared.

The news reached Knox the next day, which was the Sabbath. He was heart-broken at the loss, both to the nation and to himself personally: and broke out in his sermon in praise of Moray and all he had done for the country.

Three weeks later the body was brought to Holyrood, and carried from there in solemn procession to St. Giles'. Kirkcaldy of Grange came in front, bearing Moray's royal banner, the Lion Rampant: eight great lords were his pallbearers: and all Scotland mourned. As Knox preached his funeral sermon, thousands wept. He lies buried below the south aisle of the church: and there you can still read Buchanan's Latin epitaph.

In October of that year Knox took a stroke. He was soon preaching again: but it is possible that he never fully recovered. In December he had a bitter quarrel with Kirkcaldy.

Kirkcaldy, with Lethington's support, was now holding the castle for the Queen's party. He rescued by force some of his men from the Tolbooth, and Knox denounced him from the pulpit. It would have been bad enough in some unregenerate man, said the preacher: but it was a double grief to see 'sic stars fall from heaven'. The words were exaggerated to Kirkcaldy, who complained to the Kirk Session of Edinburgh and demanded an apology. Knox explained himself once more in the pulpit: Kirkcaldy came to St. Giles' the next Sunday, for the first time for over a year. Unfortunately, he came with his tail of men-at-arms with him; and Knox understood this as intimidation, and preached on pride, transgression and judgement, so the breach became final.

Kirkcaldy's men, against his orders, killed the next regent within six months. The country had returned to the days after Flodden, in which Knox's life had begun. Once more there was an infant King, and warring nobles and a distracted country. Only now there was the Kirk of Scotland: but Knox had to fight for it up to his last breath.

He had always been a target himself. At the time of Bothwell's reconciliation a cook called MacEchearn had run down the High Street shouting: 'Loving-to-God! Knox's quarter is run, he is scourgit through the town!' Various people had accused him of frequenting brothels, or conniving at murder, or practising witchcraft: and each time he had painstakingly pursued them and nailed the lie. Now he continued to denounce the Queen: and her party attacked him with placards and abuse and accusations of sedition, which he answered from the pulpit.

He had learnt, he said, from Isaiah and Jeremiah, who also spoke to their times, 'to call wickedness by its own terms – a fig, a fig, and a spade, a spade'. Mary's pride remained: and 'sovereign to me she is not.' Nor was he 'a man of law that has my tongue to sell for silver, or favour of the world'. When they attacked him for the *Blast*, and for praying for Queen Elizabeth, he protested hotly. He would 'give him a lie in his throat that either dare, or will say, that ever I sought support against my native country. What I have been to my country, albeit this unthankful age will not know, yet the ages to come will be compelled to bear witness to the truth.' He asked his accusers to be as plain with him as he was with his answers: 'for to me it seems a thing most unreasonable that, in my decrepit age, I shall be compelled to fight against shadows, and howlets that dare not abide the light'.

The Hamiltons joined Kirkcaldy in the castle, and the prudent captain fortified all the high points round, including the steeple of St. Giles', to Knox anger. A very loud cannon, mounted on the church, was nicknamed 'John Knox' by the soldiers: but it was considered a just judgement when it burst and injured them. Knox's sermons continued to be so outspoken that neither he nor his congregation were altogether safe. A musket-ball was actually fired in through his study window: and his people finally persuaded him, as much for their own sake as his, to cross over to St. Andrews. On 5 May, 1571, he took ship at Leith with his little household: and so journeyed back to the little city that had played so big a part in his life.

Here the stones still bear their witness: for Beaton's great castle is tumbled down, the rich abbey is a heap of ruins: but the monuments to Patrick Hamilton, George Wishart, Walter Myln and others still mark the places where they suffered.

Knox passed here the last full year of his life, preaching on the prophecies of Daniel. The counter-Reformation had begun: and he had time to correct and publish an answer, written some time before, to the accusations of a 'new-start-up-Jesuit'. He knows, he points out, as much as any of the lives and laws of Popes and Cardinals: and also of the writings of the early Fathers. Where, the Jesuit had jeered, was this 'eight year old Kirk' of Scotland compared to the fifteen hundred years he claimed for Rome? They were part still of the one Catholic and Apostolic Church, returned Knox:

'. . . We answer for our entrance, and say, that before fifteen hundred years our Kirk was in Jerusalem, in Samaria, in Antioch and wheresoever Christ Jesus was truly preached, and his blissed evangel obediently received, whether it was amongst the Jews or Gentiles. There we say was our Kirk, which is not bound to any one place but is dispersed upon the face of the whole earth; having one God, one faith, one baptism and one Lord Jesus, Saviour of all that unfeignedly believe.

'. . . Yea, we are further bold to affirm, that if ever it shall please God to bring the Kirk of Rome to her original purity, that she shall not be ashamed to reverence the pure Kirk of Scotland as her dearest sister, and next resembling her in all things, before that pride and avarice . . . corrupted her ministers, and that the inventions of men were preferred to God's simple truth. We say yet again, that when soever the Kirk of Rome shall be reduced to that estate in the which the Apostles left it, we are assured that she shall vote in our favours. . . .'

Knox had his own views on the pastoral humility shown by the Pope at Cnossa. '... understand, that the preaching ministers within the Realm of Scotland are oxen, ever labouring under the yoke, and that into the husbandry of the Lord'. As for the charge of schism and sectarianism among Protestant countries: 'Albeit that in all ceremonies there be not uniformity: yea, and albeit that in some heads of doctrine also ... yet will we not break brotherly concord, providing that we agree in the principals'.

He is magnificent on the everlasting vexed question of apostolic succession, quoting the Geneva Bible:

'We find, that He sends not his afflicted Kirk to seek a lineal succession of any person before that He will receive them; but He, with all gentleness calleth his sheep unto him self, saying: "Come unto me all ye that labour and are laden, and I will ease you." And again: "All that the Father giveth me shall come to me: and him that cometh to me I cast not away."

'O golden and most comfortable sentence, pronounced of Him who cannot lie! Here is no mention of any succession that we should claim to before that we be received of him who is the Head of the Kirk. ... And therefore we can not but wonder, why that mortal man shall crave of us that which neither God the Father, his Son Christ Jesus, neither yet the holy Apostles in their ministry craved of any Realm or Nation. ...'

Knox dedicates this work to 'the Faithful, that God of his mercy shall appoint to fight after me'. ... His Preface begins: 'Wonder not, gentle Reader, that sic an argument should proceed from me in thir dolorous days, after that I have taken good-night at the world, and at all the fasherie of the same'. ... He wished to spend his last days in prayer and in peaceful meditation. 'Call for me, dear Brethren, that God in his mercy will please to put end to my long and painful battle'. Yet he must finish his task. So this work includes his memorial to Mrs. Bowes, his statement on her troubles and one of her letters. It also has a beautiful and personal prayer, headed: 'John Knox with deliberate mind to his God'.

'Be merciful unto me, O Lord ... In youth, mid-age and now, after many battles, I find nothing into me but vanity and corruption. For, in quietness I am negligent, in trouble impatient, tending to desperation: and in the mean state I am so carried away with vain fantasies that (alas) O Lord, they withdraw me

from the presence of thy Majesty. Pride and ambition assault
me on the one part, covetousness and malice trouble me on the
other. . . .' It ends with a prayer for his 'desolate bed-fellow,
the fruit of her bosom, and my two dear children, Nathaniel and
Eleazer.'

It was in these last days that the democracy of his Kirk was first
broken by the making of bishops. The Gaelic by-word 'tulchan'
bishops has stuck to them: tulchans being calf skins stuffed with
straw to make cows let down their milk. These bishops were men
of straw made by the nobles so that they could milk the Kirk of
her patrimony. Knox 'opponed himself directly' to this, and with
all his last powers.

'I charge and command you,' he wrote to the Assembly of
August 1571: 'that ye take heed to your selves, and the flock over
the which God has placed you pastors. To discourse of the
behaviour of yourselves, I may not: but to command you to be
faithful to the flock I dare not cease. Unfaithful and traitors to the
flock shall ye be before the Lord Jesus, if that . . . ye suffer
unworthy men to be thrust into the ministry of the Kirk. . . .'

He utterly refused to inaugurate a gentle creature personally
known to him as Bishop of St. Andrews. When it was said that he
had really wanted to be bishop himself, he retorted from the
pulpit that he had refused a greater Bishopric, offered to him once,
with the favour of greater men. Perhaps his mind ran back over
the odd quirks of fate. A few weeks before his death the new
English ambassador saw him 'so feeble as scarce can he stand
alone', and sent to Cecil Knox's greetings, and his thanksgiving
for the gospel 'truly and simply preached throughout Scotland'.

'He said further, that it was not 'long of your Lordship that he
was not a great Bishop in England; but that effect grown in Scotland, he being an instrument, doth much more satisfy him.'

His last work for the assembly was reading a sermon of
Ferguson, minister of Dunfermline, which he subscribed: 'John
Knox, with my dead hand, but glad heart, praising God that of
his mercy he leaves such light to his kirk in this desolation.'

He consoled himself now with the students: with that eternal
scarlet tide that flows about the grey walls of the little town. He
went to a play they had got up. And in especial he loved to walk in
St. Leonard's Yard, and to call them over and exhort them to learn

well, and to know God and His great work in Scotland: and to
bless them. His own nephew Paul, Williams' son, was a divinity
student then. And Andrew Melville, after parish minister of
Anstruther, has left the most vivid portrait of him:

'Of all the benefits that I had that year, was the coming of that
most notable prophet and apostle of our nation, Master John
Knox, to St. Andrews. . . . I heard him teach there the prophecies
of Daniel, that summer and the winter following. I had my pen
and my little book, and took away sic things as I could compre-
hend. In the opening of up his text, he was moderate the space of
an half hour: but when he entered to application, he made me so
to grue and tremble, that I could not hold a pen to write. He was
very weak. I saw him, every day of his doctrine, go "holy and
fairly", with a furring of martens about his neck, a staff in the ane
hand, and guid, godly Richard Bannatyne, his servant, holding
up the other oxter, from the abbey to the parish kirk, and by the
said Richard and another servant' – Jamie Campbell perhaps –
'lifted up to the pulpit, where he behoved to lean at his first entry;
but, ere he had done with his sermon, he was so active and
vigourous, that he was like to ding the pulpit in blads and fly out
of it.'

It was in St. Andrews that the student George Wishart had
caught 'the reek of Patrick Hamilton'. He had touched Knox, in
his own going: and now Knox, once also a student and preacher
here, was at his own end to touch his own successor. Among the
final year students was one Robert Bruce, a descendant of King
Robert the Bruce, born in Airth Castle, and own nephew to
'Lusty' Livingstone, one of the Maries. His elder brother was a
priest, and he was going in for law, and destined for a brilliant
career at the bar and at court: till there came a night, in the years
ahead when he stood at an Assize of the Soul. So, all unknown
either to Knox or to the lad, it was on him that his cloak fell. His
sacrament sermons, preached in St. Giles' are one of the treasures
of the Church of Scotland.

By the spring of 1572 Knox never left 'his bed and his book' but
for the weekly preaching. At the end of July there was a truce in
the civil war, and the congregation of Edinburgh sent him, for the
last time, a call: begging him to return to them, and signing it:
'Your Brethren and Children of God'. Weak as he was, he would

not go until they had promised that he might still speak freely his judgement on those still holding the castle.

Before he left St. Andrews he wrote an affectionate farewell to Christopher Goodman. Then he set out on his last journey. As far as can be judged, he returned now to the Mosman's house in the Canongate: to what is now known, and shown to visitors, as 'John Knox's House'. His original Manse is believed to have been on the site of the present town buildings, opposite St. Giles'.

His voice was so feeble that he could only preach in the part of St. Giles' known as the Tolbooth, to those who could hear him, With the permission of the assembly, the Church called Lawson of Aberdeen to be his colleague and successor, and Knox also wrote to him:

'Belovit Brother: seeing that God of his mercy, far above my expectation, has called me once again to Edinburgh, and yet that I feel nature so decayed, and daily to decay, that I look not for a long continuance of my battle, I would gladly once discharge my conscience into your bosom ... that we may confer together of heavenly things; for into earth there is no stability, except the Kirk of Jesus Christ, ever fighting under the cross, to whose mighty protection I heartily commit you.' It carries a postscript: 'Haste, lest ye come too late!'

Before Lawson could respond, news reached Edinburgh of the appalling Massacre of St. Bartholomew's Eve on 24 August, 1572. In this attempt to wipe out the Huguenots wholesale France washed its very streets in blood. The butchery was merciless, from Admiral Coligny to children and infants, with every possible savagery and brutality shown. Knox, 'creeping on his club' up to St. Giles', summoned up his strength to denounce the evil rulers who had planned and ordered it. The French ambassador demanded an apology from the Regent, but was refused, and left Scotland. In Rome, the Pope ordered a solemn thanksgiving for the mass murder. Nothing that Knox had feared or prophesied could have equalled it.

Knox was now preaching on Matthew, Chap. xxvii, on Christ's death and resurrection, with which he had wished to close his ministry. On Sunday, 9 November, he preached-in James Lawson in the pulpit of Edinburgh: and declared, in Bannatyne's words 'the duty of a minster and also their duty to him lykewise: and so made the marriage, in a manner, betwixt Mr. James Lawson, then made minister, and the folk; and so praised God, that had given them one in the place of himself that was now unable to teach, and desired God to augment him a thousand-fold above that that he had, if it were his pleasure: and so with the common blessing ended'.

So a great soul handed over.

Two days later a fearful cough seized him: so that shortly he had to give up his usual Bible reading. It was his habit to read some chapters of the Old and New Testaments with some psalms daily: so that he read through all the psalms each month. Now his wife and Bannatyne read to him instead; and in particular John xvii, Isaiah liii and part of the epistle to the Ephesians, and some of Calvin's sermons in French.

Richard Bannatyne, who loved him, has left a minute account of his last days and hours.

He asked his wife to settle the servants wages, and calling Jamie Campbell to him said: 'Thou wilt never get no more of me in this life!' and so gave him twenty shillings above his said wages.

On the Friday he rose to go to church, thinking it was Sunday, and he had to preach on the resurrection: for his last sermon had been on the crucifixion and death of Christ. On the Saturday ministers from Leith came in, not knowing how ill he was: and he came to table for them and 'caused pierce ane hogshead of wine which as in the cellar, and willed the said Archibald to send for the same so long as it lasted, for he would never tarry till it was drunk. He thought Sunday was the first day of the fast proclaimed for the French massacre: but Fairley of Braid reassured him, and persuaded him to take a little meat.

On Monday, while his mind was still clear, he 'earnestly desired the Kirk (I mean, the elders and deacons) that he might bid them his last good night', and so they came. He spoke to them at some length on his ministry: and answered an accusation of Maitland of Lethington made against him even at this hour. Then he asked Lawson and an elder to carry a last appeal to Kirkcaldy in the castle: 'That man's soul is dear to me, and I would not have it perish if I could save it'. Then, with psalms and prayers and his last blessing 'they departed with tears'.

Kirkcaldy might have listened to Knox, but Lethington over-persuaded him. Yet Knox's last message was to comfort Kirkcaldy's last hours.

After seeing the session, Knox was much worse 'for he never spake almost but with great pain; and yet very few come in (that he saw) to whom he gave not some admonition'.

The Lord Boyd came and said: 'I know, Sir, that I have offended you in many things, and am now come to crave you pardon.' After which, 'they were alone'. The Lord of Morton also saw him privately, and Lord Lyndsay and the Bishop of Caithness. Glencairn came several times. Ruthven only once, and then when he offered to do anything was told: 'I care not for all the pleasure and friendship of the world.' To a gentle-woman, who desired to praise God for what he had been, and so to praise himself, he answered :'Tongue! tongue! lady; flesh of itself is over proud. . . .'

If his wife or Bannatyne paused in their reading to ask him if he heard, he would say: 'I hear, I praise God, and understand far better'.

'Ilk ane bids me good-night, but when will you do it?' he said to Fairley of Braid.

On Friday, 21 November, he told Bannatyne to order his 'kist' – coffin. Thereafter he slept little, but filled his hours with prayer and meditation. As he lay quietly, sometimes as if asleep and sometimes with breath shortened by pain, he would constantly break out: 'Live in Christ! 'Or with short prayers, such as: 'Lord, grant true pastors to they Kirk' . . . or 'Lord, I commend my spirit, soul and body, and all, into thy hands!'

On Sunday he said to an elder: 'I have been in meditation this last two nights of the troubled Kirk of God . . . I have called to God for it . . . and have prevailed! I have been in heaven and have possession, and I have tasted of these heavenly joys, where presently I am!' And thereafter said the Lord's Prayer and The Belief, with some paraphrase upon every petition and article of them; and in saying 'Our Father which art in heaven,' he says, 'Who can pronounce so holy words!'

On Monday, which was his last day on earth, he had that access of ease which sometimes precedes the end. He insisted on rising, and putting on his doublet and hose, and sat in his chair for half an hour: 'and thereafter went to bed, where he wrocht in drawing of his end'. When the goodman of Kinyeancleuch asked him if he had any pain, he said it was not a painful pain: 'but sic a pain as, I trust, shall put end to this battle'. He also told him: 'I mun leave the care of my wife and bairnies unto you. . . .'

He asked his wife to read from 1 Corinthians, Chapt. xv, of the resurrection: and said to her: 'Is not that a comfortable chapter?' And a little after: 'Now, for the last, I commend my soul, spreit and body' (pointing upon his three fingers) 'unto thy hands, O Lord.'

He was come, like Mr. Valiant-for-Truth, to the deepest part of the river. He must have felt the rising tide of mortal weakness, the nearness of great darkness: in Galt's phrase, 'the clay-cold fingers o' Daith handling his feet'. But he had been here before. Did he hear for a moment the North Sea slapping on the galley's hull, the distant sweetness of St. Andrews bells? 'Go read,' he whispered to his wife,' where I cast my first anchor'. So she read the seventeenth chapter of St. John; the great prayer of the Shepherd:

'These words spake Jesus and lifted up his eyes to heaven and said: Father, the hour is come: glorify thy son, that thy son also may glorify thee.

As thou hast given him power over all flesh, that he should give eternal life to as many as thou hast given him.

And this is life eternal, that they might know thee, the only true God, and Jesus Christ, whom thou hast sent. . . .'

The Royal Mile must have been strangely silent as the short November day ended. There was silence too in the room where Knox lay: no movement save when they wetted his mouth with a little weak ale. They said the usual evening prayers, which he heard. Then suddenly he gave 'a long sigh and sob' and whispered: 'Now it is come!'

Bannatyne, flinging himself down by the bed, said: 'Now Sir, the time that ye have long called to God for, to wit, an end of your battle, is come! And seeing all natural power now fails, remember upon these comfortable promises, which often times you have showen to us of our Saviour Jesus Christ. And that we may understand and know that ye hear us, make us some sign. And so he lifted up his one hand and incontinent thereafter rendered the spreit and sleepit away. . . .'

He was buried with national mourning in the churchyard behind St. Giles': and the Regent said at his grave: 'Here lies one who never feared the face of man'.

.   .   .   .   .

It is all a public thoroughfare now. The advocates of Edinburgh park their cars over the graves and the tablet that used to mark Knox's last resting place may now be seen within the Church where he exercised his great ministry.

In November 1965 the statue of John Knox which had stood in the Albany Aisle inside the Church was unveiled on the south west corner wall outside the Church. Among those present that day was Master John Welsh Stewart Macfie a direct descendant of the great Reformer.

EPILOGUE

Crown Rights

A WEEK after Knox's death his two sons were admitted freshmen of John's College, Cambridge, where Lever, once Knox's colleague at Frankfort, was now master. Knox had arranged this: and he had left them Marjorie's dowry, eked out to £500 Scots, and his two silver cups and some silver spoons and salt-cellars, and some of his books. They did well, both being Fellows, Eleazar being rector of Clacton in Essex in the Armada year. They both died fairly young, and were unmarried. Paul, brother William's son, was also remembered in the will. Everything else was left to his wife and three daughters. It was so little, that next year St. Giles' granted her a pension.

The year after, she married a Border laird. The eldest girl married a son of Fairley of Braid, the second one Zachary Pont, minister of St. Cuthbert's. The youngest, Elizabeth Knox, married John Welsh, a Covenanting minister from Kyle. They were exiled by James VI for opposing episcopacy: and only returned from France to London when Welsh was very ill. He was told he might live if he could get back to his Ayrshire moors. So Elizabeth waylaid the King with a petition. When he heard who her parents were, he cried: 'Knox and Welsh! The De'il himself never made such a match!'

' 'Deed, Sire, and he wasna speired!' (That is, asked to leave).

He finally said her husband would be pardoned if he would submit to the bishops: and surely there was a flash of her father's eyes as she snatched up the corners of her apron, crying: 'I had rather kep' his head in this!'

So Welsh died in London. His wife and family later returned to Ayr. (From them Jane Welsh Carlyle claimed descent: and, as it happens, she and Thomas both lie in Knox's old church of St. Mary's, Haddington).

'No Bishop, no King!' was how James VI and I summed up the struggle for the soul of Scotland, which his mother had lost. It is the very sword-point which divided the country, and began the revolution in England. It was one of the factors for which Charles I lost his head, and James VII his crown.

James VI fought to force episcopacy on Scotland: and Lawson, Knox's worthy successor, fought back to preserve 'the Crown Rights of the Redeemer'. Lawson died in exile and poverty in London. After him, Melville told the King to his face:

'Sire, there are two kings and two kingdoms in Scotland: there is James Stewart and his kingdom, and there is Jesus Christ and His kingdom the Kirk, whose subject King James VI is: and of that kingdom not a lord nor a head, but a member.' Melville was imprisoned, and died in exile.

Then, when the Kirk had reached a low ebb, there came Robert Bruce, once of St. Andrews, now forsaking the law and the court to stand at the head of the family table in St. Giles'; and to break the Bread of Life to the people with such a grace and glow of love that its light has never been wholly lost. Some of his phrases, as when he speaks of the Sacrament as giving men 'a better grip of Christ' passed into the vernacular. The latest (1958) edition of his sermons still catches the ardour of them. He too was exiled.

It was for this that Knox spent his sweat and his soul: that the sacrament be given back to Scotland. It lays an exacting burden on the ordinary folk of each generation, thus called to be 'Bishops and Kings' in their faith. It lays a life-long responsibility on the parish minister called to be head of each unruly kirk family: but that is still the most jealously-held honour in Scotland.

Democracy, the 'vain imagination' of the sixteenth century, has often been counted out as impracticable, impossible: but for Scotland it is still essential. Whenever the Church even begins to compromise over it, the Table begins to lose its meaning, the Bread its Word of life: and the nation shrivels with the Kirk. It has to be re-fought at every step, in every life-time. It is the inescapable legacy to us all of our father in God, the dour little man who was content to be known as plain Mr. Knox.

Notes

NOTES